Michael Price

Wireless Home Networking

In easy steps is an imprint of In Easy Steps Limited
Southfield Road · Southam
Warwickshire CV47 0FB · United Kingdom
www.ineasysteps.com

2nd. Edition

In Easy Steps Limited supports The Forest Stewardship Council (FSC), the leading international forest certification organisation. All our titles that are printed on Greenpeace approved FSC certified paper carry the FSC logo.

Mixed Sources
Product group from well-managed forests and other controlled sources
www.fsc.org Cert no. SGS-COC-005998
© 1996 Forest Stewardship Council

Printed and bound in the United Kingdom

ISBN 978-1-84078-365-0

Contents

1 Home and Wireless Networks

We look at home networks, how they operate and what forms they take, review the benefits and drawbacks of wired versus wireless networks, and then examine wireless home networking and its sharing of resources, devices and Internet access.

What is a Home Network?

A home network is a combination of two or more computers that can share information and resources. These resources can include devices such as printers or services such as Internet access.

Don't forget

When you have several computers that are not connected to one another, it becomes difficult to share data, devices or services.

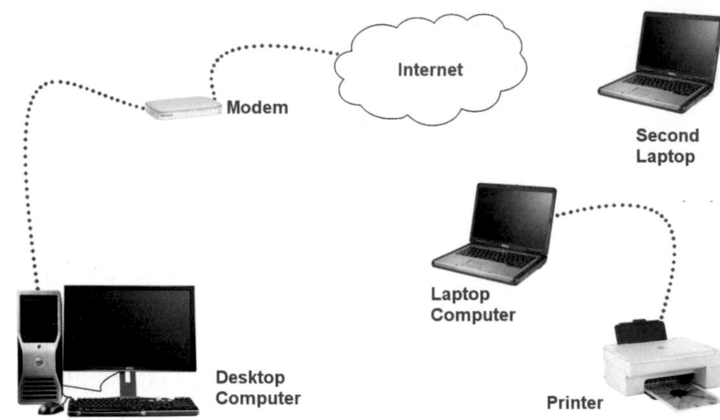

Without a network, Internet access is available on only one PC at a time. If you want to use a printer connected to another computer, you have to transfer the associated files via a floppy disk, CD or a data storage device such as a USB flash drive. Digital music, video, and photos can be enjoyed only on the PC containing the relevant media files, since the files concerned are usually too large for convenient copying.

Hot tip

When you establish a home network,each computer can access the Internet simultaneously. The data and devices on any one computer can be available to every computer. So you can be more productive, or simply have more fun.

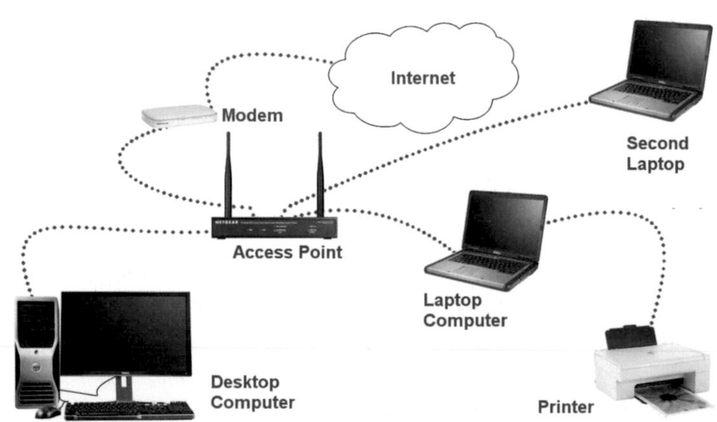

When you connect the computers in a network environment, these computers can share any of their resources, including hard disk drives and other storage facilities, as well as the printer and Internet connection.

Network Connection Methods

In order for the computers to share their resources, they must be connected together. There are a number of ways in which this can be achieved, including:

1. Wired Ethernet – special purpose networking cables
2. Phoneline Network – telephone cables around the home
3. Powerline Network – power cables around the home
4. Wireless Network – radio wave transmissions

Don't forget

Networking isn't just for computers. You can connect networked enabled storage devices or printers directly to the network. You can connect TVs and multimedia devices. Networked games consoles allow you to participate in multi-user video gaming sessions.

Network Adapters

There's a need for a network connection device or adapter in each computer. The form this will take depends on the type of network connection method being used.

Network Router or Switch

It is usually necessary to have some form of router or switch that has the role of distributing the various bits of information to the appropriate destination, e.g. between the Internet and a specific computer, or between two computers. Again, the devices needed depend on the connection method.

Which Method is Best?

Each method has its own strengths and weaknesses. We will look at each of these network connection methods in turn and identify the advantages and disadvantages associated with each.

Wireless Fidelity or Wi-Fi

As you'll see, we reach the conclusion that wireless networking, using radio wave transmitters and receivers instead of cables, is the ideal setup for the home user (see page 13). It allows you to access the network and its resources from anywhere in the house, without having to worry about cabling.

However, Wi-Fi achieves its full potential away from home, at hotspot locations such as coffee shops, hotels and airports that provide the necessary wireless access points. All you require is a wireless adapter in your laptop computer.

Wired Ethernet

Wired Ethernet has been the predominant network method in the past and so has built up a number of advantages.

1. There is usually an existing Ethernet adapter built in to your desktop or laptop computer
2. Ethernet networks are relatively high speed at 100 Mbps (mega bits per second), or 1 Gbps (giga bits per second)
3. Devices such as network attached storage, print server and digital media receiver can connect to the wired network

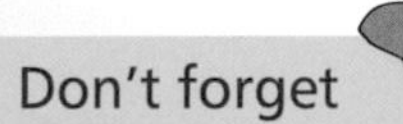

Don't forget

With switches that operate in full duplex mode, you can get up to twice the rated speed.

However, there can be disadvantages to using wired Ethernet:

1. Cabling can be expensive to install, especially when long cable runs are required, and changes are difficult to make
2. You often end up with exposed cables, which can be unsightly and create potential trip hazards
3. Cross-over cables may be required, e.g. to connect two PCs in an ad-hoc network, or to link Ethernet hubs, adding expense and complexity to your network

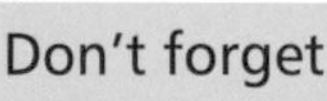

Don't forget

Individual computers will operate at the switch rate or at the network adapter rate, whichever is lower.

Standard Ethernet Cable

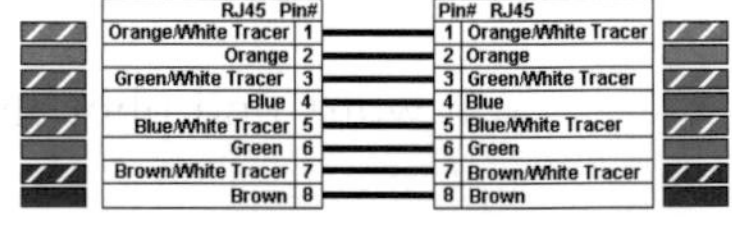

Cross-over Cable

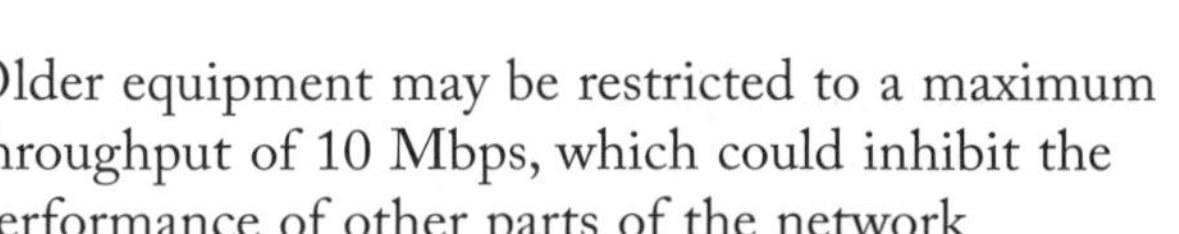

4. Older equipment may be restricted to a maximum throughput of 10 Mbps, which could inhibit the performance of other parts of the network

Phoneline Network

There are two other types of network technology that share some of the benefits of the wireless networks, in that they make use of existing wiring systems to link computers.

This uses the home telephone wiring to connect computers into a network. It is based on HomePNA technology which puts computer data on separate frequencies from voice, fax or ADSL transmissions so that these do not interfere with each other.

The benefits of phoneline networks include:

1. You need no special wiring and no switch or hub
2. Speeds of 10 Mbps to 128 Mbps are possible, depending on the implementation level you choose
3. Devices can be up to 1000 feet apart, and up to 64 devices can be connected
4. You can bridge to a wired or wireless network, and connect via a router to the Internet

There are disadvantages to using phoneline networks:

1. You won't find phoneline adapters on your desktop or laptop computers
2. There's a limited number of suppliers of these adapters and associated bridges and routers
3. You need a phone jack in each room and all the phone jacks must be on the same single telephone line

Don't forget

This method is a popular way to provide data services in hotels and convention centers.

Don't forget

There are similar devices that make use of the television coax cable system installed around the home. Coax cable allows for higher speeds and greater distances.

Powerline Network

Another way to transmit data around the home is to use the power supply wiring system. There are two types of powerline network adapters offered – Ethernet and USB.

With the USB adapter, you have one for each computer. It plugs into the power point, and connects to the computer via a USB cable. This creates an ad-hoc, peer-to-peer network. You'll need a bridge device to connect to the Internet modem and router.

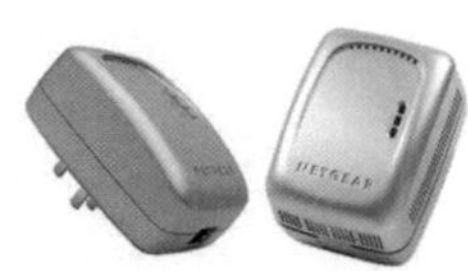

With the Ethernet adapter, you again have one per computer but the connection is via an Ethernet cable to the built-in network adapter in the computer. An additional powerline Ethernet adapter would be used to connect to the Internet modem and router.

The benefits are similar to those for the phoneline network, and in particular:

1. You need no special wiring and no switch or hub
2. Speeds of 14 Mbps to 200 Mbps are possible
3. A number of the main suppliers have products in the powerline network area

However, you can expect some problems in creating a network across your power cables. In particular:

1. The powerline network adapters must be on the same circuit breaker box
2. With the split phase wiring that is common in North America, you will have problems if some computers are connected on alternate sides
3. Your neighbors may be able to detect your powerline network signals, so an encryption password is essential

Don't forget

Originally developed in the USA, powerline networks are now available for most countries, whatever voltage their supply uses.

Beware

Your powerline network may act as a transmitter and interfere with local radio reception.

Wireless Home Networking

Wireless networking removes the constraints imposed by cabling. Some of the advantages that Wi-Fi offers include:

1. You can use your computer anywhere that you can pick up the signal from your wireless access point

2. Modern laptops have wireless adapters built in, and they can easily be added to laptops or desktops if required

3. There is Wi-Fi capability in various printers, webcams, video game consoles, while multimedia devices allow you to play digital music or view photos and videos on your home theater system and big screen TV

4. Laptops with Wi-Fi facilities can be used outside the home, via hotspots or through mobile broadband

However, there are some limitations to be aware of:

1. There are inherent security risks, especially if you install your wireless network with default settings

2. Wi-Fi connections could be slower than wired Ethernet, with nominal speeds of 11 Mbps or 54 Mbps

3. The further you are from the wireless access point or router, the slower the actual throughput achieved

For the home network, wireless is clearly the ideal solution. It is easy to set up and configure, there are no cables to install, and changes to the network are simple to apply. The performance gap between wireless and wired Ethernet has been effectively closed with the latest standards. For those situations where location or interference make one of the wired techniques more suitable, you can bridge the wired section to your wireless network.

The wireless adapters in your laptop computer continue to be useful when you are away from home, and allow you to link to the Internet via a municipal or commercial connection or through a variety of wireless hotspots (see page 161).

Hot tip 

Your wireless access point will normally provide a number of wired Ethernet connections and so supports a mixed network environment.

Don't forget 

The proposed Wireless-N standard offers 300 Mbps and a better range. Current devices built to draft specifications may need upgrading in the future.

Hot tip 

Always select Wi-Fi certified devices to avoid conflicts between devices from different suppliers.

How Networks Operate

The essential elements in a network are the network adapter (one per computer or device) and the connecting facility. This can be cable for a wired network or radio transmissions for a wireless network. For computers that are located close to one another, their network adapters can connect directly, to form an Ad-hoc network (see page 48).

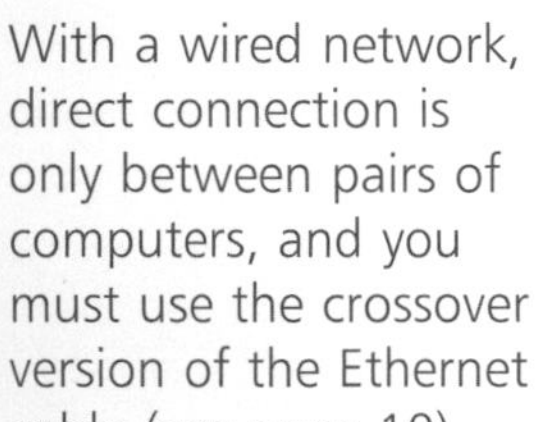

Hot tip

With a wired network, direct connection is only between pairs of computers, and you must use the crossover version of the Ethernet cable (see page 10).

For a number of computers or for greater separation, you need something to manage the multiplicity of links. This device is known as a Wireless Access Point on a wireless network. On a wired network the equivalent function is provided by a Switch.

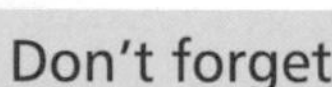

Don't forget

The wireless access point provides one or more Ethernet connections, for use during initial configuration, and to allow for the connection of modem and router devices.

If your network includes Internet access, you'll require a Cable or ADSL Modem, which could be used by any of the computers, often at the same time.

This means that multiple responses will be sent to and received back from the Internet. To manage this and make sure the responses go back to the correct computer, you need a Router to distribute each response back to the appropriate computer via the wireless access point or switch.

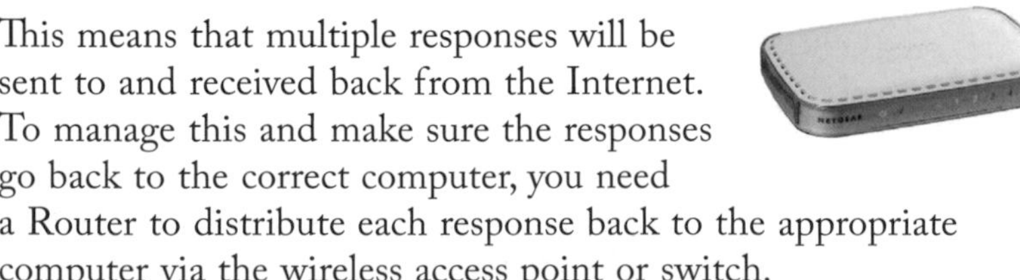

The modem and router are connected to the wireless access point to provide Internet support to the network computers.

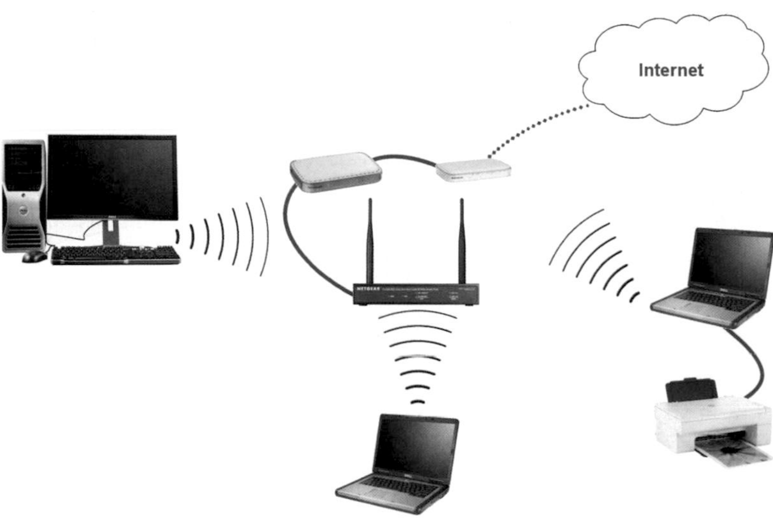

Hot tip

The router and modem use Ethernet cables to connect to one another and to the Wireless Access Point.

The modem, router and access point functions may be combined into a single device for wireless networks. Similarly you may have a combination modem, router and switch for wired networks.

Don't forget

The combination device usually includes some Ethernet ports, so your network could include computers with wired connections.

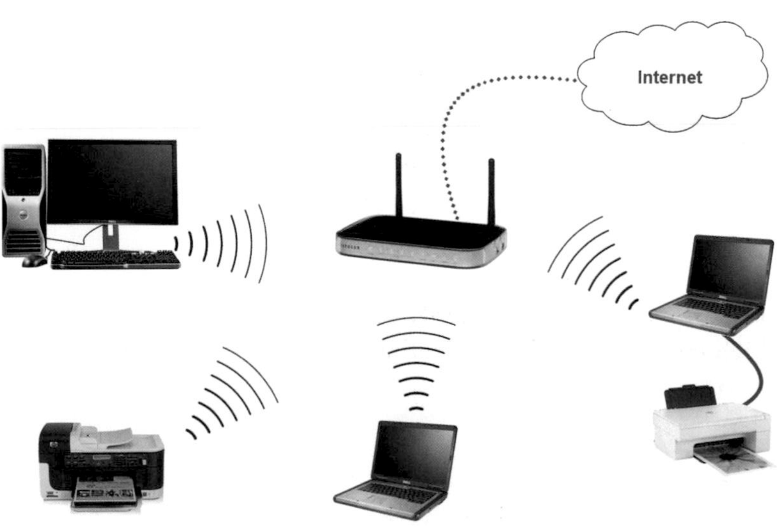

Other wireless devices such as a network printer can be added to the wireless network (see page 151).

Peer Group vs Client/Server

There are two styles of managed networks that you could choose for your home network – peer-to-peer workgroup or client/server. Either could be appropriate, depending on the extent to which you need to manage and control your network. Each provides its own set of advantages and disadvantages.

Don't forget

Workgroup networks are also referred to as Infrastructure networks, the term used in the Standards specification.

Peer-to-Peer Workgroup

A workgroup network will normally consist of two to ten computers connected together. All the software required is included in the normal Windows Vista operating system. Each computer runs its own local applications and programs, but can share its resources with all the other computers on the network.

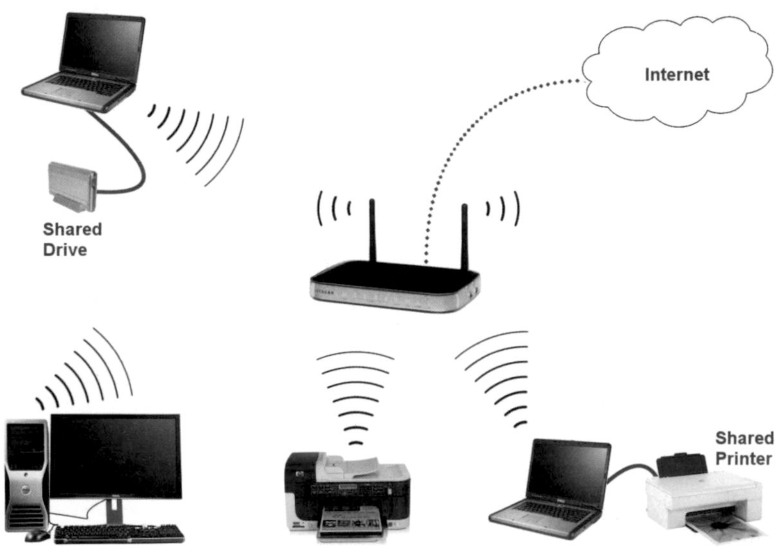

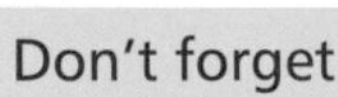

The illustrations and examples in this book concentrate on the use of peer-to-peer workgroup networking.

Sharing resources and adding new computers to the network is straightforward and uncomplicated. The network operates on the basis that all users take responsibility for the security and integrity of the network, and are required to manage their own backups. However, the consequence is that your computers are to some extent at the mercy of the least experienced or least careful user on the network.

Client/Server Domain

With the client/server network one computer (the server) shares its resources with all other computers (the clients). The clients continue to use Windows Vista, however the server requires a

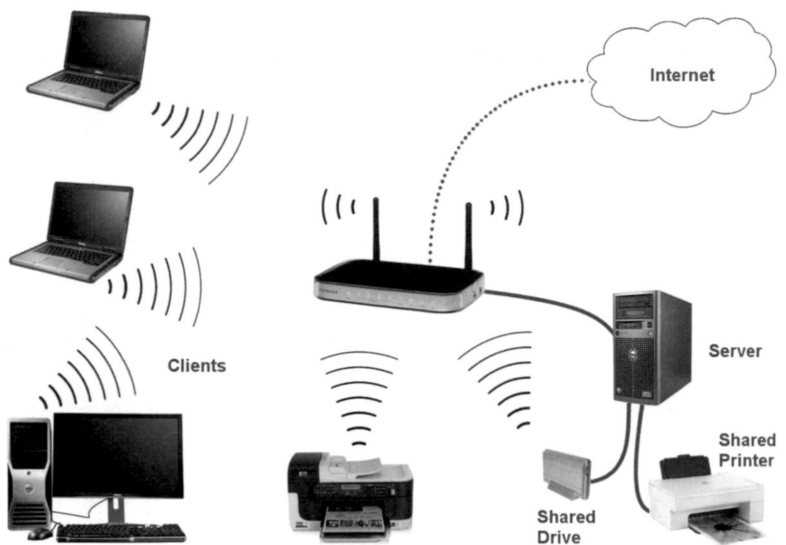

network operating system, for example Microsoft Server 2008. Data files and most of the applications are stored on the server, which has control over files, folders, printers, and other resources.

The server provides all services to the clients, and is responsible for security and authentication, managing usernames, passwords and permissions. To print a file for example, the client computer sends the request to the server, which accepts the request based on the user's permissions, then sends the print job to the appropriate printer for processing.

Choosing the Network Style

For your first network or for a small and simple network, you could start off with an ad-hoc network. This may also have a role as a temporary connection for visitors.

For most home networks, the peer-to-peer workgroup network will be the most suitable. As your requirements grow, you may decide to assign specific computers for tasks such as file sharing or printer support. This would be similar to the client/server method, but without the network operating system.

You may need more security than Windows Vista can provide, for example if you run a business from home. In this case a switch to the full client/server network with Microsoft Server 2008 might eventually become necessary.

Don't forget 

Servers would normally be connected via wired Ethernet for improved security and integrity of data. Clients may be wired or wireless.

Hot tip 

You could introduce the Microsoft Home Server (see page 130) on one computer, and allow it to manage backups and share data, without requiring the full Microsoft Server 2008 software system.

Share Resources

When you have set up your home network, you can share the resources on one computer with other computers on the network.

File and Folder Sharing

There are three ways in which you can share your files and folders:

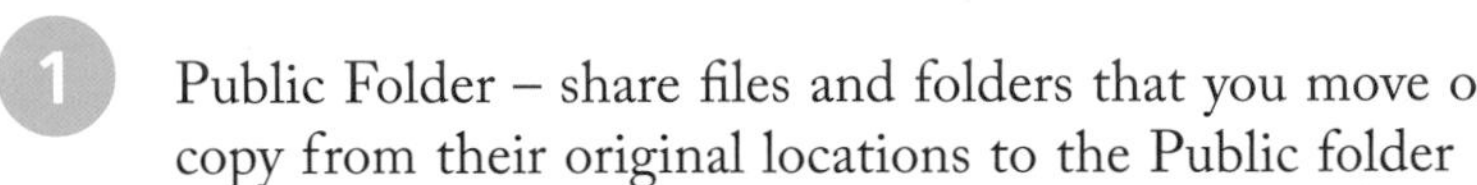

1. Public Folder – share files and folders that you move or copy from their original locations to the Public folder

There are three settings for sharing the Public folder:

- Turn on sharing so that users with network access can open files and view their contents
- Turn on sharing so that users with network access can open, read, change and create files
- Turn off sharing so that only users on the same computer can access the Public folder

The chosen setting applies to all networked users. You cannot restrict individual users or groups.

2. Any Folder – share files from any of the folders in the hard drive on your computer

This method allows you to tailor the level of access to individual users or groups of users. There are three levels of permission:

- Reader – the user has read access to the files and folders
- Contributor – the user can change files and folders, but cannot remove or delete them
- Co-owner – the user has full control over the files and folders, including change, add and delete

3. Media Files – share picture, music, video and playlist files so that they can be played on other networked computers or on networked digital media players

You can restrict which types of media files are available by default or for specific computers or devices. You can also restrict sharing to specified levels of the media file star ratings or parental ratings.

Don't forget

By sharing the root folder of a drive, you can give access to the whole of that drive (hard disk or other storage device).

Hot tip

Media file sharing is managed by the Windows Media Player on Windows Vista computers.

Printer Sharing

You can share the printer attached to one computer with users on the network. The printer is added to the Printer folder for the other computers, and can be referenced by name for printing in the same way as you use your locally attached printer.

Permissions can be assigned to each user or group of users. There are four types of printer permissions:

- Print – by default, each user can print and cancel, pause, or restart documents or files that they send to a printer
- Manage documents – users at this level can manage all jobs for the printer that are waiting in the print queue, including documents or files that are being printed by other users
- Manage printers – this permission allows you to rename, delete, share and choose preferences for the printer, and to choose printer permissions for other users, as well as to manage documents
- Special permissions – the highest level is used to change the printer owner, by default the person who installs the printer.

Password Protection

When password protection is turned on, it will limit network access to the shared folders and printers to those users who have an account and password on the computer holding those resources.

When password protection is turned off, any user on the network can use the shared printers and access the files and folders that have been shared with the Everyone group.

Hot tip

It doesn't matter what type of printer you have, as long as the printer is installed on your computer.

Don't forget

You cannot share your software defined printers such as the Fax printer or the Microsoft XPS Document printer.

Network Attached Devices

When you share a resource that's attached to one of the computers on the network, that computer must be left running in order to allow other users to access the resources, and it is usually necessary to disable power saving modes such as hibernation. The alternative is to attach the resource directly to the network.

Print Server

Some printers have an Ethernet port or a wireless adapter, either built-in or as an add-on option. This means that they can be directly attached to the switch or wireless access point and accessed as a network printer.

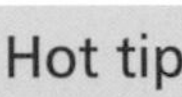

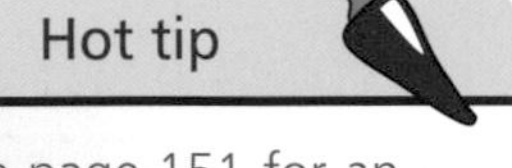

Hot tip

See page 151 for an example of installing, configuring and accessing a wireless printer.

If there's no network adapter offered, then you can use a separate print server device that includes a parallel port or a USB port for printer connection plus a wireless or Ethernet network connection.

The print server is attached to the switch or wireless access point, and the printer is attached to the print service device. The printer can now be directly accessed by computers on your network.

Network Attached Storage

Similarly, you can provide file storage facilities directly on the network. A network attached storage (NAS) device contains one or more hard drives and a network adapter to connect directly to the switch or wireless access point. This means that computers on the network can store and access files without requiring any other computer to be powered up.

Many NAS devices also come with one or more USB ports, which means you can expand the device's storage space by attaching an external USB hard drive. The NAS device can also be used to network a USB printer.

Digital Media Files

Windows Vista programs such as Windows Media Player and Windows Media Center can broadcast digital media over the network, so that other Windows Vista computers on your network can pick up and play that stream. However, you can also use a digital media receiver (DMR) to access a media stream being sent over the network and then play that stream through connected equipment such as speakers or TV. Examples of DMRs include the Xbox 360, the Play Station 3 and some MP3 players or digital picture frames.

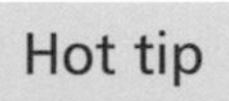

An alternative way to store and access media files is on the Windows Home Server, which can be installed as part of your home network (see page 130).

There are also specialized digital media players that can store and stream videos, music and photos from Internet sites such as YouTube and play them on your TV or HDTV.

Internet Telephony

You can use Skype software and the Internet to make unlimited free domestic and international calls to other Skype users, and low cost calls to other telephone users. Until recently such Internet calls were made and received using a headset or handset plugged into your computer. However, it is now possible to attach a wireless telephone handset so that you can make your Internet calls via your broadband modem, without being tied to the computer. Depending on the telephone type, you may be able to make and receive conventional calls on the same handset.

Internet Access

Don't forget

Sometimes shown simply as DSL, ADSL stands for asynchronous digital subscribers line. The Asynchronous term means that upload and download speeds are unequal.

There are a number of ways in which you can access the Internet from the computers on your network.

Connect via a locally attached (ADSL or cable) broadband modem

You can share access with other users on the network, but the host computer must be always on and connected.

Use a broadband modem and router on the network

This is an always-on network attached device that works independently of the computers on the network. Any one of these can access the Internet via this device.

3. Plug a mobile broadband modem into one computer on the network to provide high speed Internet access

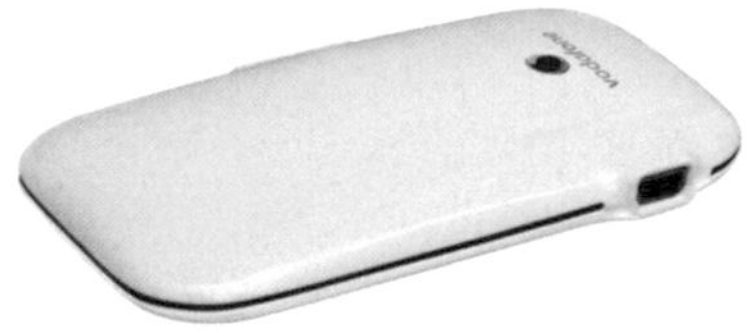

This uses the cell phone network rather than the landline. You can attach the modem to a desktop machine, but it is most useful with a laptop or netbook computer, since it can be used anywhere that has cell phone reception, not just at home, and still receives high-speed broadband Internet access.

Use your cell phone to connect your computer to the Internet

You'd connect the cell phone to the computer using bluetooth, or infrared or a data cable. A smart phone or PDA device provides a good interface to the Internet, wherever there is suitable cell phone reception. However, this type of connection cannot be shared with other computers on your network.

Hot tip

You may be able to share the Internet access with other computers on the network, while you are at home.

2 Planning your Wireless Network

Planning for your wireless network needs to take into account your objectives and the constraints of location. In this chapter we consider layout and performance issues, and examine the range of components offered, to suit a variety of requirements.

Objectives

Before you start planning your network, you should consider the purposes that the network is to serve and understand the characteristics of the tasks involved. This will help you make the appropriate decisions concerning the type of network, the level of performance required and the components needed. This can help minimise the need to upgrade or replace equipment as your network develops.

Of course, the level of detail required in this initial planning stage will be different for a small home network supporting a few users or a larger scale network intended to support a business or organization, but the principles involved will be similar.

These are some of the factors you should consider:

You can mix operating systems on your network, but it makes things easier if the computers share the same system.

Network Size

Make an initial estimate of how large a network you will need.

1. Number of computers to be connected, and their types i.e. desktop, laptop, Windows Vista, Windows XP
2. Number of regular users, remembering that some users may need sign on capabilities on more than one computer
3. Frequency of visiting users, using their own laptops or desiring guest facilities on your computer

Resource Sharing

You should identify the resources that you are likely to be sharing:

1. Files and Folders
2. Printers and Scanners
3. Access to specific device e.g. DVD Writer

If there are just a few computers involved, and you just need to exchange files between them, then the very simplest Ad-hoc network could suffice (see page 48).

When there are up to ten computers and users involved, the peer-to-peer workgroup network should certainly meet your needs. This uses a switch or access point to coordinate the computers and devices participating in the network (see page 60).

If you are planning to share Internet access over the network, you will need a router and broadband modem, or a switch or access point that includes these (see page 15).

If you want to share data on an on-going basis, or if you want to control the use of printers etc., you might designate one or more computers to perform specific tasks.

For larger numbers of computers, or where security is an issue (see below), you can expect to move towards a client/server network at some stage, so you should make networking and purchasing decisions with this possibility in mind.

Hot tip

You can share a dial-up connection, but the low bandwidth makes this impractical. You therefore need an ADSL or Cable connection for multiple users.

Security Issues

When you consider who will have access to your network, and what type of data it will store, there may be issues related to security and integrity of data. The following are some of the warning indicators:

1. Casual users may have access to the network for example, friends of the children
2. There is personal identification and financial data on one or more of the computers
3. You have confidential data related to your business or an organization that you deal with
4. The data stored on your computers could not be reproduced if the original copies were lost or destroyed

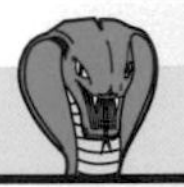

Beware

It is not always possible to control who has access to your network, so you should work on a worst-case scenario and include additional protection, just in case.

At the minimum, you need to incorporate a backup plan into your network. If you have Internet access, you'll need to protect the network from outside threats. Depending on your requirements, you may also need localized protection, and might consider limiting access, or encrypting sensitive data. For the most complete security, you might want to consider the client/server network method.

Location and Layout

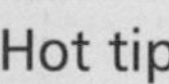

Don't forget

The type of location and layout of the area for your proposed new network will have a major influence on the network method that will be required.

If you are asked to design a network for a club or a business, you may have a set of similar computers, all lined up in a single location, where they can be connected one with another. This scenario often results in a wired network.

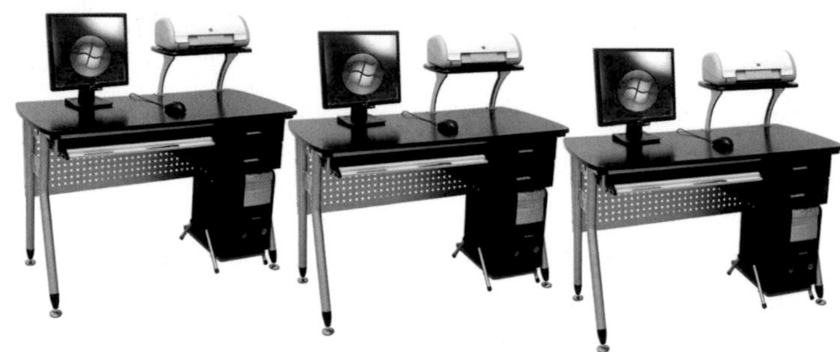

However, where members or visitors can bring along laptop computers or portable devices, it will be necessary to include some wireless capability.

In the home environment however, the computers involved are typically in different rooms, and wired connection often becomes impractical. The wireless network will therefore be the norm.

Hot tip

There's no particular problem with including a wired computer in your mainly wireless network, since it can participate equally with the other wireless computers on the network.

Often however, there will be one or two computers in easy reach of the router or modem, and for these a cable connection might be the natural choice, even though the main part of the network is wireless.

There may be network requirements with locations that are unsuitable for cable where wireless does not solve the problem. This may be a result of the distances involved, for example a loft room, or because of wireless interference from other electrical or wireless equipment in the immediate area.

In such situations you might be able to incorporate the problem locations in the network by using the phoneline or powerline methods (assuming the services are shared with the main location) along with a network bridge.

To add devices not supported by Wi-Fi or wired Ethernet, you may be able to use an alternative wireless interface such as Bluetooth, which provides short-range radio connections for devices such as cell phones and PDAs. Alternatively, you may be able to use a cable connection such as USB that will allow you to attach the device to one of the computers on your network.

You may be able to extend your network beyond the home or office, by connecting to the Internet via mobile broadband (see page 76), or via a cell phone or PDA connection.

Alternatively, you can seek out a hotspot. These are provided by a variety of organizations, sometimes free but usually at a charge and can be found at locations such as book stores, coffee shops, airports and train stations (see page 161).

Once you are connected to the Internet, you may then be able to link in to your home network, to access your data or even to run your home applications, using the remote networking capabilities of Windows Vista.

Hot tip

Another alternative is to extend the range of your wireless network by using a repeater or by including a second access point in the network configuration (see page 157).

Don't forget

You can use one of the many hotspot directories on the Internet to help locate hotspots in the region or country that you are planning to visit.

Performance Demands

Networks can be configured to support a variety of performance levels. You'll need to review the tasks that your network will support, and determine what level of performance they'll need, and hence the type of equipment will be most appropriate.

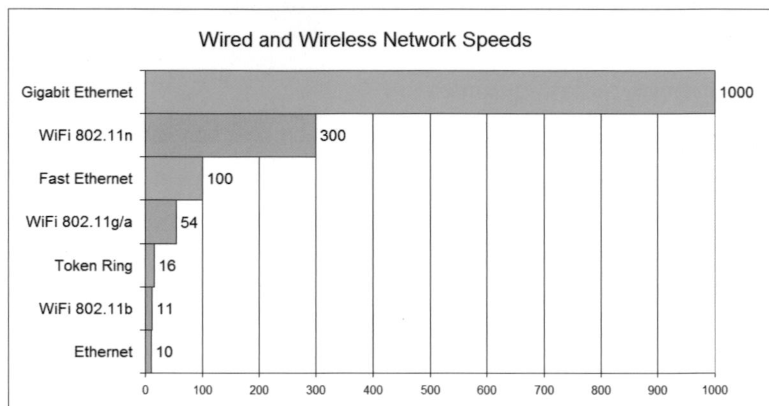

Don't forget

Speeds for wireless networks range from 11 Mbps to 300 Mbps. For comparison, speeds for wired networks range from 10 Mbps to 1000 Mbps.

This list shows typical tasks and their expected requirements, indicated as low, medium or high.

Task	Network	Internet
Application sharing	Medium	-
Business applications	Medium	Medium
Corporate/campus access	Medium	Medium
File and folder sharing	Low	-
Game playing – turn based	Low	Medium
Game playing – role play	Medium	Medium
Game playing – video and 3D	High	High
Instant messaging (IM)	Low	Low
Network printing	Low	-
Online streaming audio	Medium	Medium
Online streaming video	High	High
Playback PC-based audio	Low	-
Playback PC-based photos	Medium	-
Playback PC-based video	High	-
Video chat	High	High
Web surfing	Low	Medium

Hot tip

For some of the tasks, there are similar issues regarding the speed of Internet access, which ranges from 90 Kbps to 8 Mbps or more.

Existing Facilities

Before making your choice of networking types and equipment, you should identify the networking capabilities built in to your existing computer hardware.

For a desktop computer, check the rear panel to establish what's provided. You should find a number of USB ports, an Ethernet port and perhaps a dialup modem port. Usually, these will be part of the main system board.

Don't forget

There are usually more USB connectors on the front panel of the desktop computer.

Sometimes there will be a port included on an adapter card added to the system, for example a modem. There could even be a wireless network adapter.

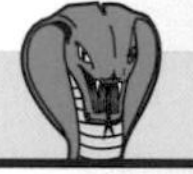

Beware

The provision of wireless network adapters as standard features is unusual for desktop computers, but they can easily be fitted as post-manufacture upgrades.

On a laptop, you'll usually find the same set of ports, on the rear panel or on a side panel. Sometimes, these ports will be supported by a PC Card that slots into the laptop.

You are most likely to have wireless connectivity also, but this is harder to spot since it is usually provided by an internal card.

There may be logos or indicator lights on the laptop to indicate the available wireless connections, or you could identify the exact model of your computer and search the manufacturer's website for the matching specification sheet.

Hot tip

You can also use details from the Vista Network and Sharing Center and Device Manager to identify network adapter types and characteristics (see page 102).

Wireless LAN Options

Don't forget

An antenna is part of the wireless adapter built in or attached to your computer, and there will be one or more antennas on the wireless access point/router.

Wireless networks operate using radio frequency (RF). When an RF current is supplied to an antenna, an electromagnetic field is created that can be picked up by other antennas in the locality. The main standards for wireless LANs are based on the 802.11 standard developed by the Institute for Electrical and Electronics Engineers (IEEE). There are four main variants in current use:

802.11b

The first widely used wireless networking standard, providing up to 11 Mbps in the 2.4 GHz band.

Beware

The 802.11a and 802.11b equipment is being phased out, so if you are building a new network, 802.11g or 802.11n are the most effective choices.

802.11a

This provides up to 54 Mbps in the 5 GHz band. This is a less cluttered part of the radio bandwidth, but the signals are more liable to absorption by office walls and ceilings.

802.11g

Like 802.11b, this uses the 2.4 GHz band, but offers up to 54 Mbps and increased range. It is currently the most common wireless networking technology.

802.11n

Another enhancement, again based on 802.11b, but offering 2.4 GHz or 5 GHz, up to 300 Mbps and up to twice the range. This standard is currently under development and is scheduled to be complete by December 2009.

Hot tip

Even though the 802.11n standard has not yet been finalized, you can buy products based on draft versions of the standard, and you can upgrade later to the final standard.

Type	Radio Band	Range Indoor	Range Outdoor	Rated Speed	Typical Speed
802.11b	2.4GHz	30 meter	100 meter	11Mbps	4Mbps
802.11a	5GHz	35 meter	110 meter	54Mbps	23Mbps
802.11g	2.4GHz	35 meter	110 meter	54Mbps	20Mbps
802.11n	2.4/5GHz	70 meter	160 meter	300Mbps	120Mbps

802.11b, g and n can all use the same 2.4 GHz radio frequency, and are compatible with each other, so you can normally use devices based on different standards within the same wireless network. However, the configuration requirements to allow for the earlier devices can reduce the overall performance of the network. 802.11a devices generally cannot connect to a 802.11b, g or n network, but some network adapters are dual frequency so could be used with either type of network.

Networking Components

For the purposes of this book, we will assume that you have decided on a wireless network. We'll start off with the ad-hoc network, then move on to the peer-to-peer workgroup.

You'll need the following categories of hardware components:

Wireless Network Adapters

A wireless network adapter is required for each computer on the network. There's a wide range of network adapters, as described on pages 33-36. These will be all that you need to support the simple ad-hoc network (see page 48).

Wireless Access Point

For a fuller function network, you'll need a device to act as the centre of your network, receiving and re-transmitting communications to link one computer with another.

Switches, Router and Modem Functions

In most cases, the wireless access point will also provide one or more Ethernet connections, so it can act as an Ethernet Switch. This means that a nearby computer equipped with an Ethernet network adapter may be attached via an Ethernet cable rather than via wireless.

The access point may also include Router capability, allowing you to connect your ADSL or cable modem via an Ethernet cable, making your Internet connection available across the network.

The wireless access point can actually incorporate the appropriate modem type, allowing it to offer the full three functions in a single unit.

If you need more Ethernet connections, you can utilise one of the Ethernet connections on your wireless access point to connect a separate Ethernet switch, letting you add 5, 8, 16 or more wired connections, depending on the switch size chosen.

Adapters for Other Devices

Finally, you may want to attach devices other than computers to your network, for example a printer or a storage device.

We look at some of the options for these components, using NetGear as our example suppliers, and select the devices that we'll use to illustrate some typical networks.

Don't forget

Though wireless is the main networking method, you'll want to retain the ability to connect using Ethernet cables, even if it's only to configure wireless access point devices.

Hot tip

In each case, you'll need to consider the level of performance required and select the appropriate model to match your needs.

Supplier Extensions

Don't forget

Network component suppliers provide components that meet the standards, but also strive to create an added edge to encourage you to stay with their brand.

NetGear offers four families of products based on the 802.11 standards, but with some extensions.

- **Wireless-G** (standard coverage, up to 54 Mbps)
- **Super G** (standard plus coverage, up to 108 Mbps)
- **RangeMax MIMO** (extended coverage, up to 108 Mbps)
- **Wireless-N** (maximum coverage, up to 300 Mbps)

This table shows the characteristics of the product families and the relative speeds and coverage, and their relative suitability for the situations and activities where they might be applied.

Hot tip

RangeMax uses Smart MIMO (Multi-in, Multi-Out) technology that uses seven internal antennas to survey the environment and adapt to detected barriers and interference.

Don't forget

You'll find similar ranges and descriptions from the other networking product suppliers.

Product Families → / Features ↓	Standard Coverage		Extended Coverage	Maximum Coverage & Bandwidth
	802.11g	Super G	RangeMax	RangeMax NEXT
	cable routers	cable routers	cable routers	cable routers
	ADSL modem routers	ADSL modem routers	ADSL modem routers	ADSL modem routers
	cards & adapters	cards & adapters	cards & adapters	cards & adapters
Speed				
Equivalent to wired 10/100 Fast Ethernet				☆
Maintains highest speeds throughout the entire home				☆
Speed vs. Standard G		2x	10x	14x
Coverage				
Standard range (typical) - 1 to 2 rooms	☆	☆	☆	☆☆
Extended range (typical) - whole home		☆	☆	☆☆
MIMO technology			☆	☆
Eliminates dead spots			☆	☆☆
Coverage vs. Standard G		4x	10x	10x
Internal antennas			☆	☆
Steady-Stream connections			☆	☆☆
Draft 11n True-Test				☆
Compatibility				
Public Hotspots	☆	☆	☆	☆
802.11b, 802.11g	☆	☆	☆	☆
Built-in laptop wireless	☆	☆	☆	☆
Security				
Double firewall (SPI & NAT)	☆	☆	☆	☆
Touchless WiFi (WEP, WPA/PSK, WPA2, PSK)	☆	☆	☆	☆
Security dashboard parental controls	☆	☆	☆	☆
Suitability For				
Internet sharing	☆	☆☆	☆☆☆	☆☆☆☆☆
Multiple users	☆	☆☆	☆☆☆	☆☆☆☆☆
Sharing photos	☆	☆☆	☆☆☆	☆☆☆☆☆
Streaming music	☆	☆☆	☆☆☆	☆☆☆☆☆
Downloading large files	☆	☆☆	☆☆☆	☆☆☆☆☆
Streaming videos	☆	☆☆	☆☆☆	☆☆☆☆☆
Simultaneous HD video streaming				☆☆☆☆☆
Simultaneous Gaming				☆☆☆☆☆
VoIP				☆☆☆☆☆
Network file storage				☆☆☆☆☆

Laptop Wireless Adapters

There are wireless adapters for laptop computers to match the various standards and extensions. These are available in several formats, but the most common is the PC Card, developed by a group called the Personal Computer Memory Card International Association (PCMCIA).

PC Card Wireless Adapters

If your laptop computer does not feature a wireless adapter, or if the adapter fitted does not meet the required standard, the appropriate PC Card adapter could solve the problem. There are Wireless PC Cards in each of NetGear families of products, including for example:

1. Wireless-G PC Card
Compatible with 802.11g and 802.11b wireless routers, and operating at speeds up to 54 Mbps

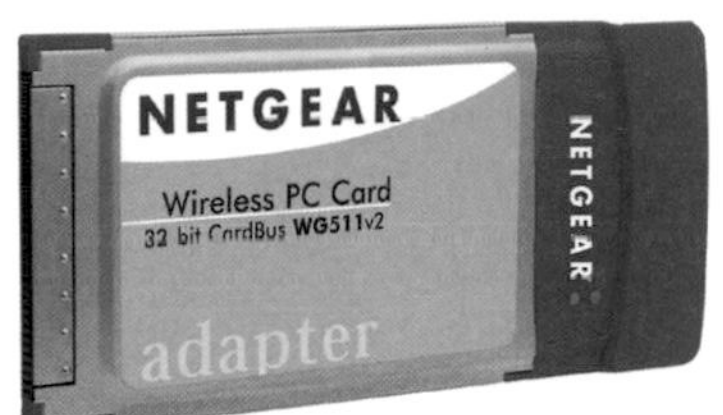

2. Super-G Wireless
An enhanced version, operating at speeds of up to 108 Mbps and with 4 times the coverage of the standard Wireless-G

3. RangeMax MIMO Wireless-G PC Card
Compatible with 802.11g and 802.11b wireless routers, operating at speeds up to 108 Mbps over an extended range

4. RangeMax Next Wireless-N PC Card
Compatible with the draft 802.11n and with 802.11g and 802.11b, and operating at speeds up to 300 Mbps

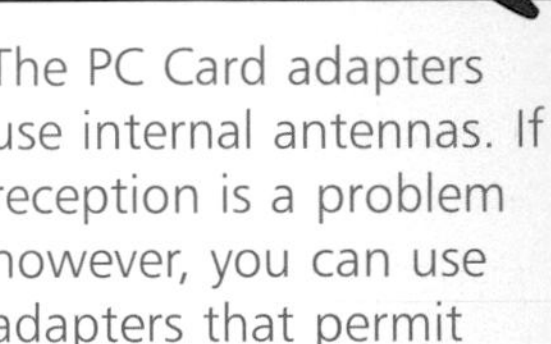

Hot tip

The PC Card adapters use internal antennas. If reception is a problem however, you can use adapters that permit an external aerial to be attached.

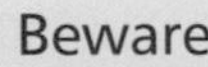

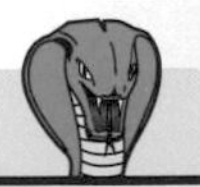

Beware

To achieve the enhanced performance, these adapters must be used with matching routers, so they are at their best in networks that obtain all the equipment from the same supplier.

Hot tip

The ExpressCard combines the portability and hot plugging capabilities of the PC Card with the performance benefits of the PCI adapter.

ExpressCard Wireless Adapters

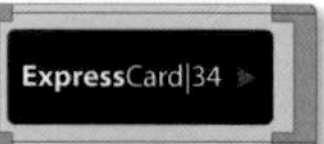

Your laptop may have ExpressCard in place of the more usual PC Card. ExpressCard operates at 2.0 Gbps via PCI Express and 480 Mbps via USB 2.0, with this bandwidth dedicated for each slot. In contrast, PC Card shares a total 1.06 Gbps bandwidth. In addition, ExpressCard uses lower voltages (1.5 and 3.3 volt versus 3.3 and 5.0 volt).

Though not widely available, there are some ExpressCard wireless adapters, for example:

1. LinkSys Dual Band Wireless-N Express Card
This allows you to connect your laptop to a network on either the 2.4 GHz or 5 GHz frequency and to operate at speeds up to 270 Mbps. It offers its best performance with the LinkSys Dual Band Wireless-N routers, but works with any Wireless-G, B and A networks.

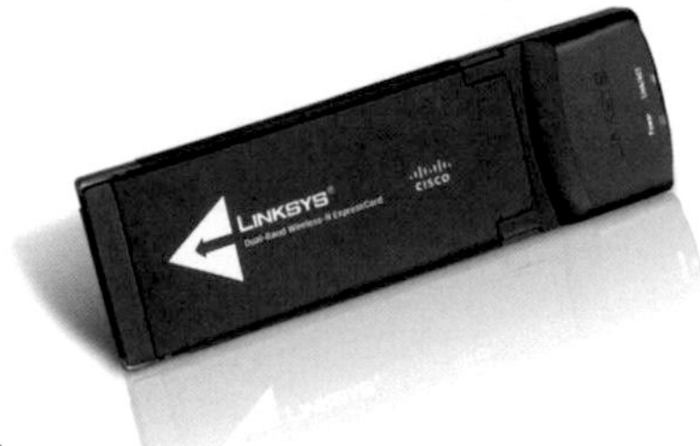

Don't forget

These converters can of course be used with any PC Card, not just wireless adapters. Also, there are similar converters for the ExpressCard format.

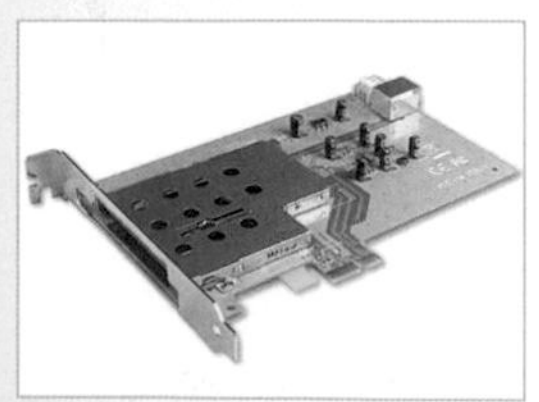

PC Cards on a Desktop Computer

If you have a PC Card wireless adapter and want to use it on a desktop computer that doesn't support this interface, you can install a PC Card to PCI converter into a PCI slot to provide one or more PC Card slots at the rear of the system unit.

Desktop Wireless Adapters

For desktop computers you'll find wireless adapters for all the standards and extensions, the main format being the internal adapter card designed for the PCI interface. This is perhaps the most effective way to add wireless capability to your desktop computer because it connects directly with the computer's data bus. NetGear offer a range of PCI wireless adapters, including:

Don't forget

There is an extended version of PCI known as PCI Express. The PCIe interface provides superior performance over the standard PCI interface. However, PCIe wireless adapters are not readily available.

1. Wireless-G PCI Adapter Supporting 802.11g and 802.11b networks at speeds up to 54 Mbps

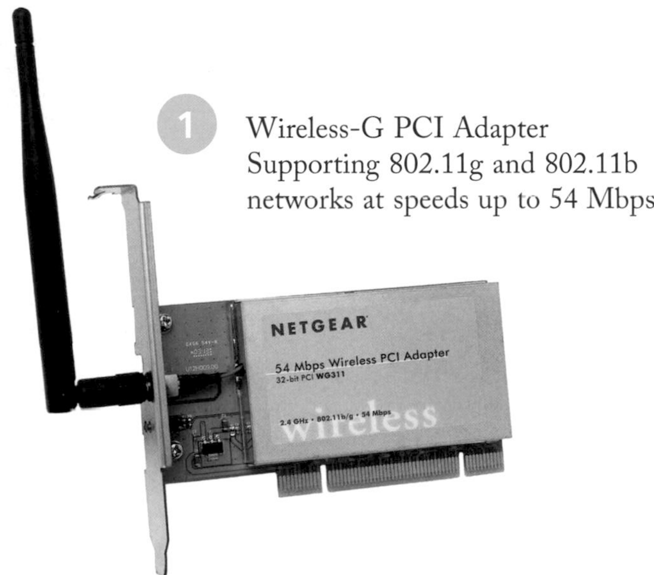

Hot tip

There are also Super-G and RangeMax MIMO Wireless-G PCI adapters that operate at 108 Mbps and offer enhanced coverage.

2. RangeMax Next Wireless-N PCI Adapter Compatible with 802.11n, 802.11g and 802.11b wireless routers, and operating at speeds up to 300 Mbps

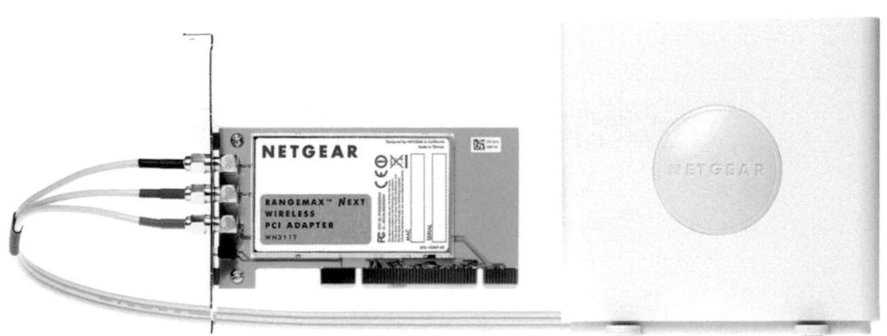

Don't forget

The Wireless-N PCI adapter has a separate desktop or wall-mountable antenna connected by leads to the PCI adapter itself.

As with all the enhanced adapters, the maximum performance levels require use with matching NetGear Wireless-N routers.

USB Wireless Adapters

The alternative format for both desktop and laptop computers is a USB wireless adapter. These cover all the options you might need, and are available for all the networking standards. NetGear offer a range of such adapters, including:

1. Wireless-G USB 2.0 Adapter
   This supports 802.11g and 802.11b networks, and operates at speeds up to 54 Mbps

2. Super-G Wireless USB 2.0 Adapter
   Providing enhanced performance, up to 108 Mbps

3. RangeMax MIMO Wireless-G USB 2.0 Adapter
   Operating at speeds up to 108 Mbp, with up to ten times the range of the standard Wireless-G

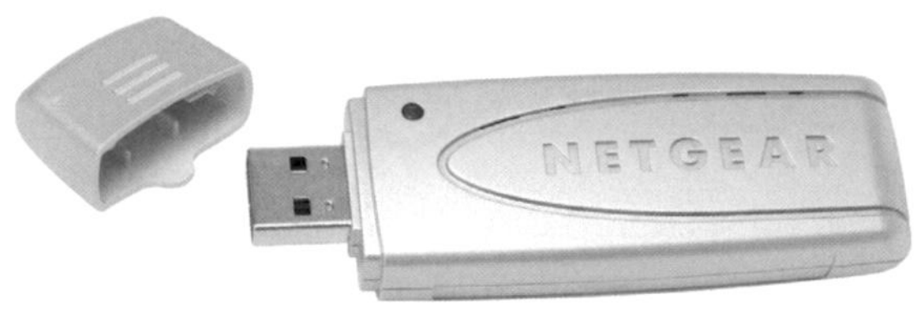

4. RangeMax Wireless-N USB 2.0 Adapter
   2.4 GHz or 5 GHz bands, at speeds up to 300 Mbps, and with an external antenna

Hot tip

The Super-G version looks just the same, but operates at twice the speed of the Standard G adapter.

There's also a RangeMax Wireless-N adapter in the USB stick format with micro antenna.

Wireless Router/Gateway

For anything other than a simple ad-hoc network, you need a device to handle the interconnections between the computers and other devices on the network. As with the adapters, there are devices to provide Network-G, Network-N and Dual Band in compliance with the wireless standards. There are also enhanced versions to implement improvements and extensions that are specific to the supplier.

For NetGear, this means devices to support its four families of products (Wireless-G, Super G, RangeMax MIMO, Wireless-N). These devices are designed to perform the functions of:

- Wireless Access Point
- Wireless Broadband Modem Router
- Wireless Cable Router

Taking the Wireless-N products as an example:

Wireless-N Access Point

This is used to extend an existing home wireless network and is normally used in conjunction with a wireless cable or telephone router. You must connect your laptop and desktop computers using compatible Wireless-N network adapters, to achieve the highest levels of performance and range. However, the wireless access point is also backwards compatible with Wireless-G and Wireless-B.

A single gigabyte Ethernet port, is included. This can be used for configuration and to allow connection to your wired network.

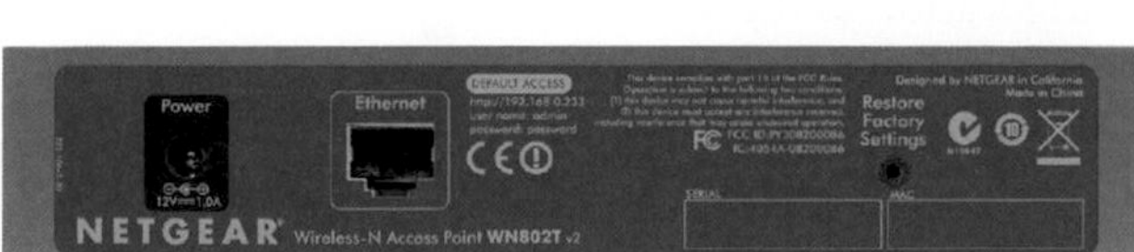

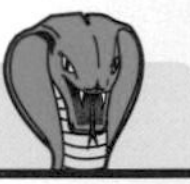

Beware

This device is Wi-Fi certified for draft 2.0 of 802.11n, so it requires a 802.11n draft 2.0 certified notebook or wireless adapter to perform at full capacity.

Hot tip

Other wireless access point models feature Wireless-G, Super-G or dual band support.

Wireless-N Cable Router

Use this device when you have Cable access to the Internet and wish to create a wireless network. It supports Wireless-N network adapters and is also compatible with Wireless-G and Wireless-B, and it has internal antennas.

Four 10/100 Mbps Ethernet ports are included, used for initial configuration and for connection to a wired network.

Don't forget

This router may also include a RangeMax Wireless-N USB adapter (see page 36).

This device downloads and installs firmware revisions to keep itself up to date.

Wireless-N Router with Built-in ADSL Modem

This is a complete solution for wireless home networks with telephone line broadband. It provides the wireless access point, the router and the ADSL modem. It has all the required security features including firewall. It is compatible with Network-N and with Wireless-G and Wireless-B. It incorporates two external adjustable antennas.

Hot tip

This router and the associated USB adapter mentioned above are used for the example network.

Four 10/100 Mbps Ethernet ports are included, used for initial configuration and for connection to a wired network. There is also a version with a set of gigabyte Ethernet ports included.

Other Devices

You can connect other devices to your wireless network, to add extra functions and services. As an illustration, here are some of the add-on products available from NetGear.

Digital Entertainer HD

This digital media receiver automatically finds all the digital media files on your home network and organizes them into an easily accessible library.

It connects to your Network-G compatible router (or you can use a wired Ethernet connection) and supports functions such as:

- Playback protected media files downloaded from the Internet
- Schedule TV recordings as a personal video recorder (PVR)
- Access USB devices (e.g. flash drive, digital camera, iPOD)
- View your computer desktop remotely on your TV

You don't need a hard disk on your digital media receiver, you can add storage directly to your network, for example using one of the ReadyNAS devices from NetGear.

ReadyNAS Duo

This storage device connects to the network and is simultaneously accessible on all connected Windows (or Macintosh) computers. It contains a hard disk (500 GB, 750 GB or 1000 GB depending on the model) and an optional second hard disk drive can be installed. The spare hard drive will keep an extra copy of all the data and instantly take over if the first hard drive should fail.

Hot tip

This allows you to stream movies, videos, music, Internet radio, and photos from your computers and storage devices at up to 1080p resolution on your HDTV.

Don't forget

The PVR function requires you to have a TV tuner card installed in your computer.

Beware

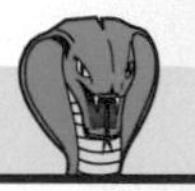

Storage devices are connected via the Ethernet port on your network router, even on wireless networks, to improve the level of data integrity.

Don't forget

The Smart Wizard set-up function automatically guides you through the configuration of the printers.

Wireless Print Server

This device allows you to connect one or two printers to your wireless-G network, without using Ethernet cables. You can place your printers anywhere in your home or office – they don't have to be next to any of your computers. Just plug the printers into the print server's USB ports.

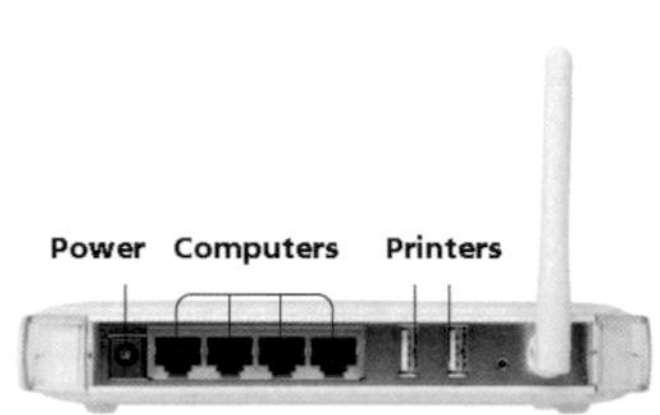

The print server has four Ethernet ports, so can also act as a wireless Ethernet bridge, connecting a cluster of up to four computers and laptops to the wireless network, using their built-in Ethernet adapters.

If you are involved with HD video or with high-performance network gaming, you might want use the 5 GHz Wireless-N band to support the associated devices. The 5 GHz band offers more wireless channels than the 2.4 GHz band, giving an enhanced connection. To link these devices into your network, you need a bridge, for example:

Don't forget

When Wi-Fi devices share the 2.4 GHz band with cordless phones, Bluetooth devices, microwave ovens and baby monitors, this could generate wireless interference.

5 GHz Wireless-N Access Point/Bridge

This access point/bridge allows you to connect any 5 GHz Wireless-N or 5 GHz Wireless-A device to your existing home network. This could include digital video recorders (DVR), digital media adapter (DMA) and a game console. It works with Xbox, PlayStation, Wii, TiVo HD, Slingbox, and digital set-top boxes among other equipment. It also supports laptop computers fitted with wireless-N adapters.

This bridge provides an easy way to upgrade to Wireless-N without disconnecting your existing wireless router.

3 Wireless Adapters & Ad-Hoc Networks

Start by identifying an existing wireless adapter or installing the software and attaching a wireless adapter to your laptop or desktop computer. Then you'll be able to set up ad-hoc networks to share files and printers or to play games. Or you can move on to the next chapter to set up a full network.

Identify Network Adapters

Hot tip

If there's no Network on your Start Menu, click Start, begin to type Network Center and select Network and Sharing Center from the shortlist displayed.

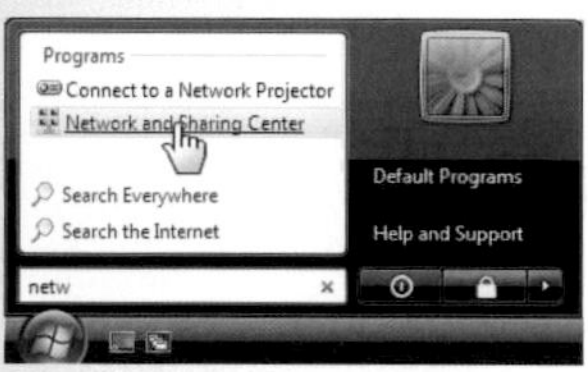

Before you can create your wireless network, you must have a wireless adapter installed in each computer. This may already be installed, especially with laptop computers. To see what network components are defined in any computer that is operating under Windows Vista:

1. Click Start, select Network and then click the Network and Sharing Center button

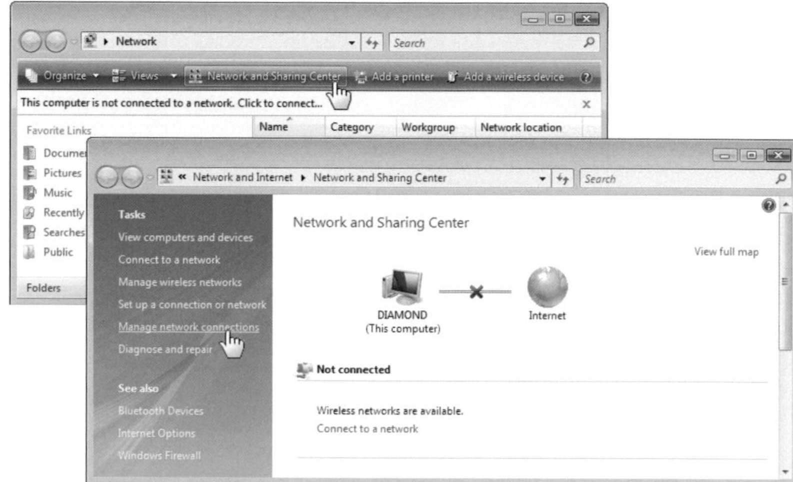

Don't forget

This is a new installation so there are no networks currently defined, though Vista tells you that there are wireless networks available.

2. Click the task shown as Manage network connections

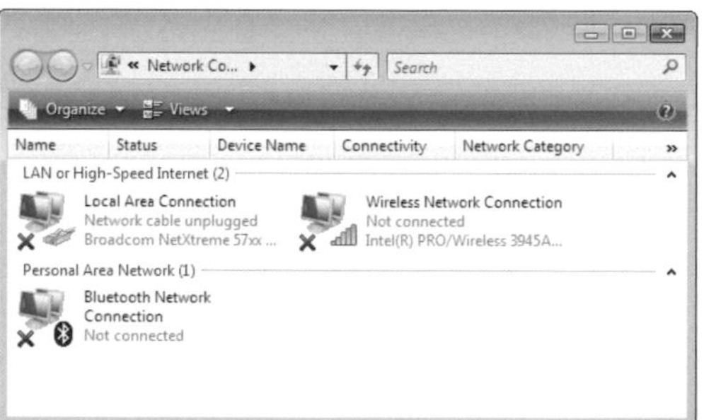

Hot tip

This panel shows that none of the network adapters are connected to a network and there is no Internet connection defined.

This displays all the network adapters that are defined in the system. For the example computer, a Dell M1710 laptop, there are three network adapters identified – Bluetooth, Wired Ethernet and Wireless.

To get more information about these adapters, you can use the Device Manager and see what has been defined:

1. Select Start, Control Panel, System and Maintenance, then select the Device Manager task

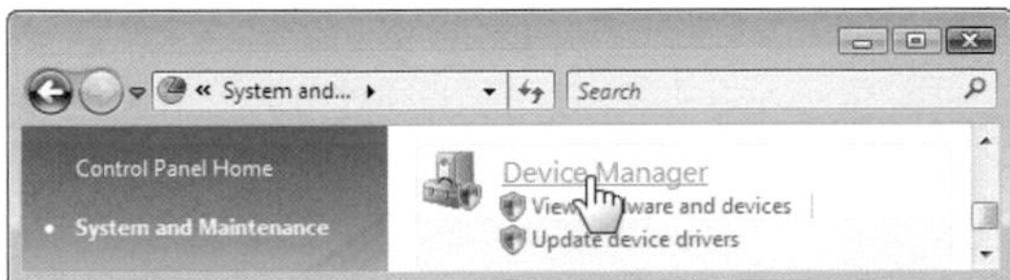

2. Locate the entry for Modems and click the [+] symbol to expand the list of devices

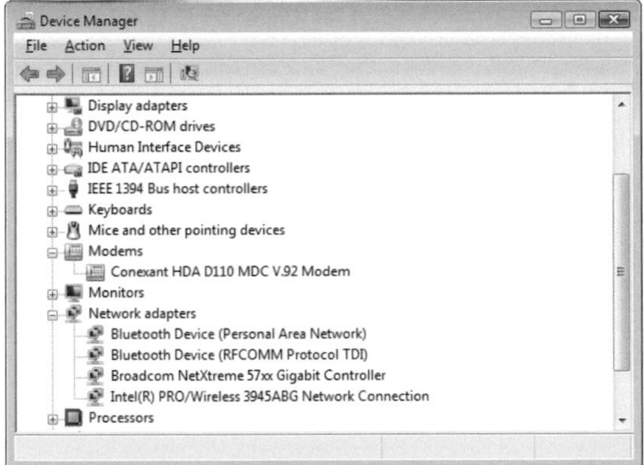

3. Locate the Network Adapters entry and expand the list

On this example laptop computer, there's a dial-up modem that could be used for Internet access, a Gigabyte Ethernet adapter for connection to a wired network and some Bluetooth devices, very useful when you need to attach cell phones, PDAs and similar devices that are without built-in Wi-Fi support. However, the most important device for wireless network purposes is the Intel Wireless 3945ABG, supporting Wireless A, B and G.

Since you already have a wireless adapter, you can now set up an ad-hoc network, join an existing ad-hoc network or establish a full workgroup network.

Hot tip

You could select Start, type part of Device Manager then select the associated entry from the list displayed at the top of the Start Menu.

Don't forget

The device entry in the Device Manager list often helps identify specific features of the device concerned, since these are usually incorporated into the device name e.g. Intel 3945ABG.

Beware

If the wireless adapter included with the laptop does not match the level needed, you may need to install a separate wireless adapter, for example a Wireless-N adapter.

Installing a Wireless Adapter

Hot tip

The example computer used is a Dell Dimension Model E520 running Windows Vista Ultimate.

Don't forget

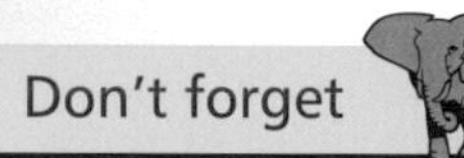

This computer may already be connected to a wired network. You will still need a wireless adapter, in order to participate in an ad-hoc network.

You won't always find an existing wireless adapter, especially with desktop computers. To view adapters in the example computer:

1. Open the Network and Sharing Center

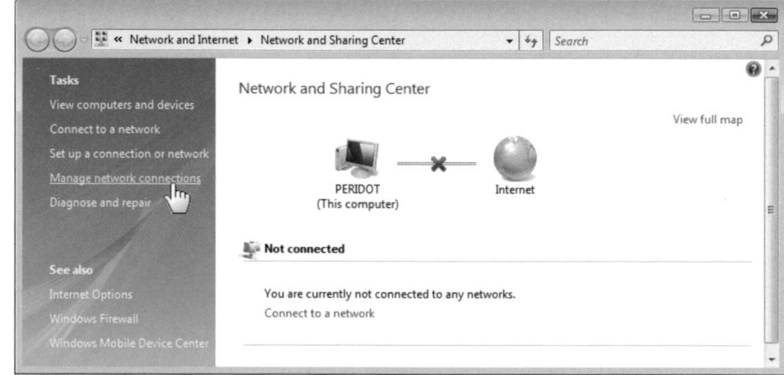

2. Select Manage network connections, and you'll see just the one network adapter for wired Ethernet connection

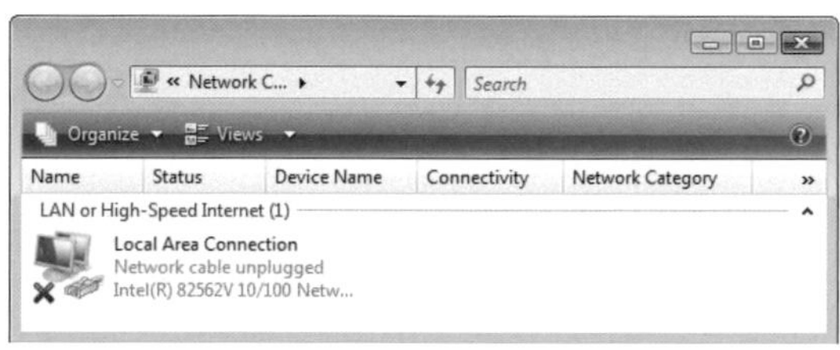

3. Device Manager will show a dial-up modem and the Ethernet adapter, but no Bluetooth or Wireless adapters

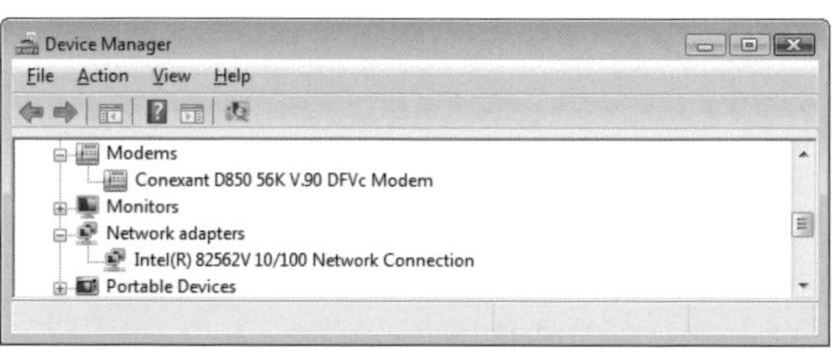

To create an ad-hoc network using this desktop computer, or to incorporate the desktop computer into an existing ad-hoc network, you first need to install a wireless adapter.

You start by installing the software drivers and utilities for the device, before you attach it to the computer. For example, to install a USB adapter, as an example the Netgear RangeMax Wireless-N USB 2.0 adapter (WN111) on a desktop computer:

1. Insert the Netgear WN111 Resource CD and click the entry to Install Software

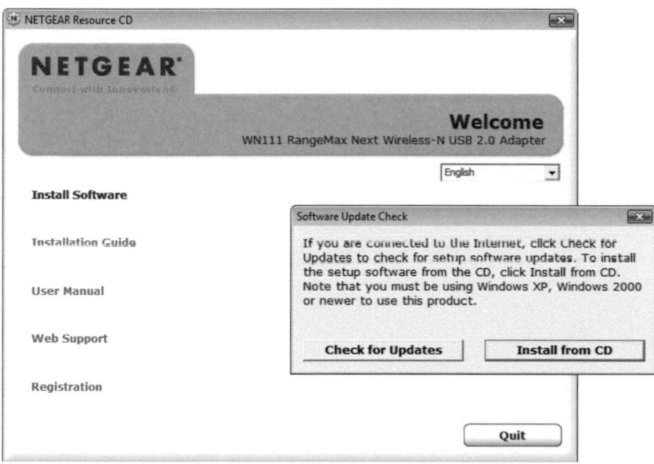

2. If you are connected to the Internet, click Check for Updates, otherwise you should choose to install from CD

3. Follow prompts from NetGear Smart Wizard to install the wireless adapter software on your computer

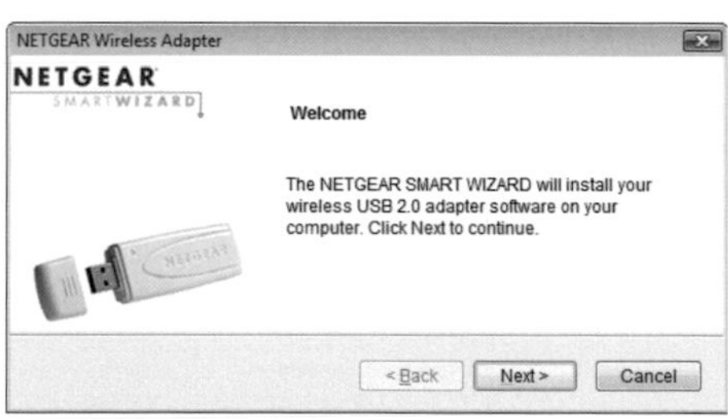

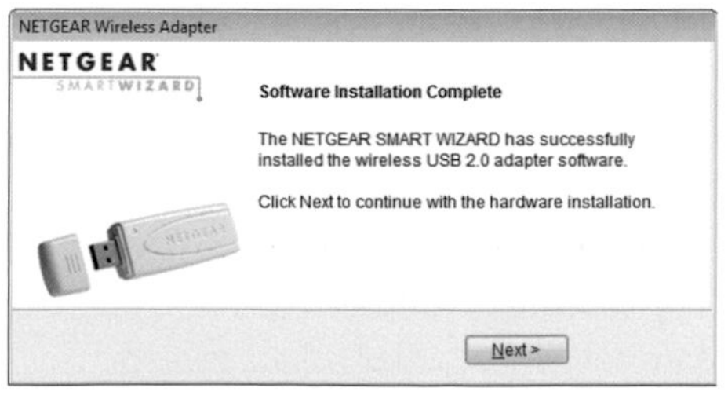

4. Click Next to continue with the hardware installation

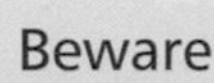

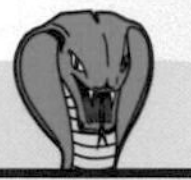

If the AutoPlay panel is displayed, you must click the option to Run Autorun.exe to show the NetGear Welcome panel.

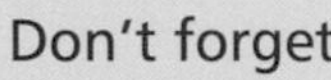

The process will be similar for wireless adapters from other suppliers, though the details will vary.

Attaching the Adapter

Hot tip

Some USB wireless adapters include a cradle so you can position the adapter on your monitor or laptop to maximize reception.

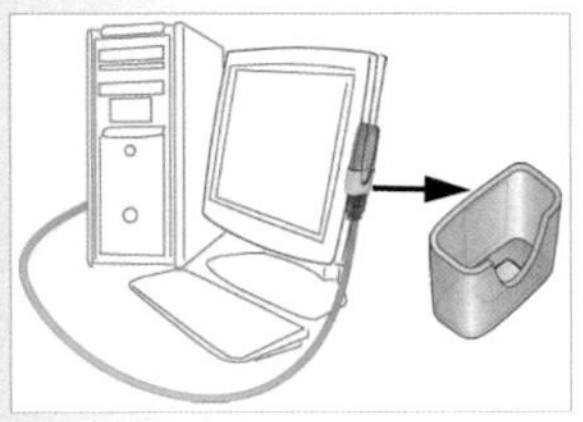

1. Choose an available USB port on your computer

2. Connect the USB cable to the WN111 and insert the other end of the cable into the selected USB port

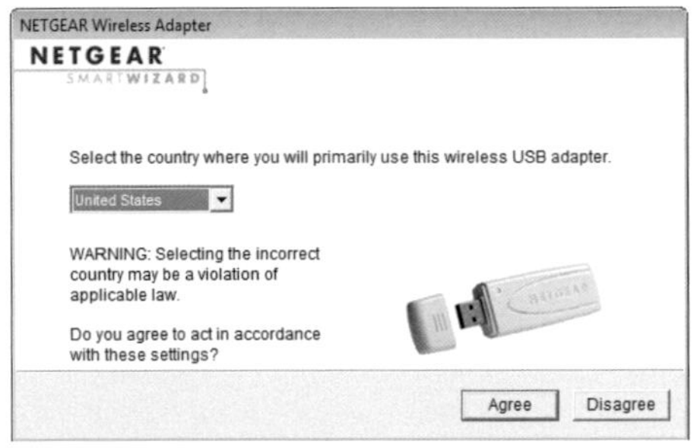

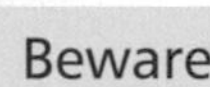

Beware

The channels available and the permitted output vary by country, so you need to specify your location when you install Wi-Fi hardware.

3. Choose the location where you'll normally use the adapter to ensure you comply with the local wireless regulations

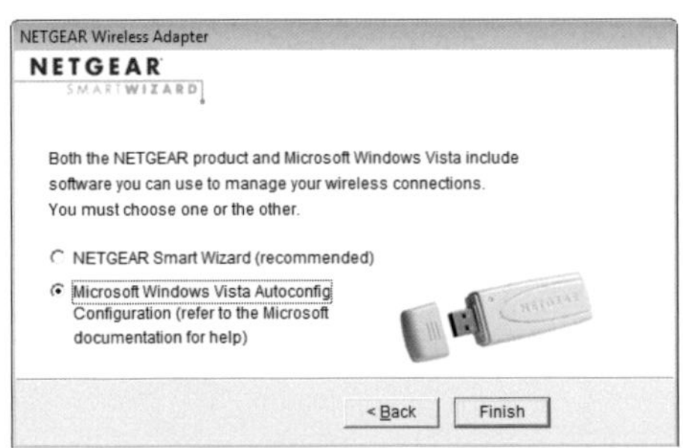

Don't forget

All the suppliers have their own configuration software. If you have a mixture of suppliers, they may be easier to manage if you use the Windows configuration software as your standard.

4. If you have NetGear equipment only, choose NetGear Smart Wizard to manage wireless connections. Otherwise use Windows Vista Autoconfigure, then click Finish

Set Up a Network

When you have a wireless network adapter in your computer, either pre-installed or added as an extra, you can begin the process of creating a network:

1. Open the Network and Sharing Center and click Connect to a Network

2. Windows will search for any networks available

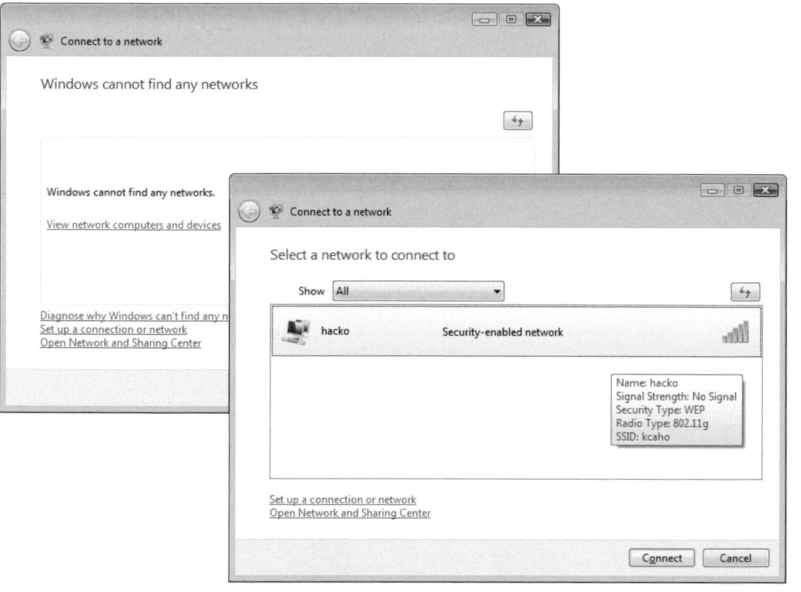

3. Select the option to Set up a connection or network

Hot tip

You follow a similar process to create or connect to an ad-hoc network or a workgroup network.

Beware

Even if you have no networks defined, Windows may detect a network in the area, in this case a neighbor's network, though with a very weak signal. This has been set up as a secure network, so isn't accessible without the appropriate credentials.

Create Ad-Hoc Network

To view the network adapters on your computer select Manage network connections from the Network and Sharing Center.

At this stage you have a wireless adapter defined but are not connected to any network.

When you select Set up a connection or network, Windows will display the options that are available to you.

The wireless network options only appear when you have a wireless network adapter in the computer.

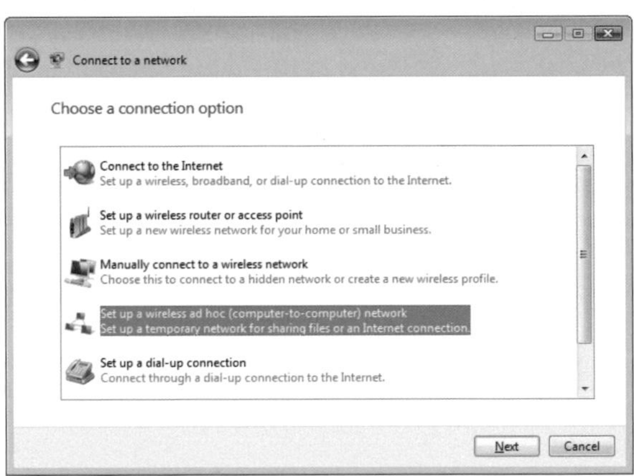

1. Choose the option to Set up a wireless ad-hoc (computer to computer) network and click Next, then Next again

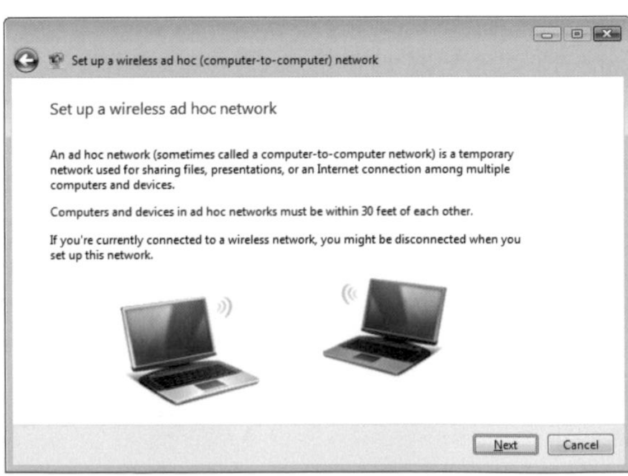

To set up a wireless ad-hoc network:

1. Specify a network name containing 1-32 case-sensitive characters, for example Tempnet1

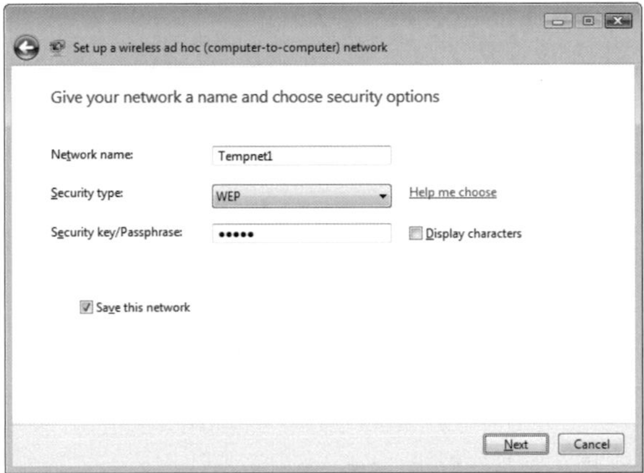

2. Choose the security type from the selection offered, for example WEP (wired equivalent privacy), and provide the security key or passphrase

3. Click Save this network to allow for automatic connection, if desired, then click Next

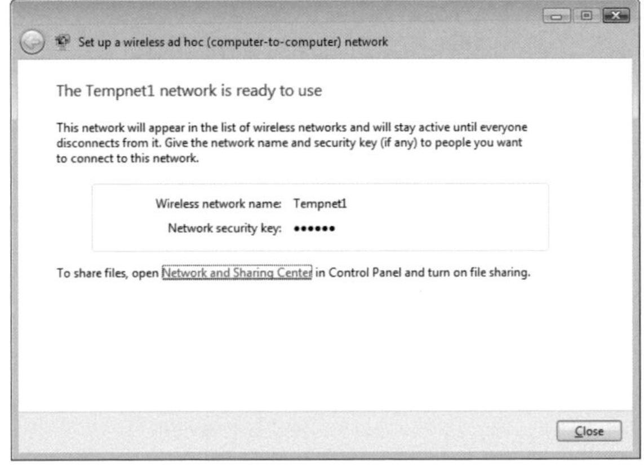

4. Click Close and the network waits for users to connect

Beware

If you click the box to Display characters, the actual password will be shown on all the screens presented during set up.

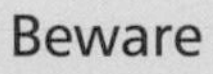

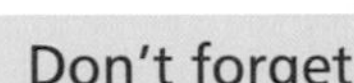

Don't forget

For WEP the security key consists of 5 or 13 case sensitive characters, or 10 or 22 hexadecimal digits.

Hot tip

If you have an Internet connection, via a modem or wired connection, you'll be offered the opportunity to turn on Internet Connection Sharing.

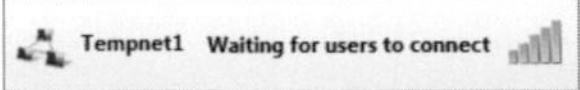

Join Ad-Hoc Network

Wireless enabled computers in the neighborhood can connect to an active ad-hoc network.

Hot tip

If the wireless adapter is already connected to a network, select Connect to a network from the Network and Sharing Center, to disconnect from the old and connect to the new network.

1. Click Start, Network and click on the message bar, select Connect to a network and choose the ad-hoc network

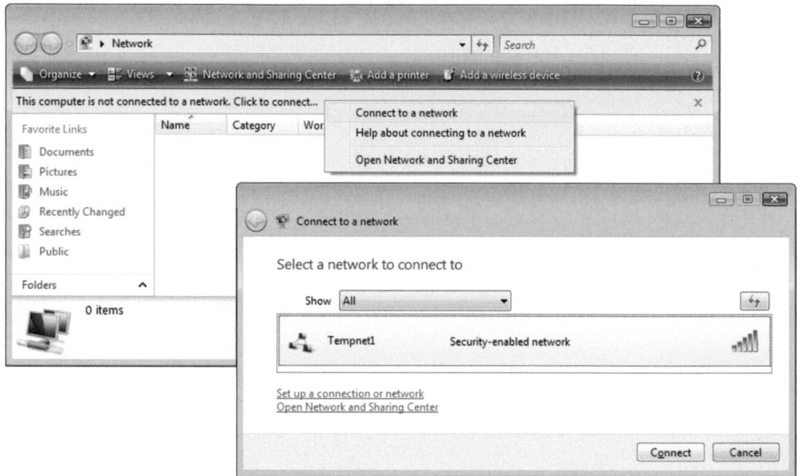

Don't forget

You can save the network definition if you are likely to reuse it in the future.

2. Enter the security key or passphrase and click Connect

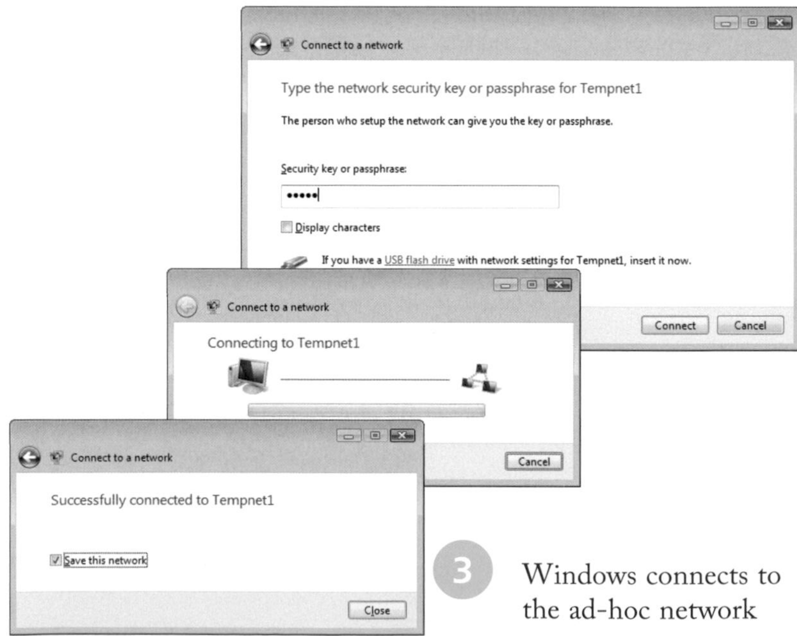

Don't forget

The wireless adapter in the computer must support the type of wireless security selected for the ad-hoc network.

3. Windows connects to the ad-hoc network

Open the Network and Sharing Center, and you'll see Windows seeking to identify the new network

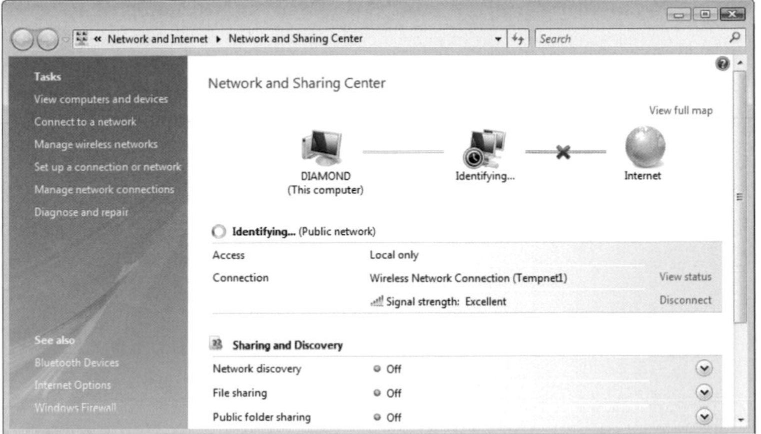

If you haven't specified Save this Network, the ad-hoc network will be set up, on a temporary basis, as Unidentified with Public location.

1. Windows asks for the location – Home, Work or Public

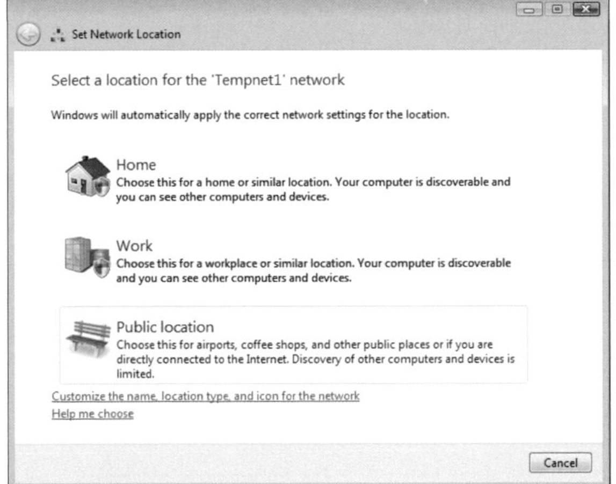

You should choose the more restricted Public unless you are going to share files or printers, since this is the safest mode of operation.

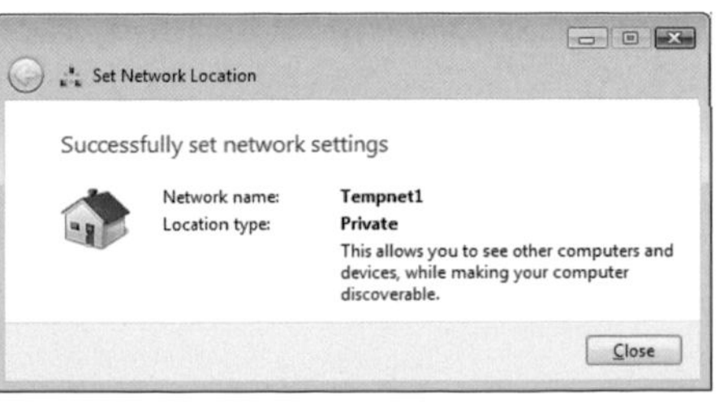

2. When Windows has applied the settings for the location, click Close

Share Files and Printers

Hot tip

The Network and Sharing Center will also show details of any other wireless or wired network connection active on the particular computer.

Don't forget

To see the computers currently connected in the ad-hoc network, select View full map.

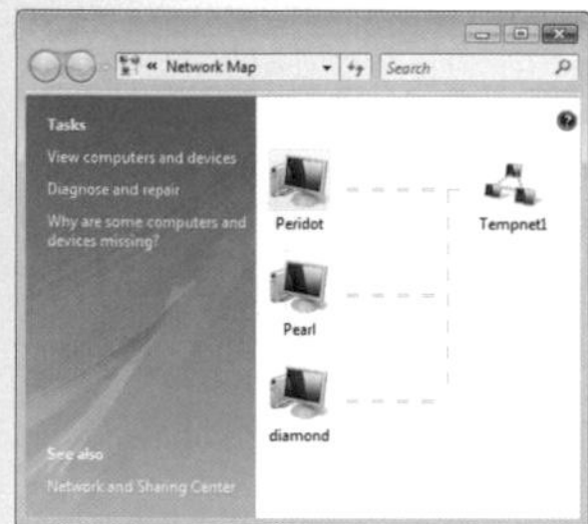

When you select Home or Work, Windows turns on Network discovery, File sharing and Public folder sharing. These settings are displayed in the Network and Sharing Center.

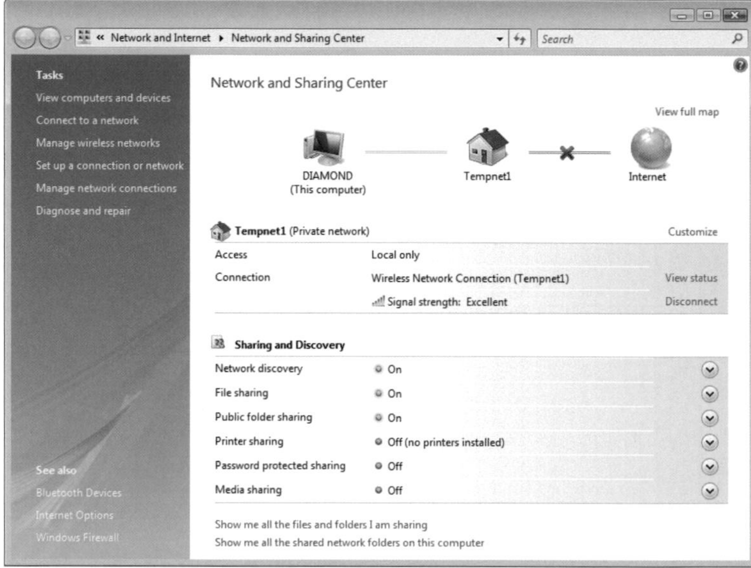

If there's a printer, Printer sharing is also turned on. Password protected sharing and Media sharing are both turned off.

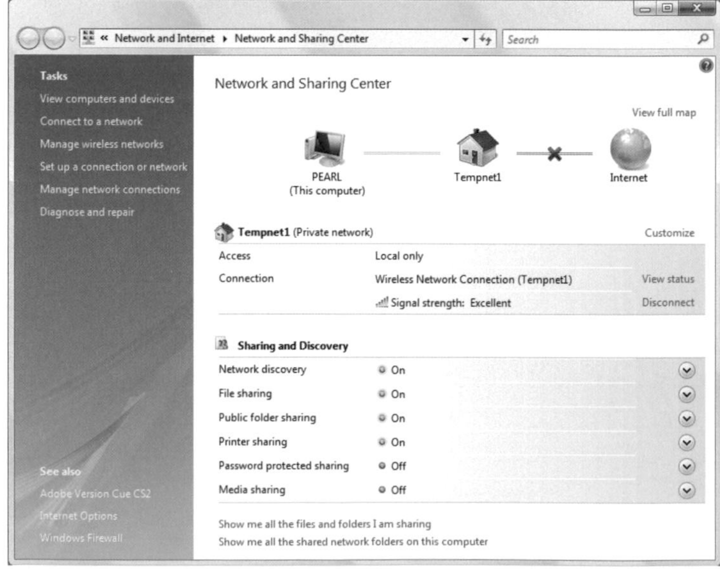

In the Printer folder for the computer (Pearl) with the shared printer, you'll see Windows has applied the Sharing option to the default printer and also to the other printers defined (in this example these are software devices for PDF and OneNote).

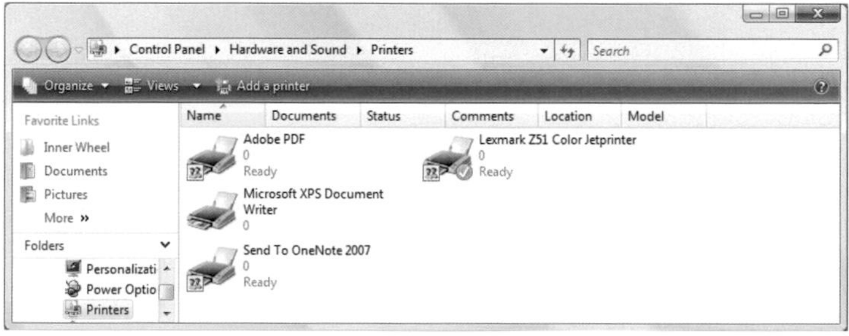

Hot tip

The People flag attached to the printer icon indicates that sharing has been applied to that device.

1. Click View Computers and Devices in the Network and Sharing Center and double-click the computer (Pearl)

Don't forget

All the computers that are currently connected to the ad-hoc network will be displayed.

2. You'll see printer devices and the Public folder

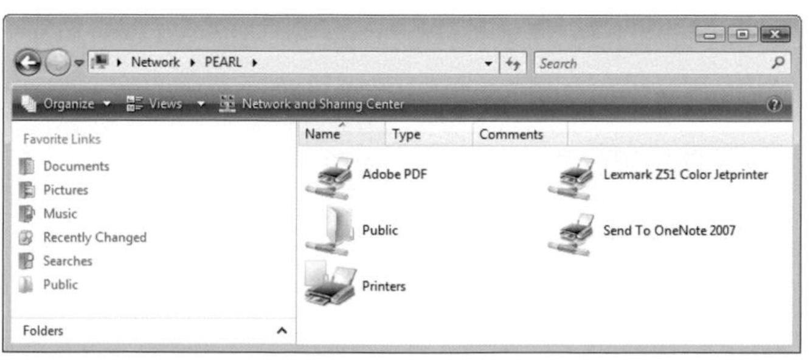

Beware

There may be other drives and folders shown as shareable. However, these are not accessible in the ad-hoc network environment.

Internet Connection Sharing

Hot tip

If there is an Internet connection, for example via a wired router/modem, you can share this when the ad-hoc network is created.

1. Click the option to Turn on Internet connection sharing

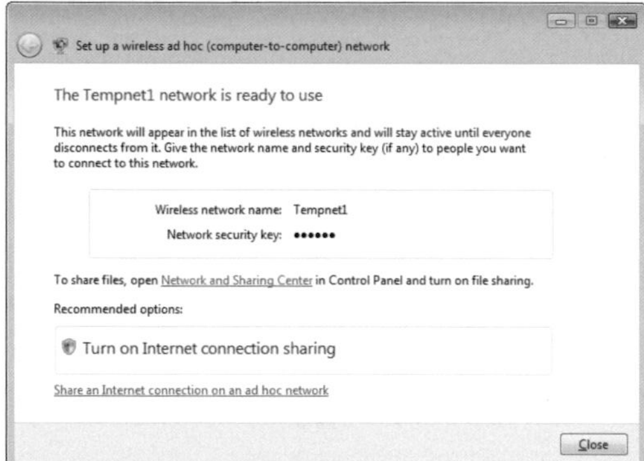

2. The Network and Sharing Center will show a connection for the Internet and one for the ad-hoc network

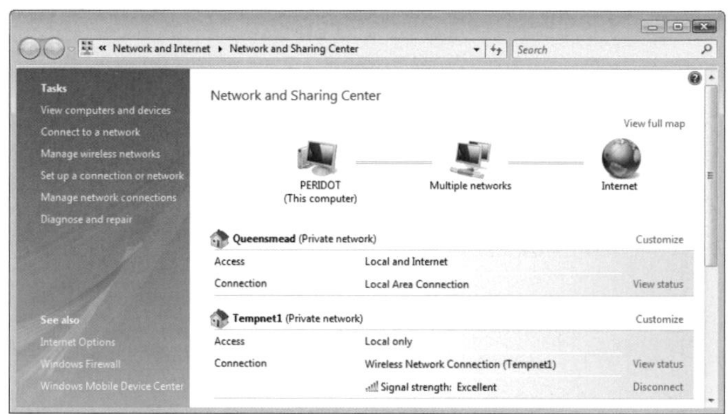

3. A second computer connected to the ad-hoc network will have access to the Internet via the originating computer

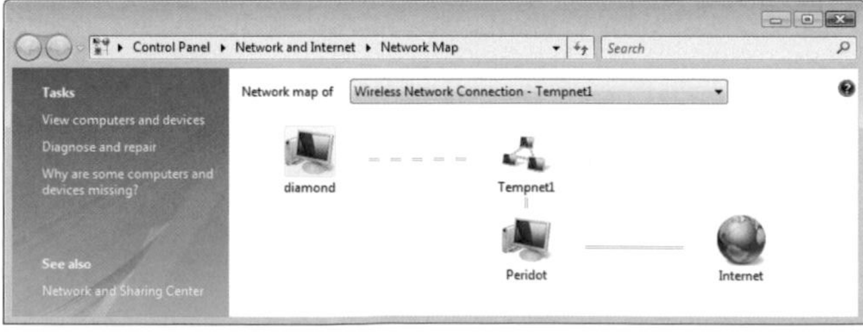

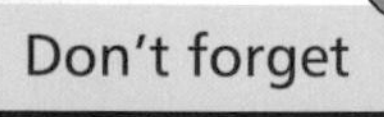

Don't forget

This is meant for use with temporary networks. You'd use a wireless router or access point to make an ongoing connection to the Internet.

Game Playing

Whenever you and some friends are in the same location with your wireless enabled computers, you can set up an ad-hoc network and participate in a multiplayer game, for example Checkers or Chess from Style-7.

1. Visit the Style-7 website at www.styleseven.com and click the link for the Chess-7 game

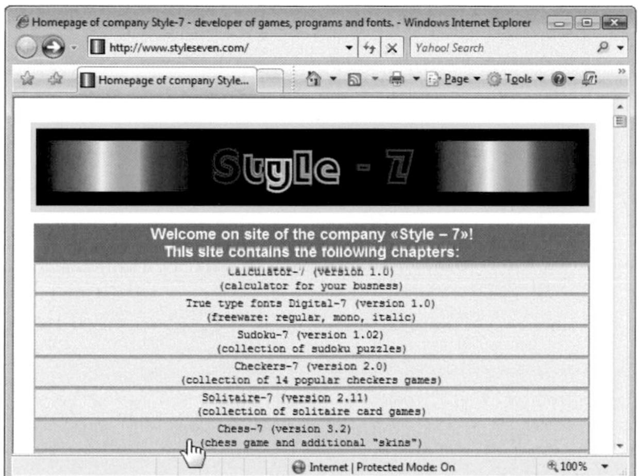

Hot tip

These examples are games for two players. Games such as Counter Strike and Age of Empires support larger numbers of players.

2. Scroll to the Download section and click Chess-7 to download the seven day trial version

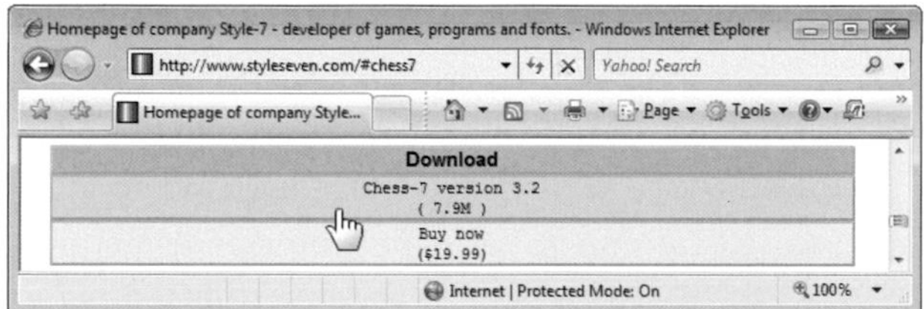

3. Download and save the Chess-7.exe installation file, and share copies with anyone who wants to play over the ad-hoc network

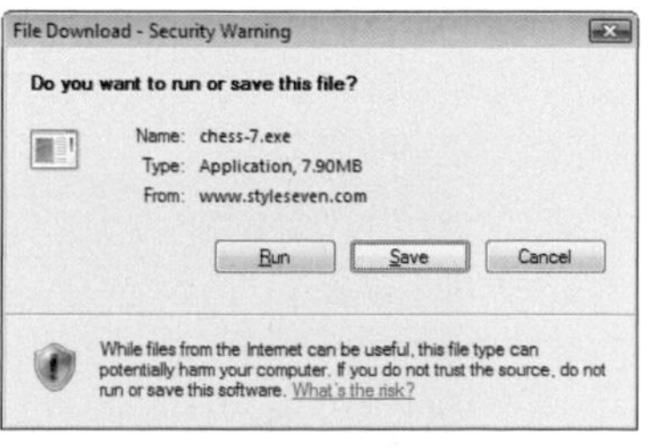

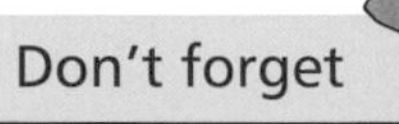

Don't forget

The Chess-7.exe file must be run on each computer to install the game. It is added to the All Programs, Style-7, Chess-7 folder on the Start menu.

Find the IP Address

You'll need to know the network address for the server computer.

1. In the Network and Sharing Center click View Status for the ad-hoc network wireless adapter

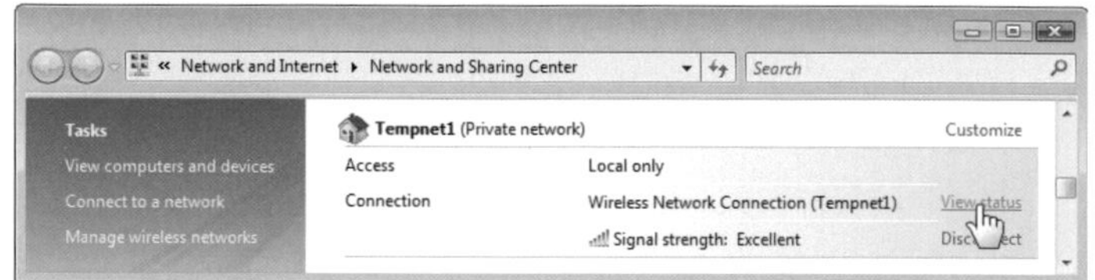

Hot tip

To play a game over the network, one computer usually acts as the host or server, while the others are clients.

2. The Wireless Network Connection Status panel shows the connection speed and signal quality.

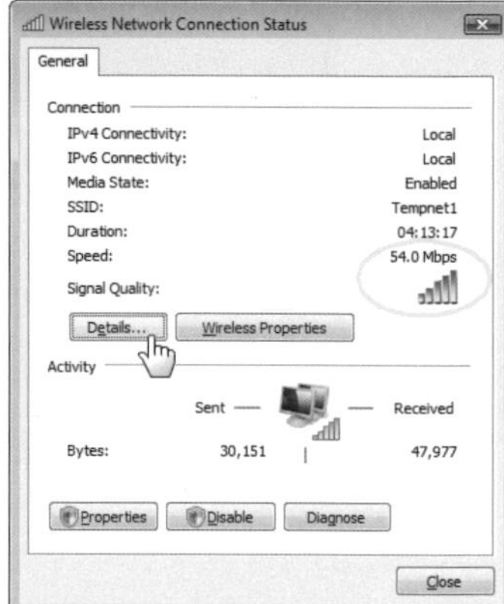

3. Click the Details button to display the Network Connection Details panel

Don't forget

The IP or Internet Protocol address is a logical number associated with the wireless adapter.

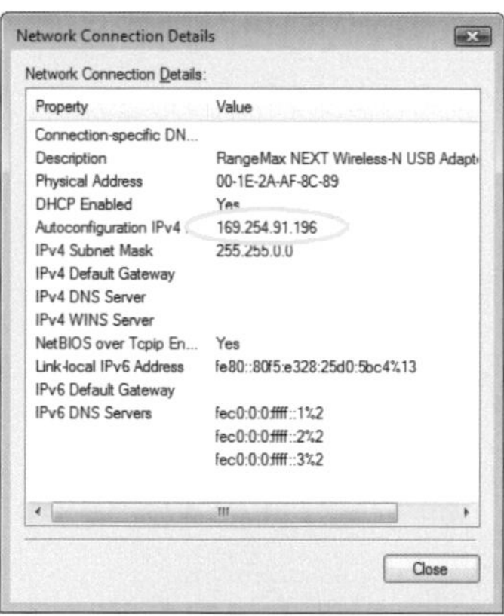

4. This shows the local IP address assigned to the wireless adapter in this case 169.254.91.196

5. You can also show the IP values on the computer by typing Ipconfig at the command prompt

Beware

There may be other IP addresses associated with the computer, for the Wired Ethernet adapter or for the router/modem. You need the wireless IP address for ad-hoc network gaming.

Playing the Game

1. Start the program on the server, select Game and click Network

Game
New... CTRL+N
Network... CTRL+K
Exit ALT+F4

2. Start game as Server, specify the server's IP address and click Start

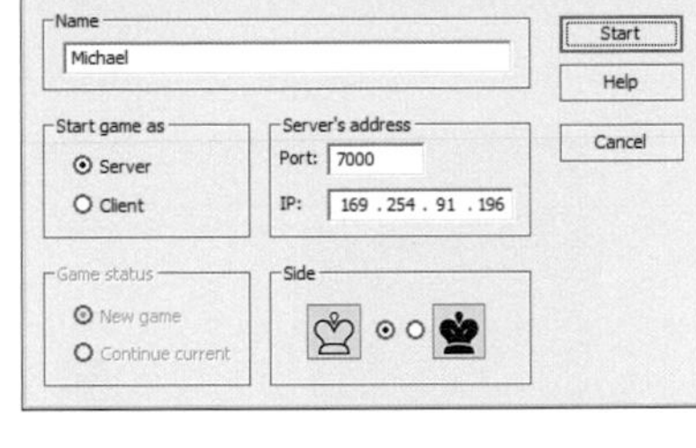

3. The server will wait for the Client to start

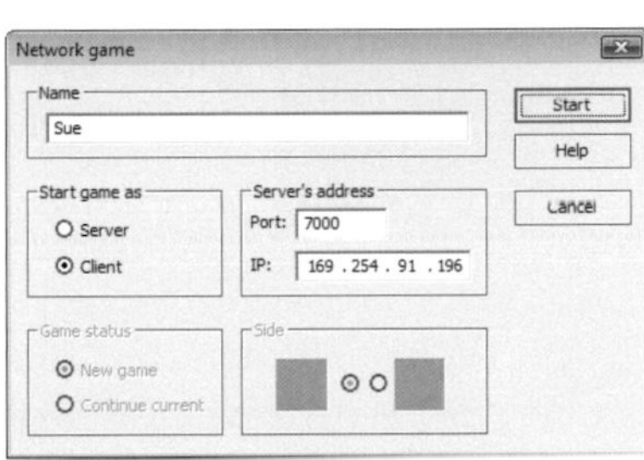

4. On the other PC select Start game as Client, specify the server's IP address and click Start

5. Take turns to make your moves to complete the game

Beware

You must tell Windows Firewall to unblock incoming messages for this program on your private networks.

Don't forget

Moves on one computer are communicated to the other and the boards are updated on each. Records of the moves made and pieces taken are kept.

Disconnecting

The ad-hoc network remains active as long as the originating computer plus at least one other computer is connected.

1. To remove a computer from the network, open the Network and Sharing Center and click Disconnect

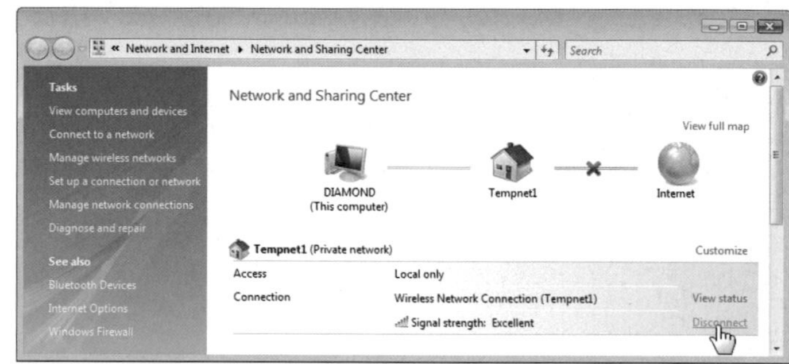

2. When all the other computers have disconnected, the originating wireless adapter remains waiting for users

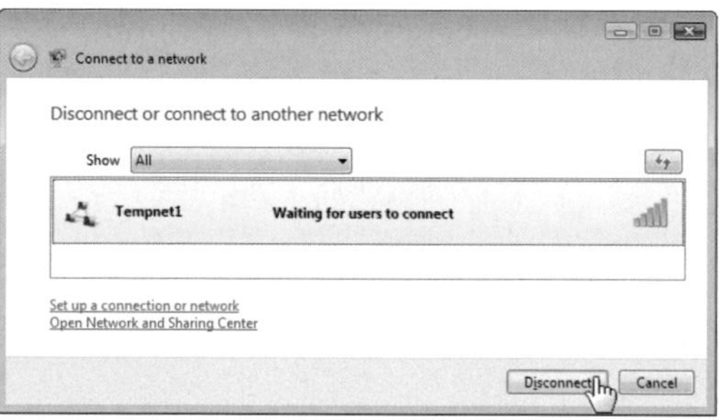

3. To terminate the ad-hoc wireless network completely, select Disconnect then click the Disconnect message box to confirm, and the network will be removed

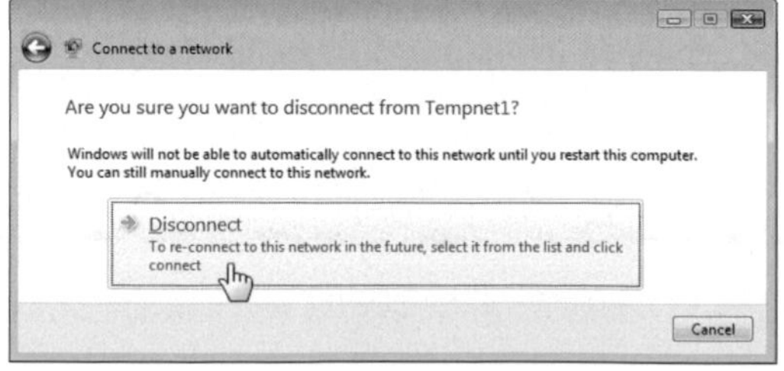

When you disconnect, the network is removed from the Network and Sharing Center.

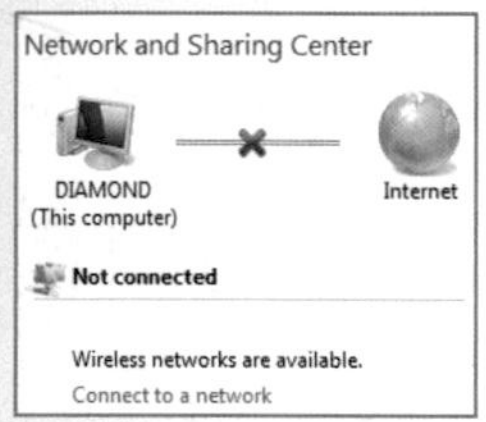

You can reconnect to the network if you saved the definition (see page 49), otherwise you'll need to redefine it from scratch.

4 Wireless Peer-to-Peer Networks

With your wireless adapters installed, the next task is to install and configure the wireless router/modem. Then you can set up the Internet connection and complete the router configuration, so you can add computers to the network for a peer-to-peer workgroup.

Wireless Router/Modem

Hot tip

For a permanent wireless home network environment, the ad-hoc network is not the most practical, since the host computer must always be powered up. There are also limitations on the level of security.

The preferred wireless network for the home is the peer-to-peer workgroup. For this you need a wireless access point or router, plus a cable or ADSL modem for Internet access. The usual approach is to install a combination device. For our example network, we will use the NetGear DGN2000 Wireless-N Modem Router, which combines a four port Ethernet switch, router function and ADSL modem.

Don't forget

The quantity and type of microfilter included will vary by region.

This is shipped with the following items:

- AC power adapter suitable for your region
- Ethernet cable
- Telephone cable
- Microfilter
- Resource CD (Installation software and manual)

Before installing your router/modem, it is very useful to make yourself familiar with the buttons and ports offered, and in particular with the LEDs provided and the signals that these offer.

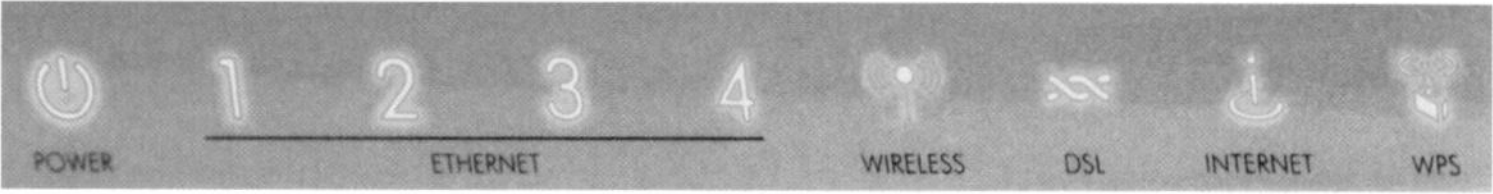

Hot tip

See the Setup Manual on the Resource CD for a complete list of the LED color and status settings.

On the DGN2000, the LEDs consist of:

- Power - Red: Power-on self test (POST) failure
- Ethernet Green: 100 Mbps, Amber: 10 Mbps
- Wireless Blinking Green means data is being sent
- [A]DSL Green: synchronized, Amber: being trained
- Internet Port Green: active Internet session
- WPS Green: wireless security enabled

On the side panel, there is a button that allows you to turn the Wireless function on and off. There's also a WPS setup button for attaching devices. Pressing both buttons simultaneously acts as a hardware reset, to return the router to the factory settings.

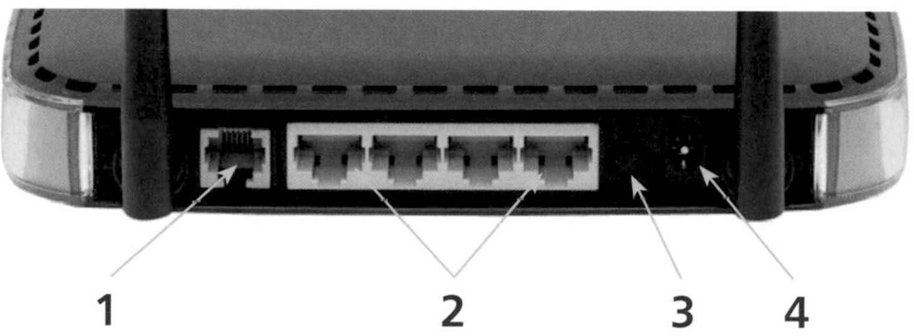

The rear panel contains the following items:

1. ADSL port (RJ-11) to connect to the telephone line
2. Four Ethernet LAN ports (RJ-45) for wired connections
3. Power on/off button
4. AC power adapter input

The ports on the router are color-coded to distinguish the Internet port from the other four Ethernet ports.

Positioning the Wireless Router

The operating range of your wireless connection depends on where you place the device. For the best results, it should be near the center of the area where your computers and other devices will operate, preferably within line of sight of these devices. It should be elevated, and kept away from electrical devices such as ceiling fans, home security systems, microwaves, or cordless phone bases. The number and the thickness of walls between the router and the computers will significantly affect the range.

Hot tip 

WPS (Wi-Fi Protected Setup) allows for simple configuration at the press of a button for devices that support this interface.

Don't forget 

One of the wired Ethernet ports is used to set up the router initially.

Beware 

Keep the router away from any large metal surfaces, such as a solid metal door or aluminum studs, or large expanses of other materials such as glass or concrete.

Installing the Wireless Router

The Smart Wizard on the Resource CD takes you through the steps required to connect your router, configure your wireless settings and access to the Internet. You need a computer with a wired Ethernet adapter to run the Smart Wizard and complete the configuration of your router.

1. Insert the Netgear DGN2000 Resource CD

2. If the CD does not start up automatically, run Autorun.exe

3. Click the Setup entry to Install Software

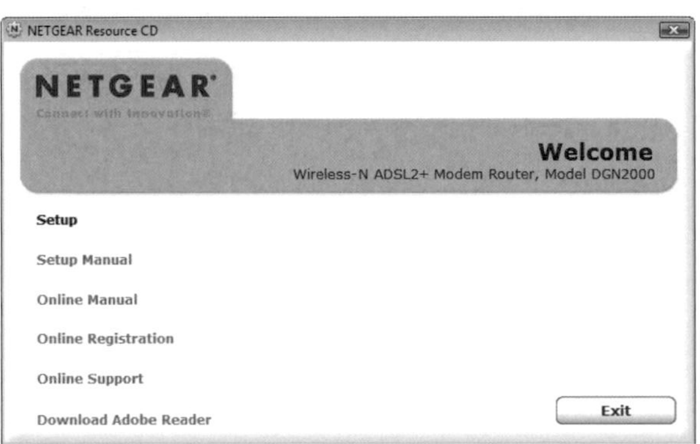

4. Before starting, make sure your ADSL Internet service connection is active and you have the configuration data

Hot tip

The wizard guides you through the setup process. It automates many of the steps and verifies that the steps have been successfully completed.

Beware

If you have a Macintosh or Linux system, you need to use the manual installation method where you log directly on to the router to adjust the settings.

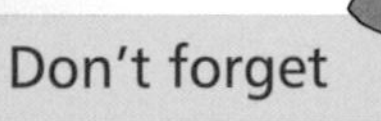

Don't forget

Close all applications before continuing with the installation.

The wizard explains everything you need to know. For example, it tells you about microfilters and shows you the types available.

1. Select the type of microfilter you have, i.e. Single or Dual

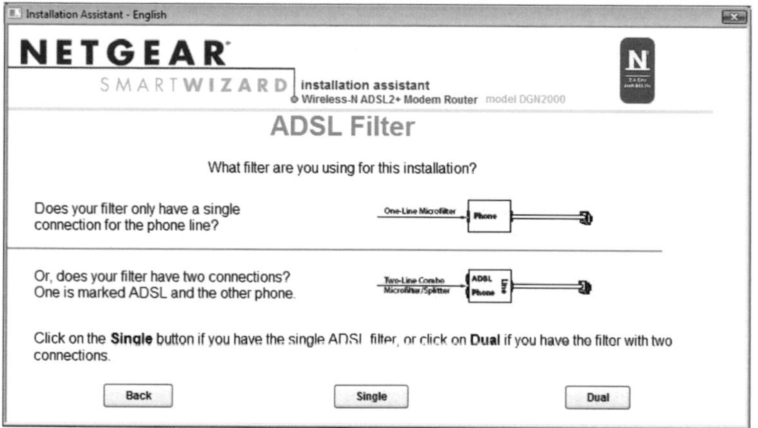

2. Follow the prompts to connect the router to the phone line and to the Ethernet port on your computer

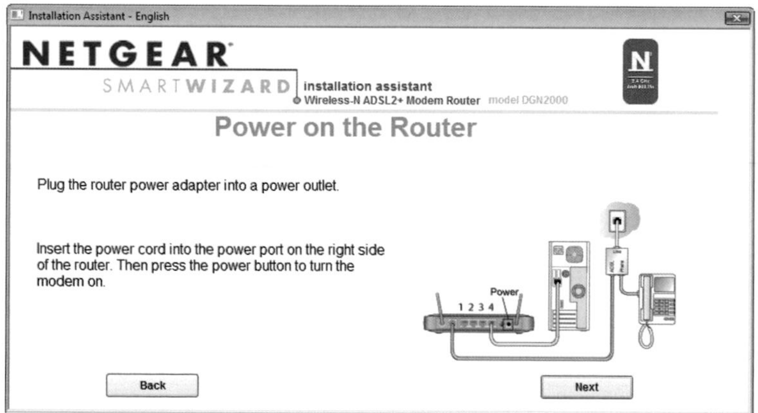

3. Plug in the power adapter, connect it to the router and press the power on button to turn on the router

The router will start up and go through the power-on self test procedure then initialize the connections.

Hot tip

Microfilters prevent noise interference between your telephone wiring and your modem. You must fit a microfilter to every telephone and telephone device that uses the same telephone line as the ADSL modem.

Beware

You must have a wired Ethernet adapter in the computer you use to set up your router. Fortunately, most computers do include such an adapter.

Don't forget

The specific details may vary but a similar installation process will be offered, whichever router you choose to install.

Verify Router Connection

The power, ADSL and wireless LEDs will light up. When the ADSL light turns solid green, the connection has been made.

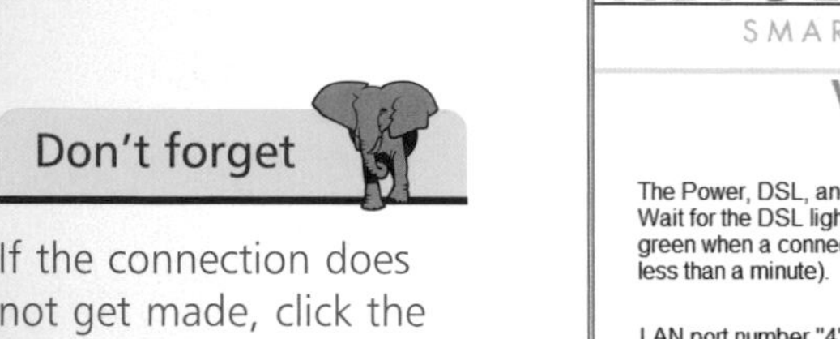

Don't forget

If the connection does not get made, click the Troubleshooting button for help and advice on resolving the problem.

1. Click Next and the Wizard will change the settings

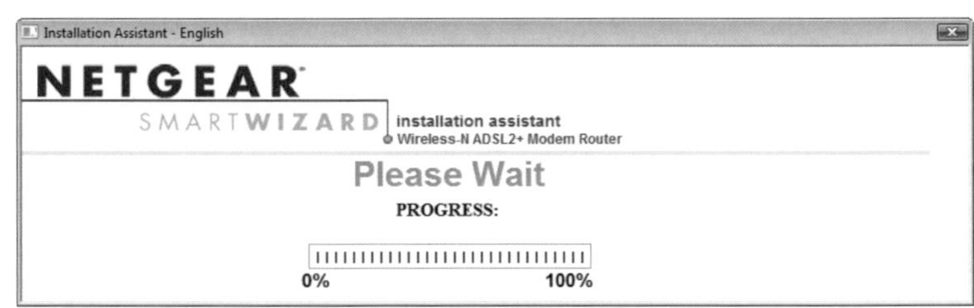

Hot tip

If there's more than one wired adapter in your computer, you may be asked to choose which one will be used to connect to the router.

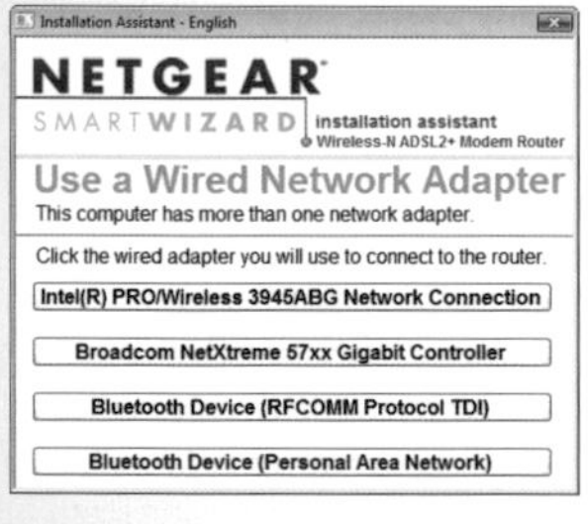

2. Select your country and language then click Next

Beware

From this point on the Configuration Assistant runs. This requires Internet access.

Administrator Password

Before configuring the Internet connection, you are given the opportunity to change the password used for administration from the default printed on the label attached to the router:

1. When prompted, enter a new password, retype it to confirm and then click Next

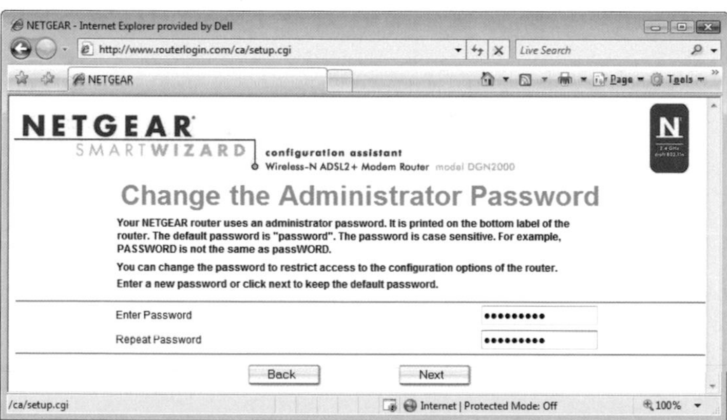

2. The Wizard will then detect your Internet connection

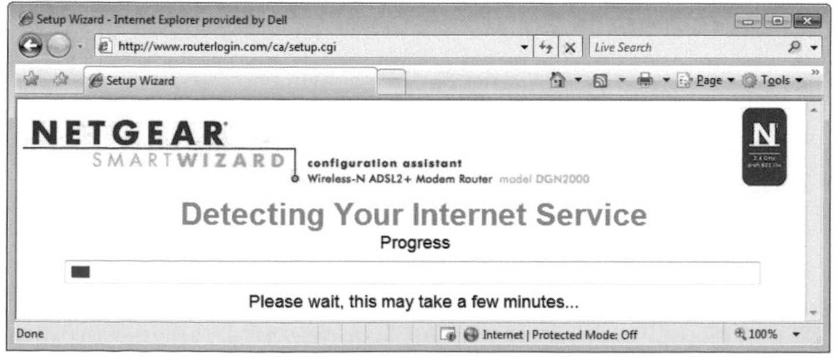

Hot tip

The label shows the router's MAC address, serial number, security PIN, as well as the factory default login information.

Beware

Pressing the two buttons on the side of the router will reset all settings, including the administrator password, to factory defaults.

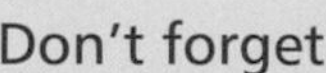

Don't forget

Your ADSL broadband service must be set up and active in order to complete the Internet connection setup.

Internet Connection Setup

ADSL in the UK uses Point-to-Point Protocol over Asynchronous Transfer Mode (PPPoA). Many other countries use Point-to-Point Protocol over Ethernet.

Your Internet sign on details are stored in the router. That is why it is essential to change the default password.

1. The Wizard will detect your Internet Service type

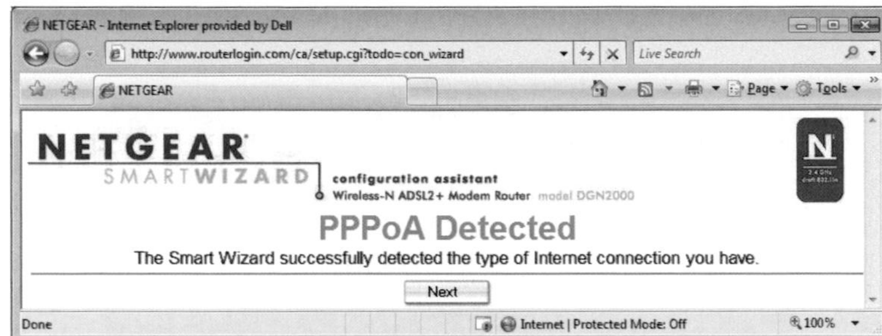

2. Enter your login details, e.g. email ID and password

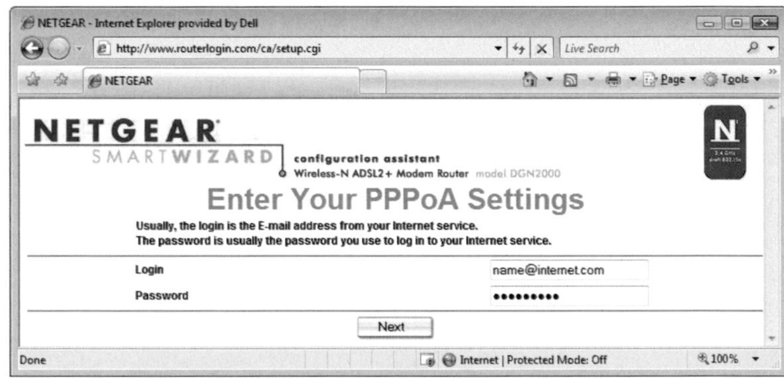

3. The router will update itself with your Internet settings

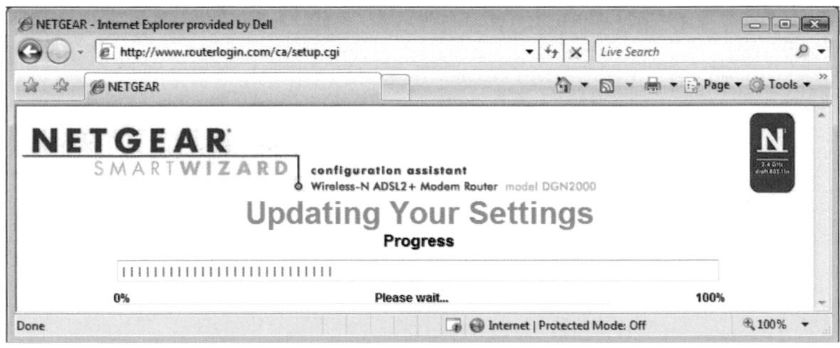

4. When this completes, wireless network can be completed

Configure Wireless Network

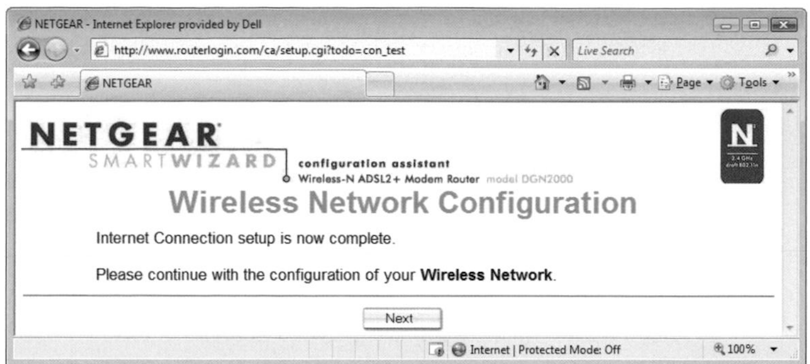

Hot tip

When the Internet connection setup has been completed, the configuration assistant moves on to wireless network configuration.

1. Select your region when prompted, then choose the wireless mode you want, either 130 Mbps or 270 Mbps

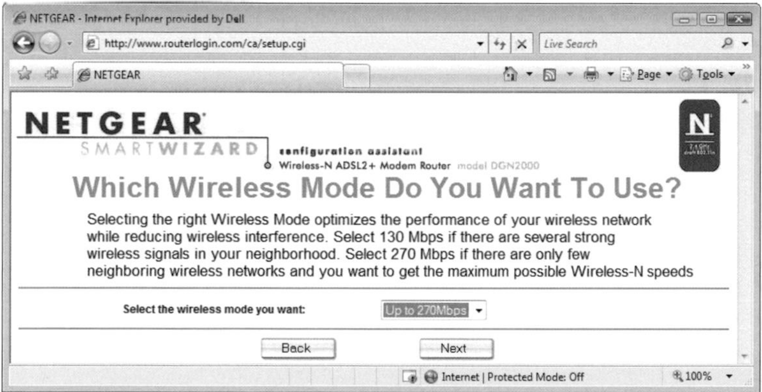

Beware

You should choose 130 Mbps if there are strong wireless signals in your area that might interfere.

2. Name your wireless network, replacing the default SSID (service set identifier) for Netgear, with a unique name

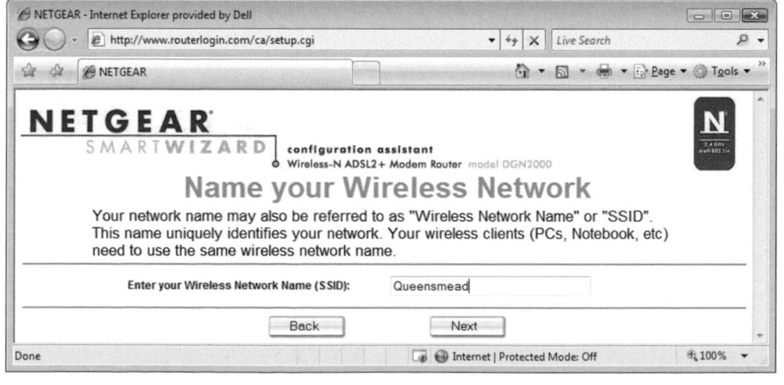

Don't forget

You must provide users of your network with the SSID and the password that you specify so that they can connect (see pages 70 and 72).

Wireless Network Security

Beware

If you don't choose to secure your network, anyone within range will be able to sign on and use your bandwidth or worse still, access your computer and data.

1 You should choose to secure your wireless network

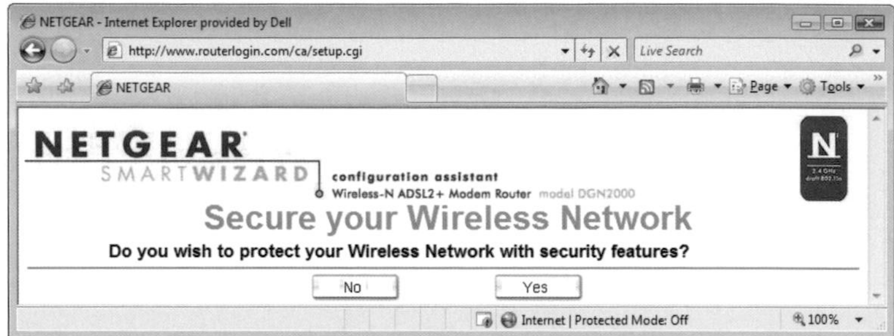

2 There are three types of wireless security offered, WPA (Wi-Fi protected access), WPA2 and WEP

Hot tip

Choose the highest level of security that is supported by your other network devices. For older devices, you'll need to select WEP.

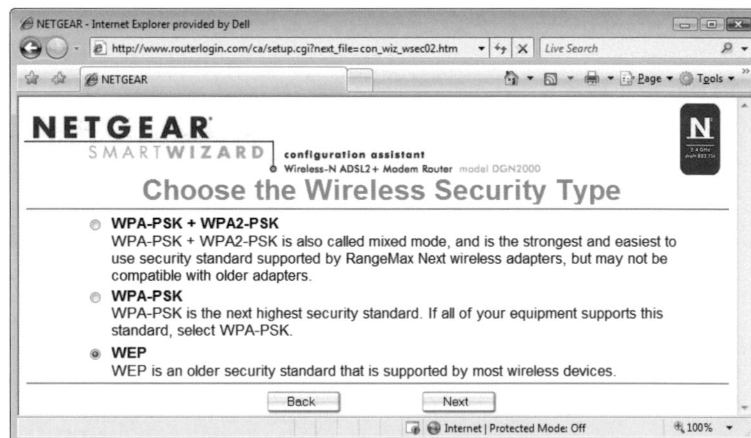

Don't forget

If this is a replacement router, and you already have a wireless key for your existing devices, use the same key when you configure the new router.

3 Enter the key that your wireless clients will be given

Router Setup Completed

The wireless network configuration is completed and a summary of your router's settings is displayed. This is the information required to connect computers on your wireless network.

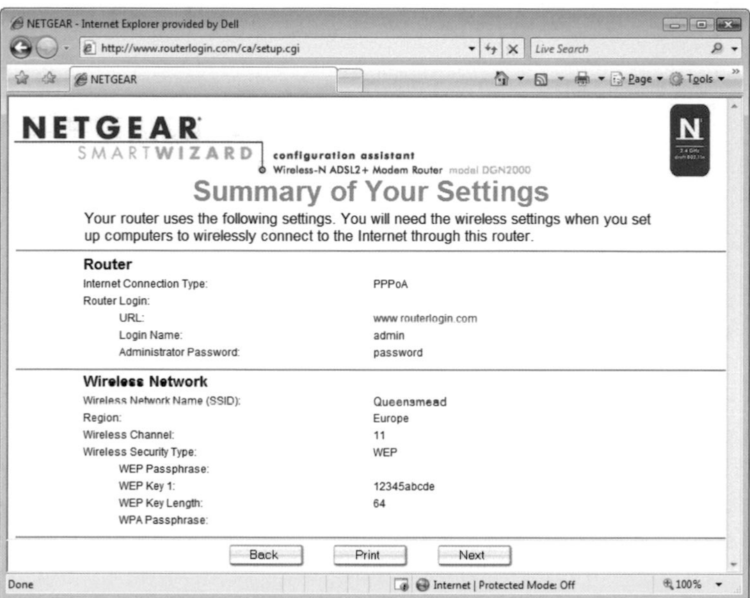

1. Click Next and the router configuration is completed

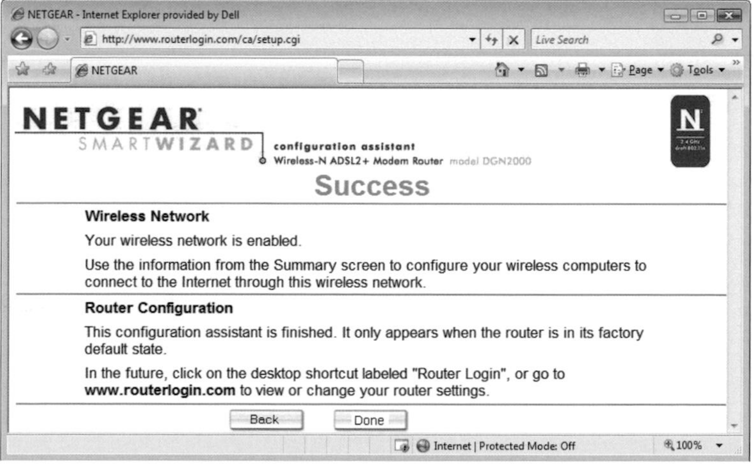

2. Click Done to terminate the Smart Wizard

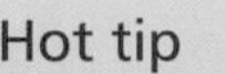

Hot tip

Click the Print button to make a permanent record of these details.

Don't forget

Click Router Login on the desktop or go to the URL www.routerlogin.com to view or change router settings.

Connect to Wireless Network

When the router is configured, remove the Ethernet cable, and set up the wireless connection for the laptop Diamond.

Hot tip

This assumes that you already have a wireless adapter pre-fitted or added to your computer.

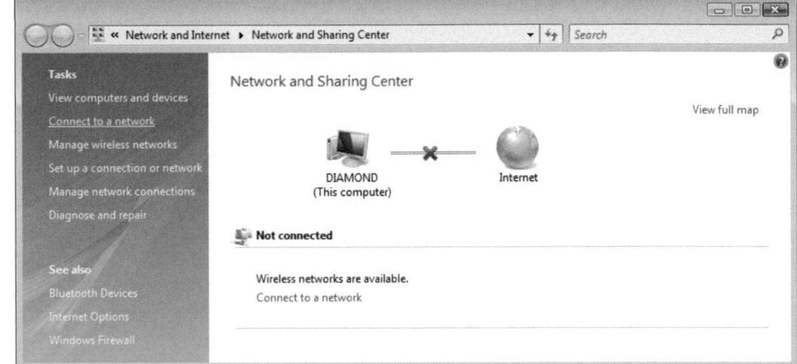

1. Open the Network and Sharing Center and select Connect to a network

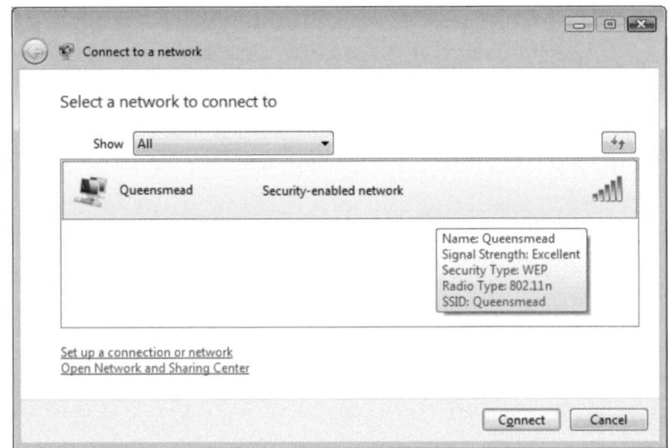

Don't forget

There may be other wireless networks in the neighborhood (see page 47 for an example).

Hot tip

If you have saved your security settings to a USB flash drive (see page 101) you can use this to provide the security credentials.

2. Select the new wireless network and type the security key

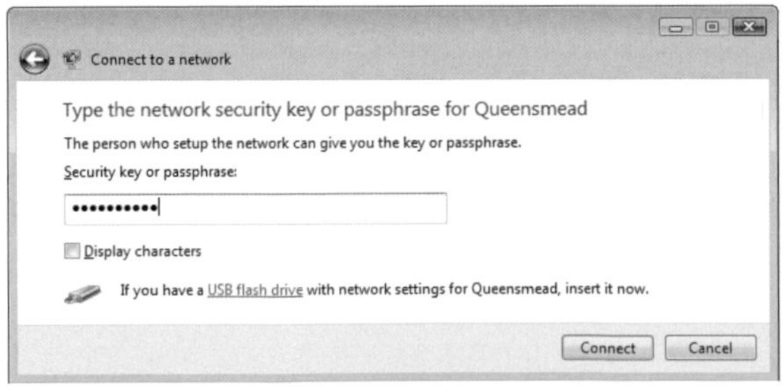

3. When the network is connected, choose to save the network and start the connection automatically

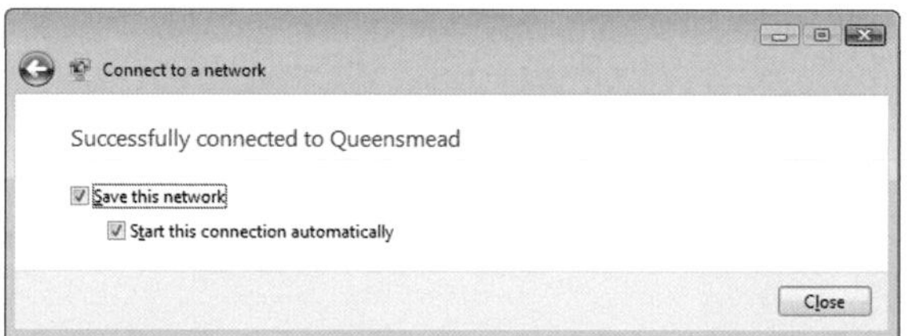

4. View the Network and Sharing Center to see the settings

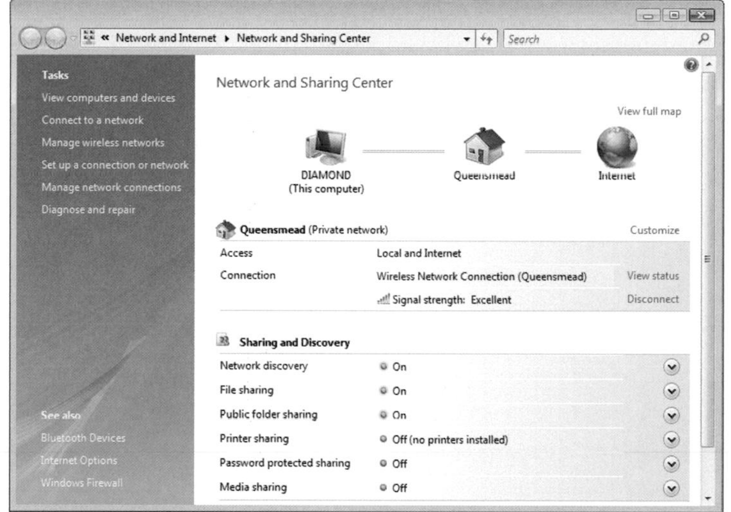

5. Click View Status to see the connection speed and signal quality.

The wireless adapter built into the laptop supports a speed of 54 Mbps

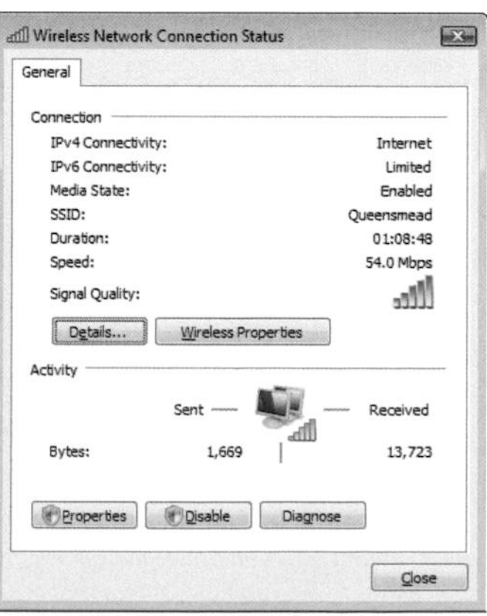

Don't forget

This allows you to connect to the wireless network whenever you are in range, without having to re-enter the security key.

Hot tip

Note that printer sharing is switched off for this computer since there is no local printer defined.

Add a Second Computer

1. Select Connect to a network on the desktop computer (Peridot), with the USB wireless adapter (see page 44)

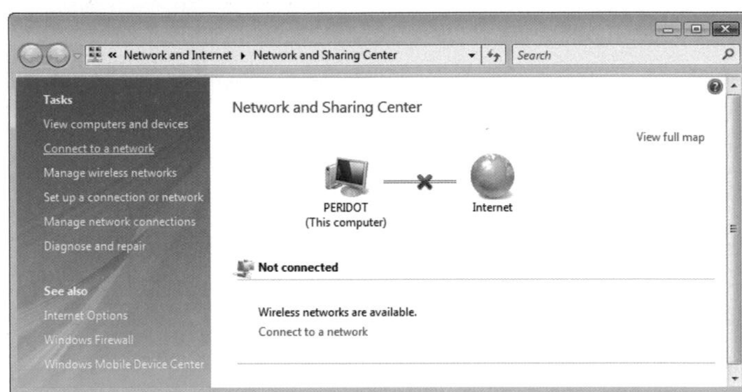

2. Select the wireless network and click the Connect button

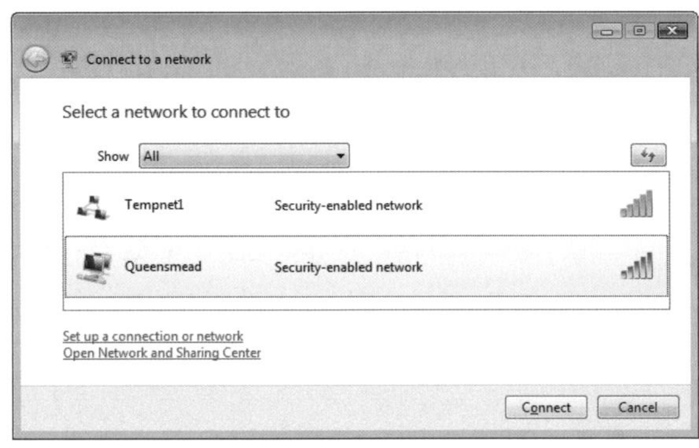

3. Type the security key when prompted and the connection to the wireless network will be established

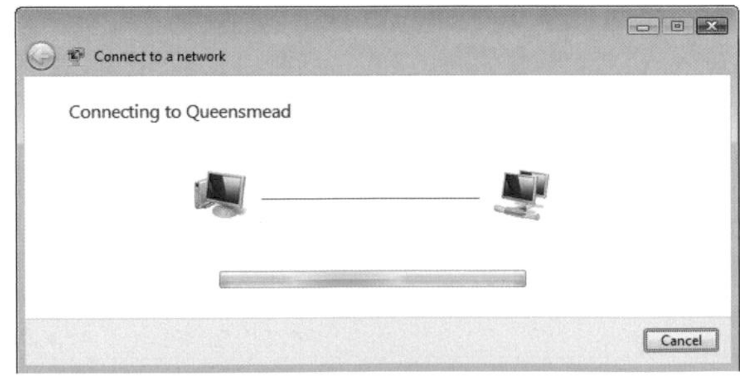

This computer uses the NetGear WN111 RangeMax Wireless-N adapter.

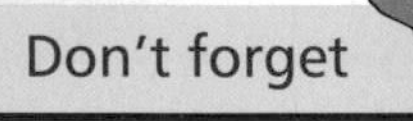

In this example there's a second wireless network defined, the ad-hoc network (see page 50).

Use your USB flash drive if you have set this up with your security details (see page 101).

4. When connected, select to save the network and to start the connection automatically

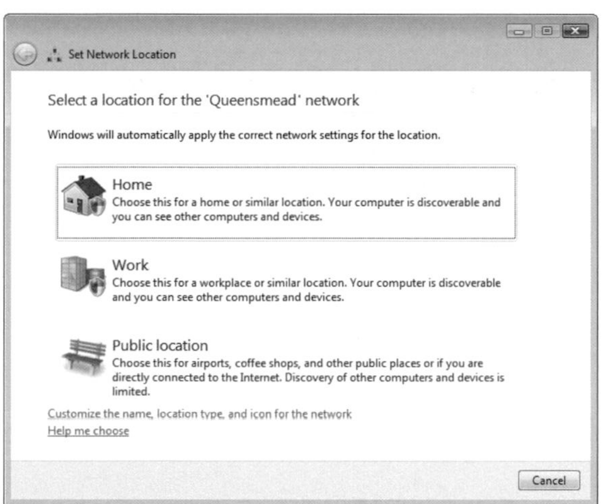

5. Select the Home location to define the network as Private

6. Select Network and Sharing Center, View Status to see the speed

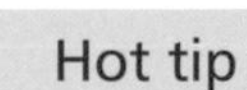

Note that printer sharing is switched on for this computer since there is a local printer defined.

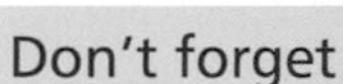

The WN111 adapter matches the DGN2000 router/modem and is able to achieve a speed of 270 Mbps.

Mixing Wireless Adapters

You can mix and match suppliers of wireless adapters. For example, the desktop computer Pearl has a LinkSys adapter

This adapter is the LinkSys WUSB600N, a Wireless-N USB network adapter with Dual Band support.

1. Network and Sharing Center, View Status shows that this adapter also achieves a speed of 270 Mbps with the NetGear DGN2000 router modem

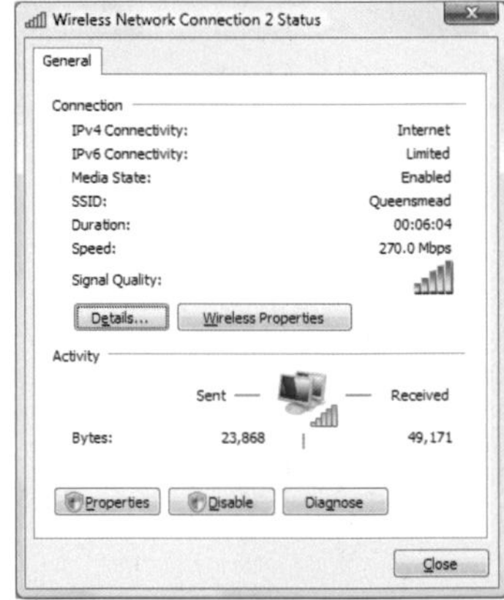

2. Click View Full Map in the Network and Sharing Center to see all the devices attached to the wireless network

Beware

You may not get the full speed from the adapter, due to the effects of distance or interference.

You could have wired Ethernet adapters as well as wireless adapters in your network.

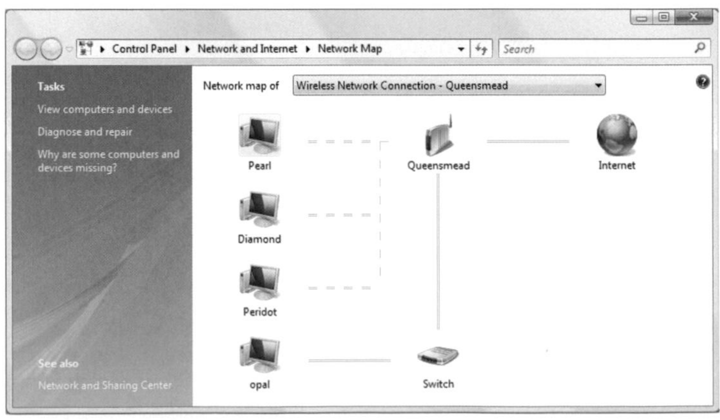

5 Networking with Mobile Broadband

If you have no landline or you travel a lot, you could set up your wireless network and Internet connection using mobile broadband, such as provided via the Vodafone modem which also lets you send SMS text messages. We also look at the 3 Mobile broadband devices and associated services.

Mobile Broadband

Hot tip

With Mobile Broadband, you can browse the Internet, collect emails or receive and send SMS text messages.

Beware

You may be provided with a cable that is double-ended. Use this when a single USB port does not provide enough power to support the modem (when using a USB hub for example).

Don't forget

The peer-to-peer network requires a telephone line or cable connection. Mobile broadband uses the 2G or 3G cell phone network to link with the Internet.

The peer-to-peer network with router and modem provides access to the Internet from anywhere within the house or office, but does not help you when you are traveling or away from your home base. However, there is another way to connect wirelessly to the Internet that you can use at home or away, in fact anywhere that you can use your cell phone.

With Mobile Broadband, the Internet can be accessed via a portable modem (also known as a mobile dongle), which is connected to your laptop via the USB port. The USB cables that are provided with the modem make it easier to reposition the modem to improve the reception.

There are also PC Card modems and USB stick modems that plug directly into the laptop.

Even easier to transport are the netbook computers with built in 3G mobile broadband facilities.

Both these methods avoid the need for cables but they may not always get the best reception.

To help investigate the mobile broadband approach, we will use Vodafone's Mobile Broadband USB Modem 7.2 (see page 79) which can attach with the USB stick or with a USB cable.

Mobile Broadband Services

These provide Internet access for laptops, PDAs, BlackBerrys and Smartphones. They offer 2G and 3G network support, which provides a speed faster than dial-up, but not as fast as what you may be used to with your cable or phoneline broadband connection. Mobile broadband services are not designed to replace the standard ISP, but are intended for low demand mobile use. Most services restrict or limit large data exchanges, such as streaming audio or video, P2P file sharing or multiple JPEG uploads. The functions typically supported include:

- Check Email – Send and receive email through your personal or your business email accounts
- Surf the Internet – Access the Internet and visit the full versions or cell-phone friendly versions of your favorite sites
- Access the Intranet – You can connect to your business Intranet through a secure connection, so you can work while you are traveling away from the office
- Connect to Wi–Fi HotSpots – Service providers may host hotspots in popular travel destinations and franchises such as Starbucks, where you can get a fast connection

Choosing your Mobile Broadband Service

The costs for mobile broadband services are similar, so coverage is usually the main factor when deciding which service is best for you. Remember that you should choose a service that provides good connections where you need them most, whether that is at home or in places or countries that you visit most often. You should also check the level of Wi–Fi access in the locations that you travel through when you are away from home or office.

Some services require you to have a voice plan with them as well, which may also influence your choice, one way or the other.

You may choose a service that offers additional facilities such as a netbook computer as part of the service, if you do not already have a suitable computer.

Finally you should take into account the level of help and support available, including telephone, email and information online such as FAQs, tutorials and documentation.

Hot tip 

If you are without a landline or cable service, the use of mobile broadband may be an economic solution that avoids the need to install those facilities.

Don't forget 

See http://cantoni.mobi/ for a list of websites suitable for mobile devices such as the iPhone, BlackBerry, Treo, or other smartphone.

Don't forget 

If you will be a light user of mobile broadband services, you may want to look for a pay as you go pricing plan.

Mobile Broadband Providers

To get an idea of the range of mobile broadband services available, http://mobile-broadband-services-review.toptenreviews.com/ provides comparison and reviews. At the time of writing, this has just six reviews. Perhaps this is indicative of a new and developing product area. You may find more when you visit.

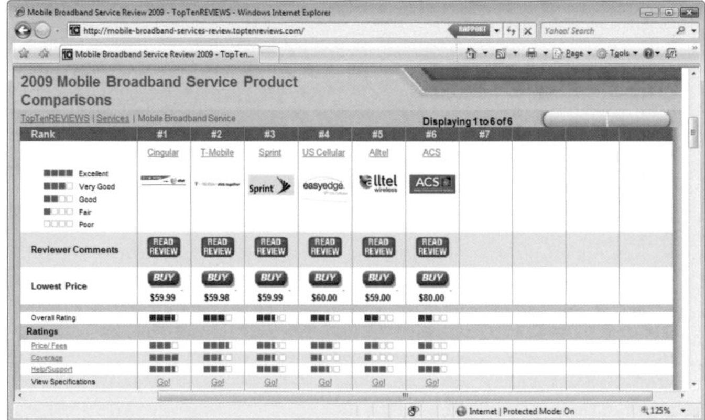

The services listed are for PC computers only, emphasizing the fact that things are more advanced for PC and Windows environments.

1. Click Read Review for more details, or scroll down to compare price, device support, coverage and tech support

You'll find similar websites for other countries. For example, visit http://www.broadband-expert.co.uk/ for UK information.

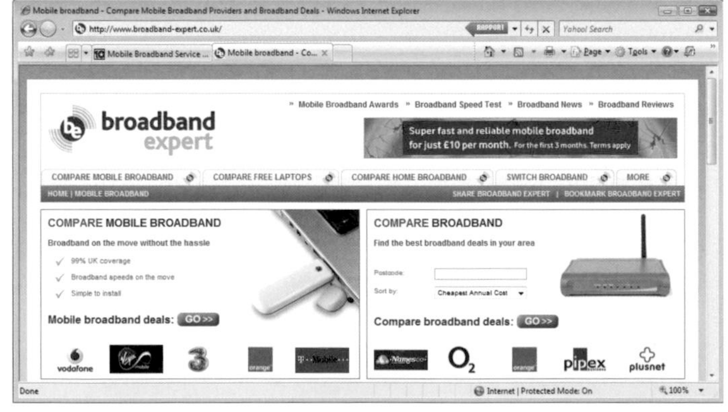

Details are also available for offers with free laptops included, and for home broadband (cable and landline) services.

2. Click the Go button for details of mobile broadband deals from Vodafone, Virgin, 3, T-Mobile, O2 and Orange

Set Up the Vodafone Modem

You'll need an activated Vodafone SIM card, which should normally be provided when the modem was purchased.

1. Plug the Vodafone Mobile Broadband USB Modem into an available USB port using the USB stick connector

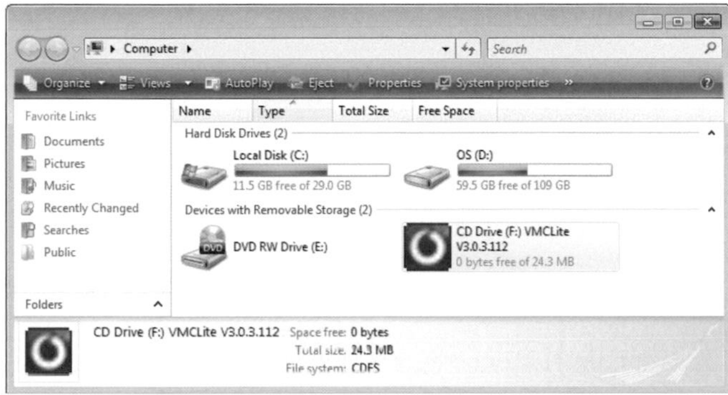

2. The storage component is added to the Computer folder as a removable CD drive, using an available drive letter

3. Depending on your AutoPlay settings, the Install program will launch immediately, or you can select it from the AutoPlay panel

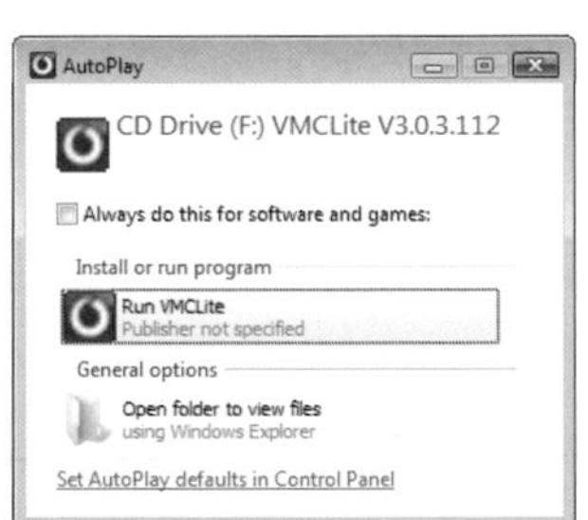

4. Specify the language to be used for the installation, e.g. UK English

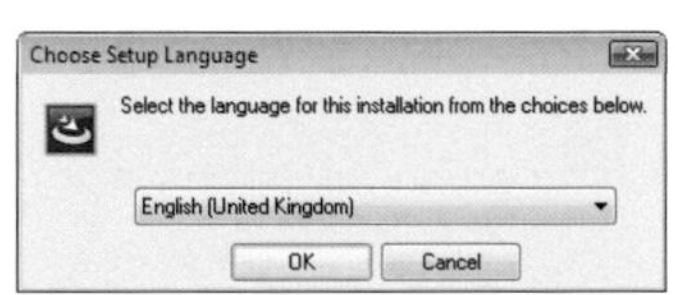

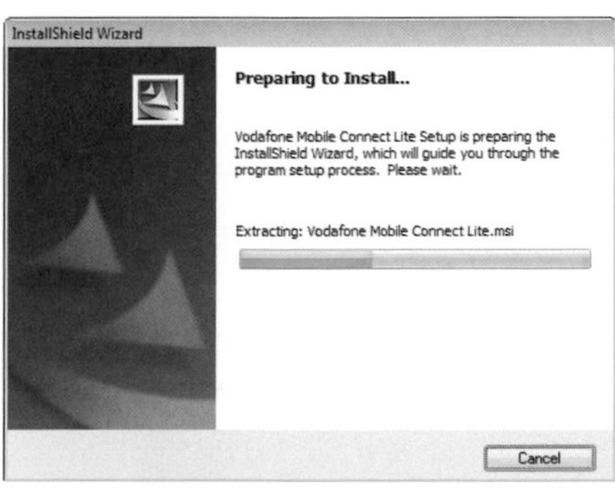

5. The files required to install and run the modem are copied to the hard disk on your computer

Beware

If the device does not power on, you may need to use the two-ended cable and two USB ports to power the modem.

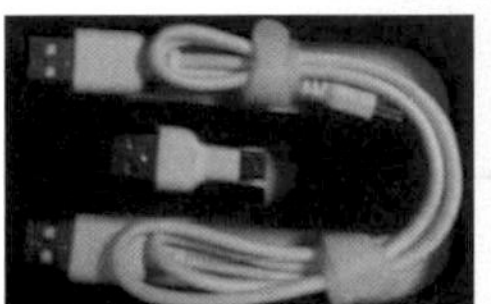

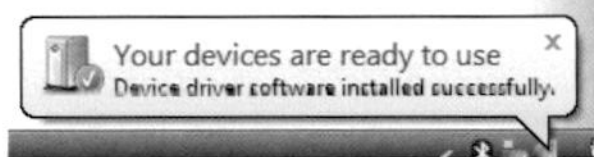

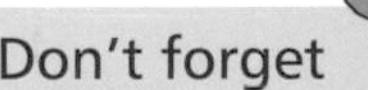

Don't forget

The first time the modem is attached to a particular system, the Install program executes. On subsequent occasions, the Vodafone Mobile Connect program runs (see page 80).

Installing the Software

The appropriate network operator for the location where you are installing the modem should be selected.

1 Confirm the suggested network operator, then click Next

2 Accept the License Agreement when prompted and click Next, and the program features will be installed

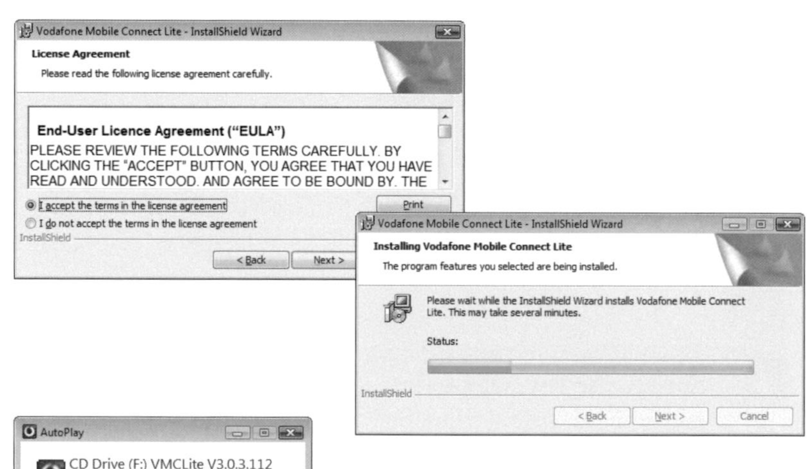

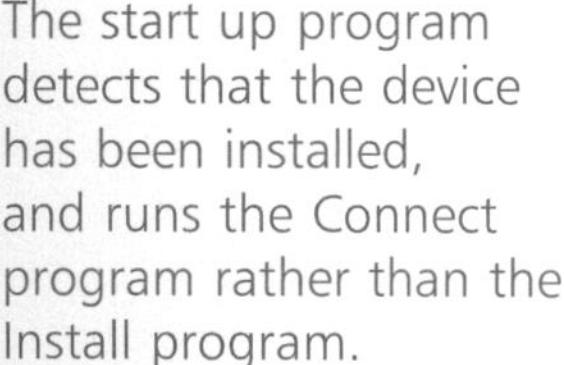

The start up program detects that the device has been installed, and runs the Connect program rather than the Install program.

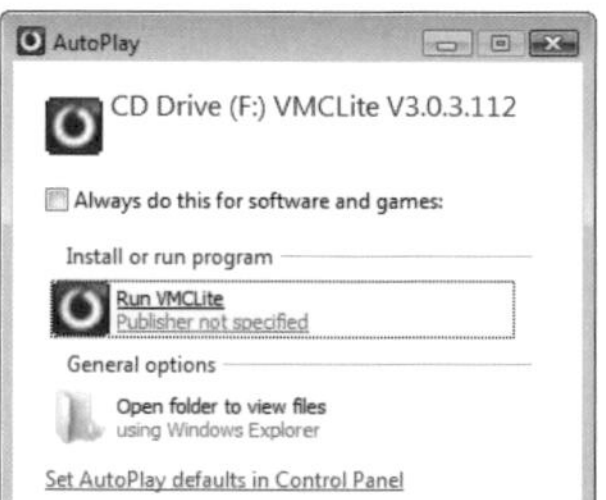

3 When the software is installed, your device is set up and the AutoPlay panel is re-displayed, this time to run the Vodafone Connect program

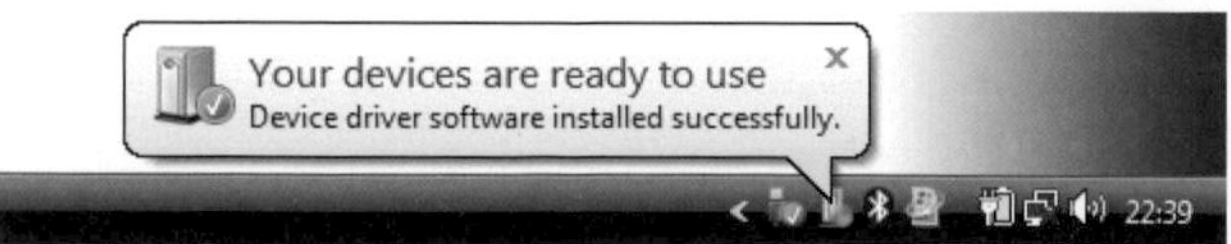

4. Select Run VMCLite and the Vodafone Mobile Connect program will start up

5. You'll be offered the option to connect to your selected network

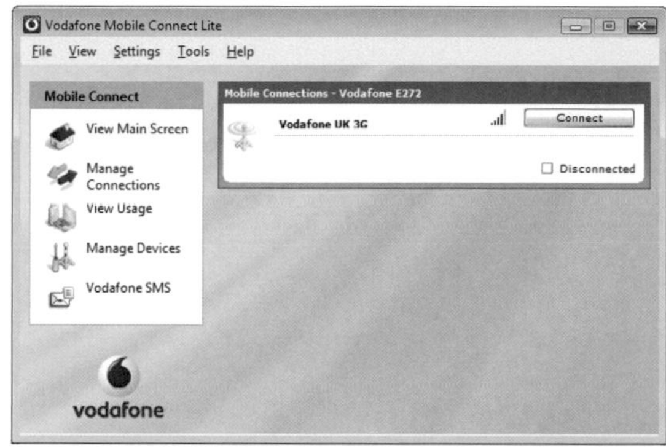

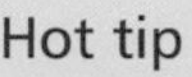

Hot tip

When the application starts, an icon is added to the system tray, where it joins the Safely Remove icon.

6. If you are not ready at this time to connect, click the [X] button to hide the application

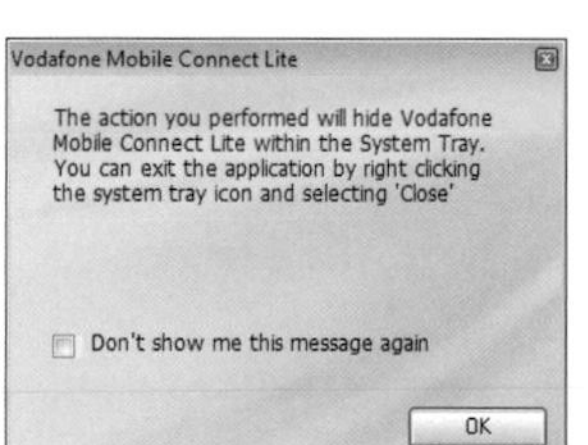

7. To exit the application, right click the system tray icon and select Close

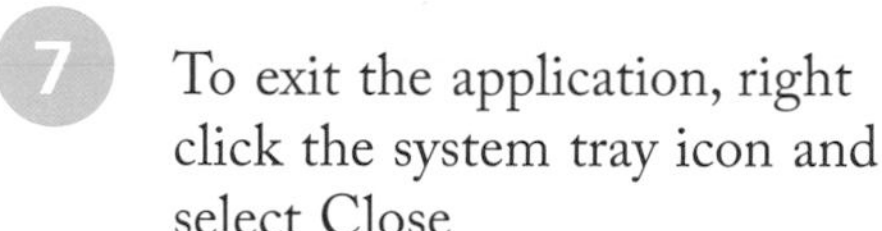

8. Before removing the modem, left click the Safely Remove icon and choose Safely remove USB storage device

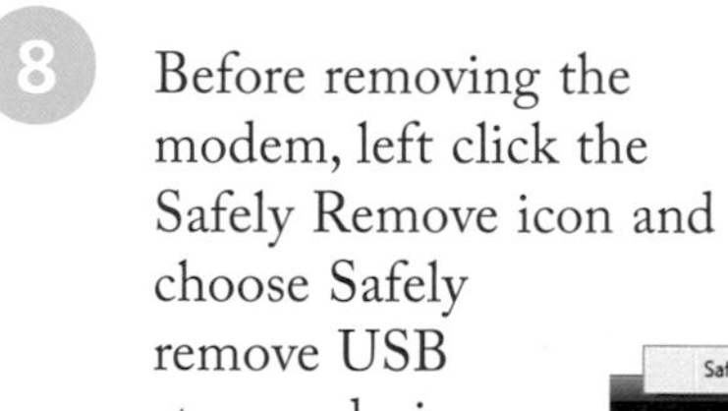

9. When prompted, remove the hardware device and then click OK

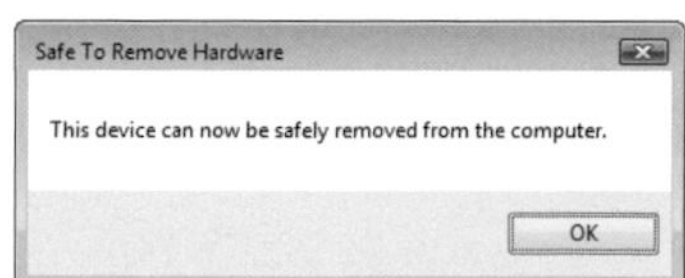

Don't forget

You'll need to go through the Close and Safely Remove steps whenever you want to remove the modem, except if you Shutdown the computer.

Get Connected

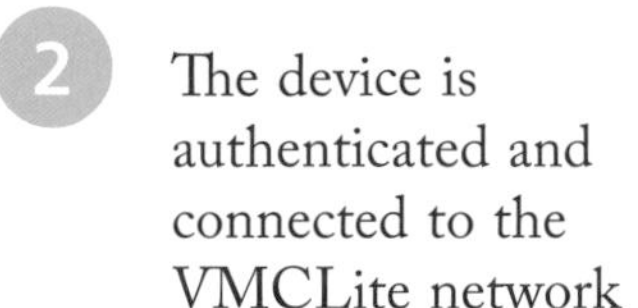

1 Connect the modem, start the Connect application and click the Connect button

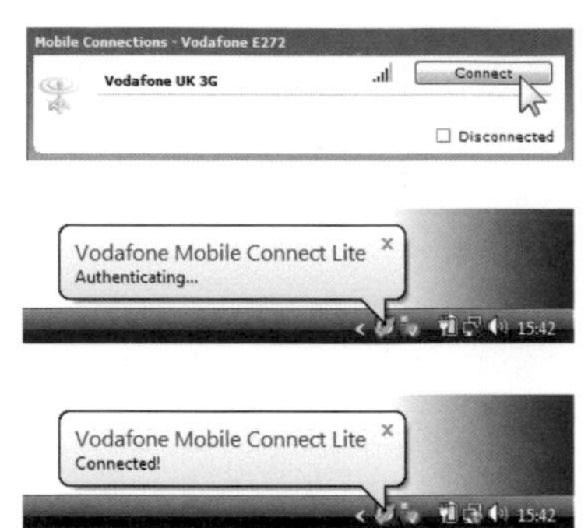

2 The device is authenticated and connected to the VMCLite network

The first time, you'll be asked to select a location for the network. Choose Public for the greatest security when you are using the modem away from home or office.

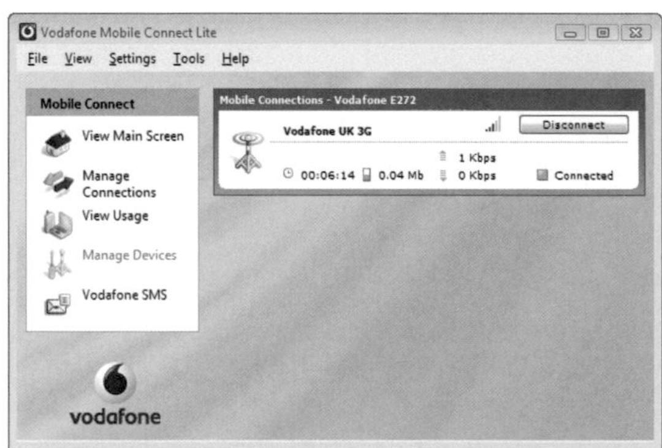

3 Visit the Network and Sharing Center to see details of the new connection

See pages 102-103 for more information about using the Network and Sharing Center in Windows Vista.

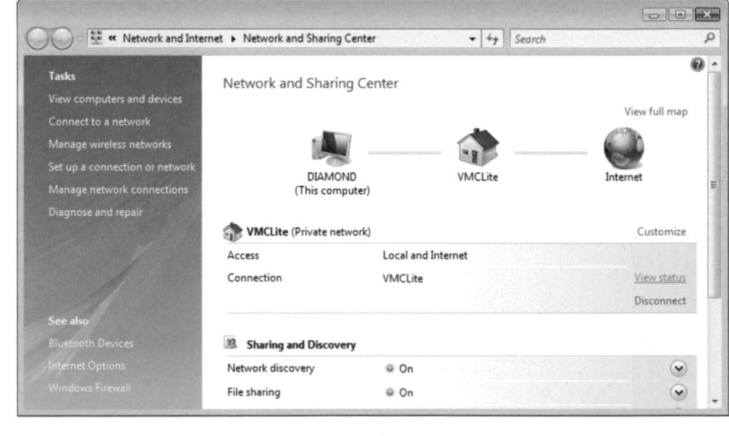

4 The network will be shown as connected to the Internet

5. For information about the network connection, click View Status

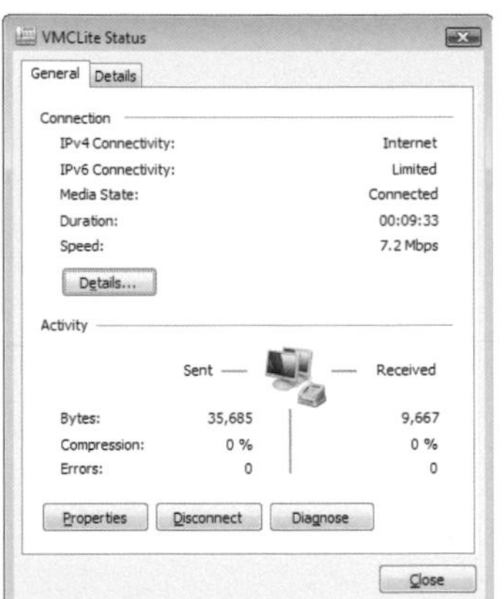

You'll see that the device is connected to the Internet at a stated speed of 7.2 Mbps. You'll also see details of the data volumes sent and received.

6. Click the Details button for more information

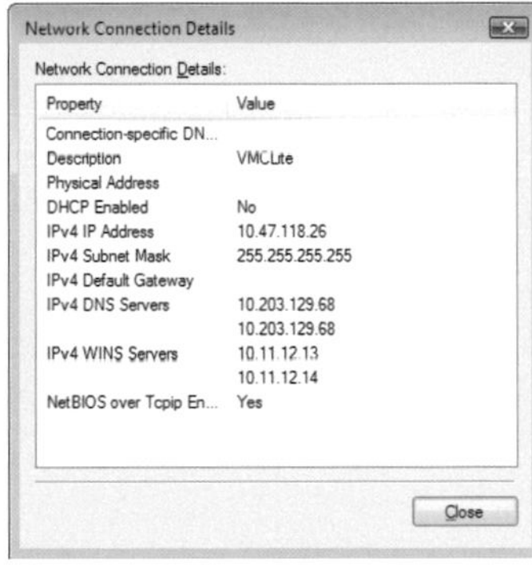

This shows the network connection details, in particular the IP (Internet Protocol) address allocated to the device. This is dynamically allocated, and may be different each time you connect to the network. It also shows the IP addresses of the host servers associated with the network service.

7. You can access your email and the Internet as desired. To check your performance, visit www.speedtest.net

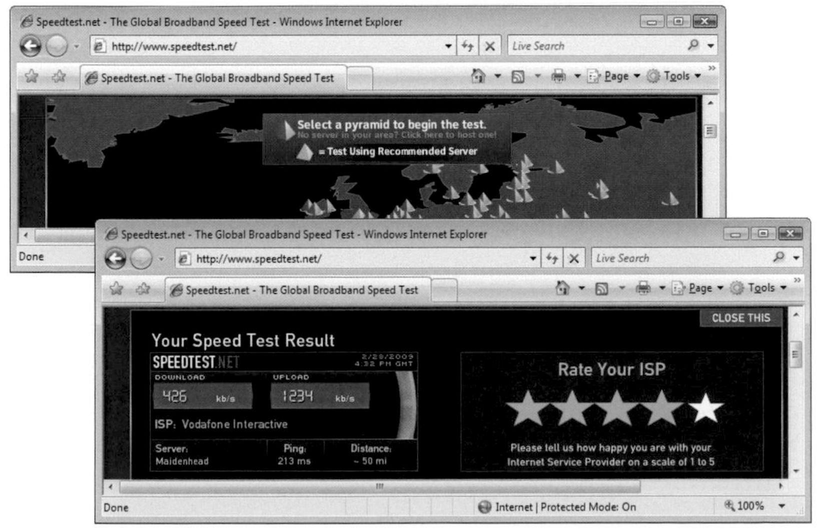

This shows the nominal maximum speed for the network. See below for an example of actual network performance.

Hot tip

The performance you'll get depends on the reception level and on how busy the network is in your area. To check actual speed, visit a website such as Speedtest.net that measures broadband performance.

Auto Connection

You can set up the mobile broadband modem to connect automatically to the network. However, you may first need to adjust the AutoPlay settings, if the AutoPlay panel displays when you plug in the device.

1. When the AutoPlay panel appears, click the link to Set AutoPlay defaults in Control Panel

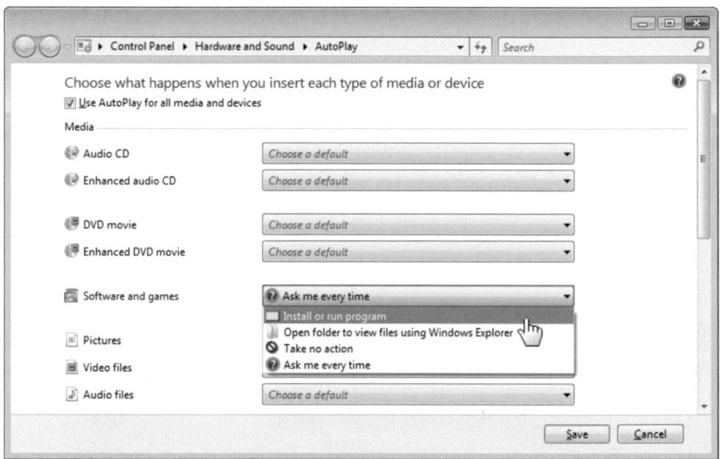

2. Click the down arrow for Software and Games Media and select Install or Run Program, then click the Save button to apply the change

From now on, when you plug in a storage device that contains a program, Windows will automatically install or run that program. When you plug in the mobile broadband modem, Windows will therefore detect and run the VMCLite program it contains.

Don't forget

You must change the AutoPlay settings and the VMCLite application settings to allow the mobile broadband modem to connect automatically to a detected network.

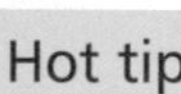

Hot tip

This change applies to other media such as CDs, DVDs or USB memory sticks that contain application programs.

Now change the settings to make the connection automatically

1. In the VMCLite application select Manage Connections

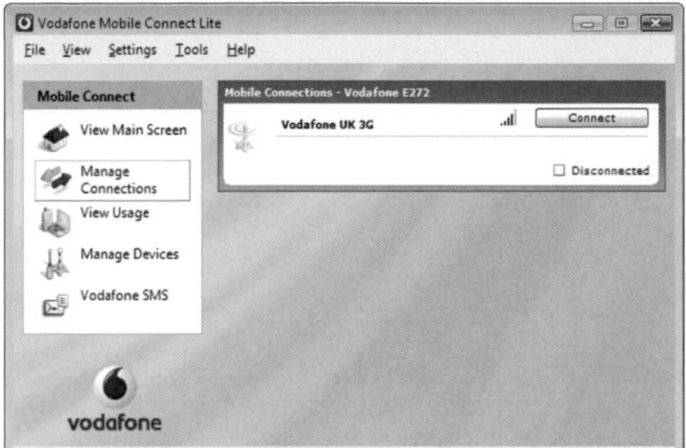

2. Click the down arrow and select Automatic Connection

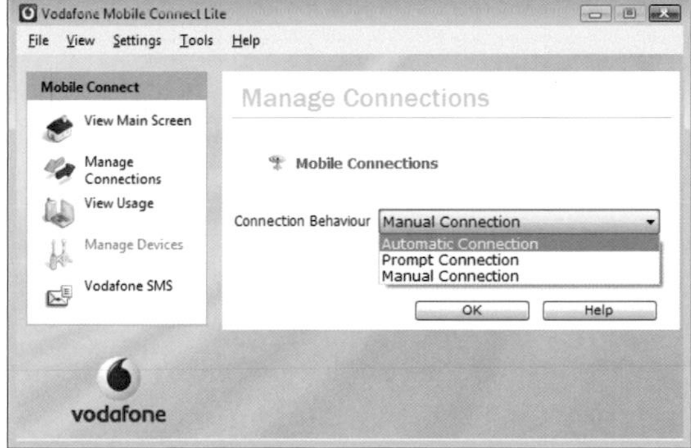

3. Click OK to save the changed settings

The application now automatically connects to a network once it has been detected. This can be after startup with the mobile broadband modem attached, or whenever the modem device is plugged into the computer.

Choosing Prompt Connection will cause a prompt to be displayed. Press Connect to link to the detected network, or Cancel to go to the main screen.

Hot tip

Changing the AutoPlay options will allow the program to start automatically, but it will still wait for you to manually connect, unless you update the settings.

Don't forget

You can still send and receive SMS text messages (see page 90) even if you don't connect to the data network.

Share Internet Connection

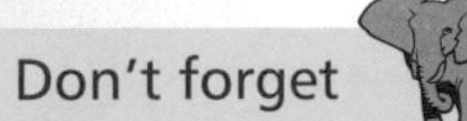

Don't forget

If you are using the mobile broadband connection at home or in a location with other computers, you can share the Internet connection.

Don't forget

You could also share the connection on a peer-to-peer network with a wireless access point.

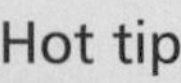

Hot tip

See pages 48-51 for more details on creating and accessing an ad-hoc wireless network.

1. Set up the mobile broadband Internet connection

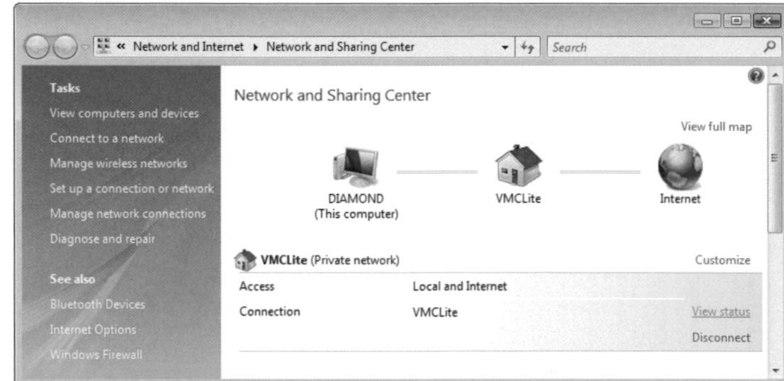

2. Create an ad-hoc wireless network on the same computer

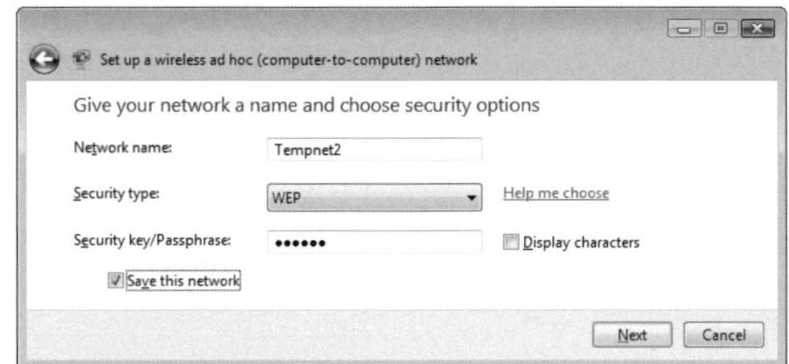

3. When the ad-hoc network is ready to use, choose to turn on Internet connection sharing

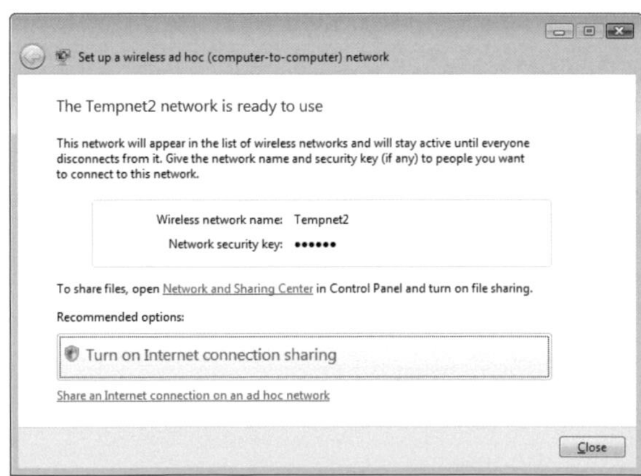

4. On the other computer, connect to the ad-hoc network

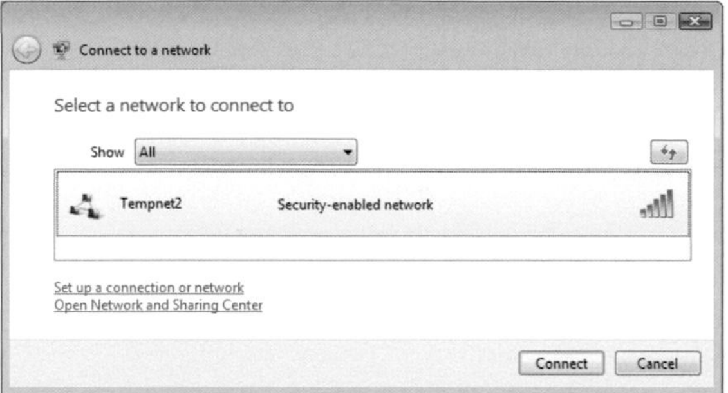

5. The network will be enabled, with an Internet connection

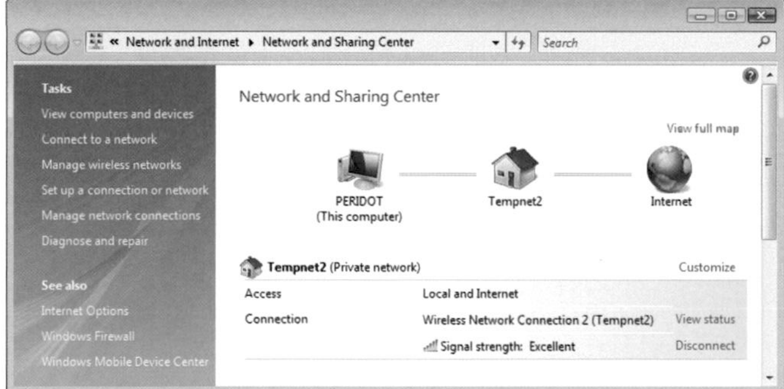

6. The ad-hoc network will appear on the first computer

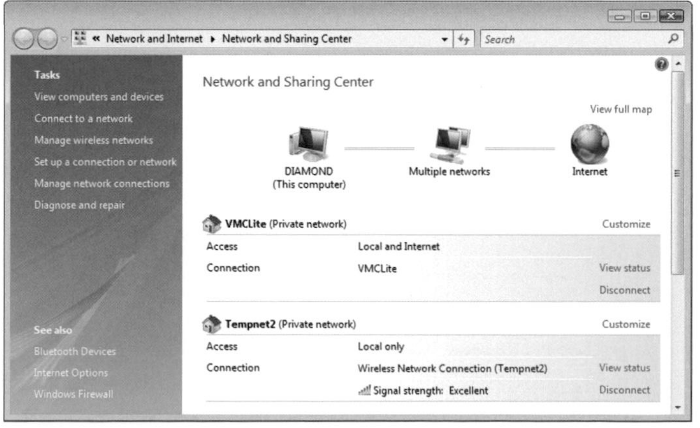

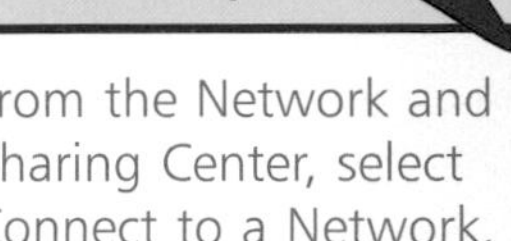

From the Network and Sharing Center, select Connect to a Network, and choose the ad-hoc network just created.

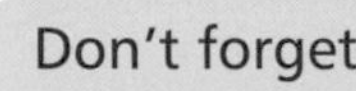

As soon as another computer connects to the ad-hoc wireless network, it will appear in the Network and Sharing Center of the originating computer.

View and Limit Usage

The Vodafone Mobile Connect Lite program provides details of your usage in terms of data volume or time

Don't forget

The charges for your mobile broadband service may depend on the amount of data that you send and receive or on the time for which your connection is active.

1. Open the VMCLite program (there's no need to Connect) and click the View Usage button

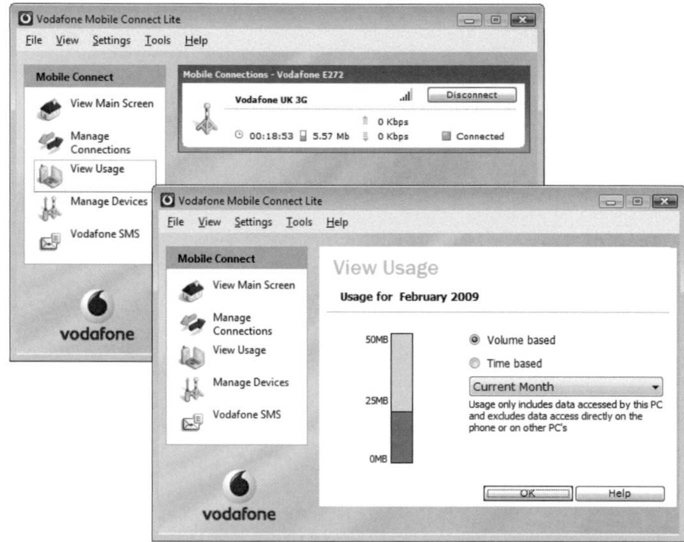

2. The Volume based usage is displayed. Click the button to display Time based

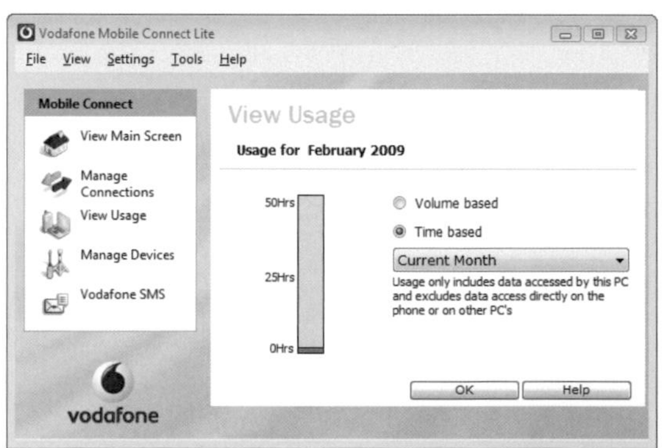

The application displays information for just the last two calendar months.

3. Click the down arrow to choose between This Month and Last Month

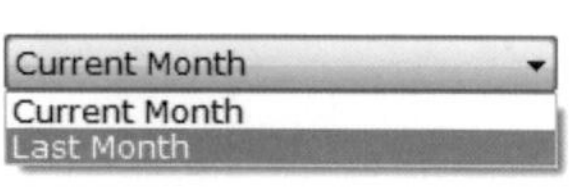

You can reset the limits in the Usage display for both time (hours) and data volume (megabytes). To adjust the levels:

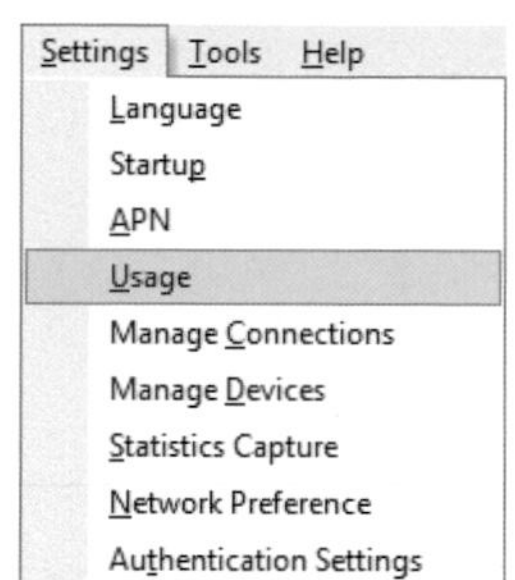

1. From the VMCLite program, select the Settings menu and then click the Usage command

2. With Volume limit selected, click in the Usage limit box and type a new level to replace the existing value (default is 50)

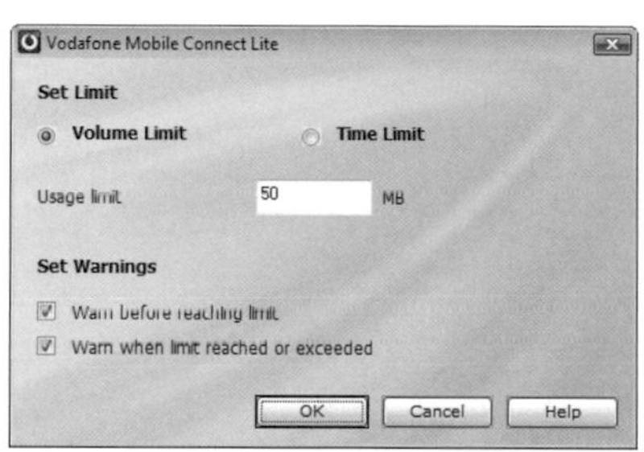

3. Click the Time limit button

4. Click in the Usage limit box and type a new level for the Time limit

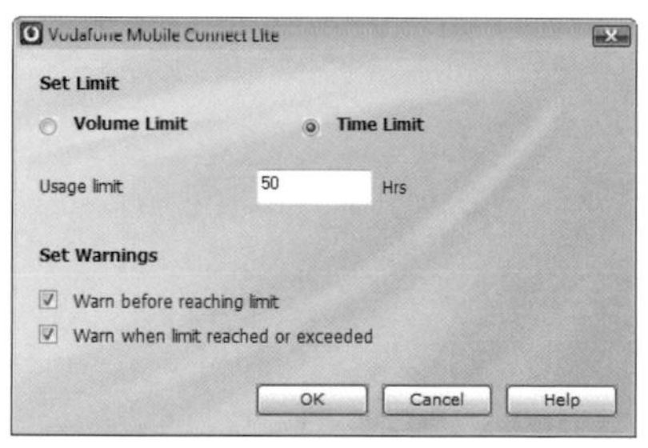

For either limit, the program will issue a warning, when you reach 95% of the limit specified. You'll also be warned when the limit is exceeded.

These warnings will appear whenever you connect to a network for which the limit has been exceeded, unless you deselect the message or increase the appropriate limit.

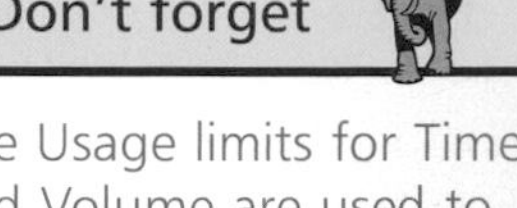

The Usage limits for Time and Volume are used to scale the charts displayed in the Usage Views.

Statistics Capture

There is a Statistics Capture command in the Settings menu. This relates to information that is collected automatically by Vodafone, to assist in demand forecasting. You do not have access to this data.

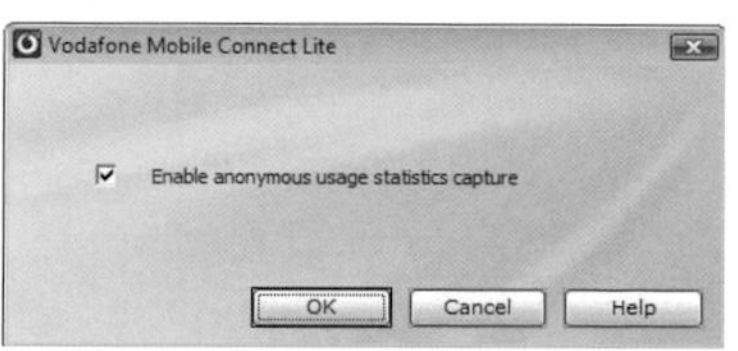

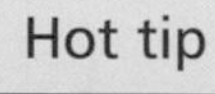

This information is collected anonymously. However, you can choose not to participate in this by clearing the Enable option.

Vodafone SMS

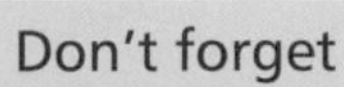

Don't forget

The Vodafone mobile broadband modem has a SIM card and an associated cell phone number, so can participate in SMS messaging.

Beware

You cannot send or receive text messages unless Vodafone SMS is active. However, you can minimize the window and still receive your SMS text messages.

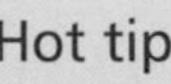

Hot tip

Telephone numbers are automatically stored with country code, so your contacts list can be used, wherever you may be.

In addition to email and Internet access, you can use the mobile broadband connection to send and receive SMS messages.

1. From the VMCLite main screen select Vodafone SMS

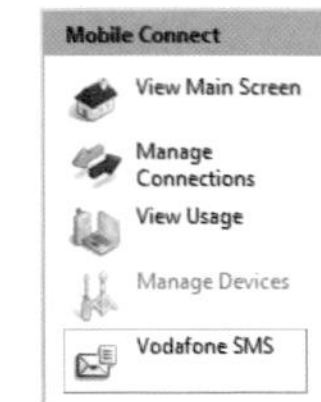

2. This opens at the Inbox and shows the SMS messages that have been received

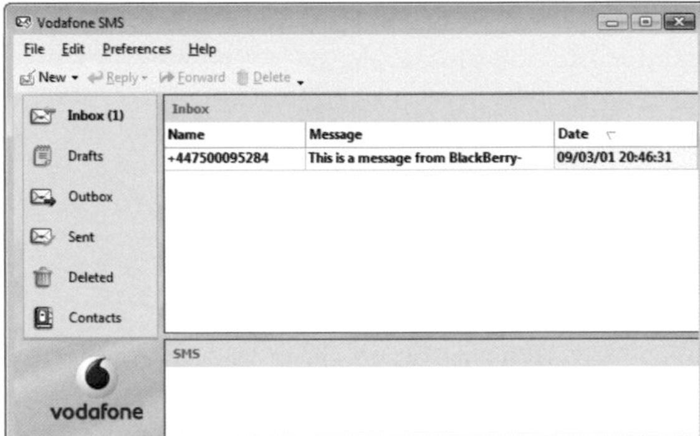

3. Select a message to see the full contents in the Viewer at the bottom of the SMS window

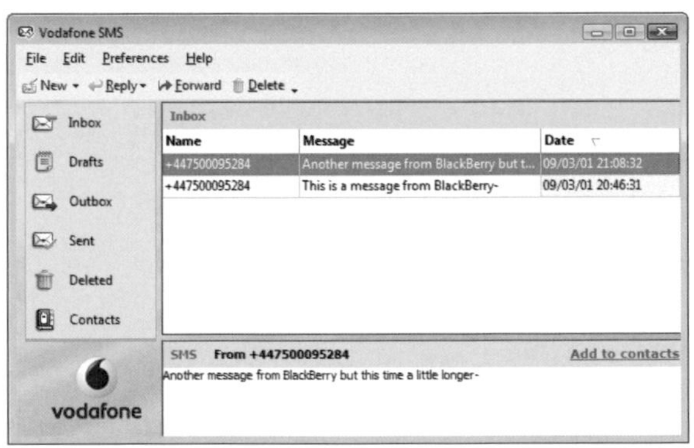

4. Click Add to Contacts, and type the name then click OK, to include the sender's telephone number in your contacts list

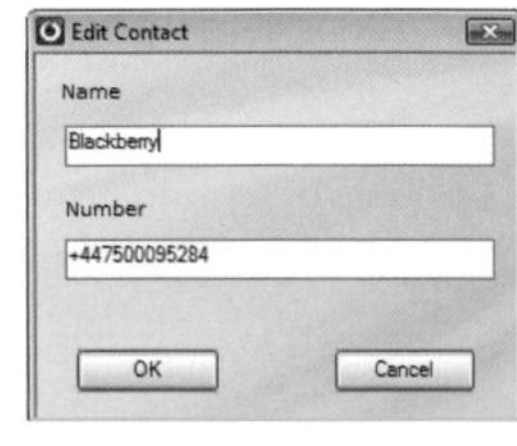

5. Click Reply, then select Reply or Reply with Original, and type a response to the sender

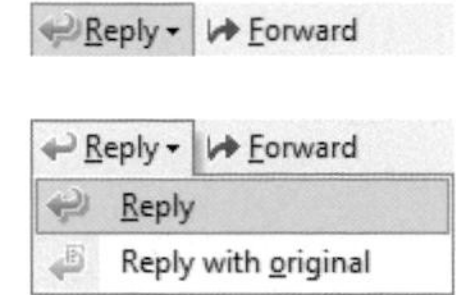

6. Click Send, then click OK to confirm

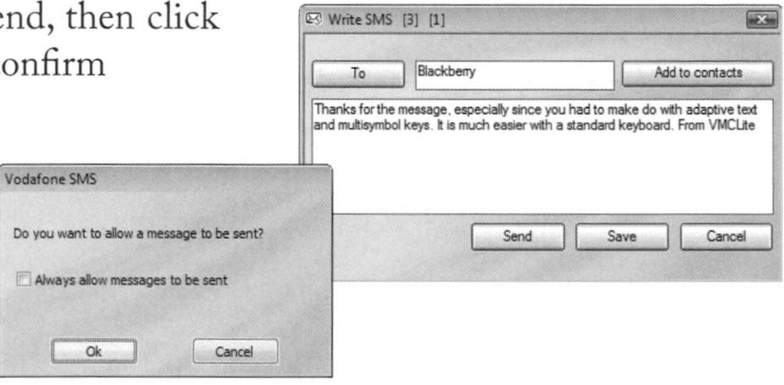

7. When you've finished sending messages, minimize the window and you can continue receiving messages

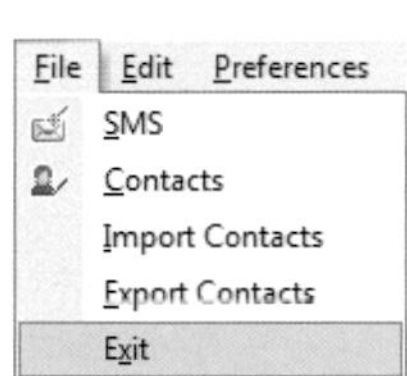

8. Select File, Exit to stop receiving text messages

Hot tip

Choose Forward to send the message to another number, or select Reply, Reply with Original to include the original text in your reply.

Don't forget

Click the box Always allow messages to be sent, and the message will go without the need for confirmation.

SMS and Data Connections

The ability to send or receive messages while you have an active data connection is device dependent. It is supported by the Huawei E272, the modem component of the Vodafone mobile broadband device. However for those devices that do not support concurrent data connection and SMS, newly created text messages will stay in the Outbox until the phone connection becomes free.

Available Data Connections

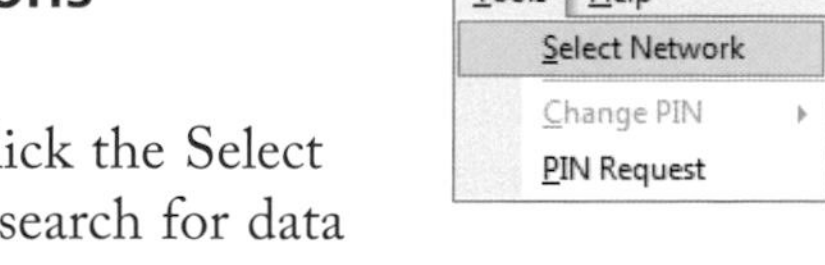

1. Click Tools and then click the Select Network command, to search for data

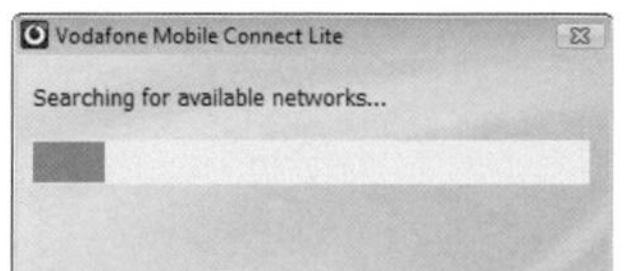

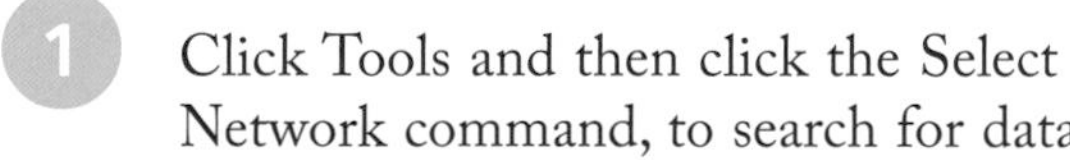

Don't forget

Networks are listed by Operator, Type and Status. In this case the Vodafone 2G network is available and the Vodafone 3G network is Current. The other operator networks are Not Allowed.

Contact Management

Beware

Deleted contacts are permanently lost. There's no equivalent of the Email Deleted Items.

The Vodafone SMS feature provides a simple name and cell phone address book that is stored locally on the computer. Tools are provided to allow you to create, edit and delete contacts.

1. Open VMCLite and select Contacts, then select New, and complete the details to create a contact entry

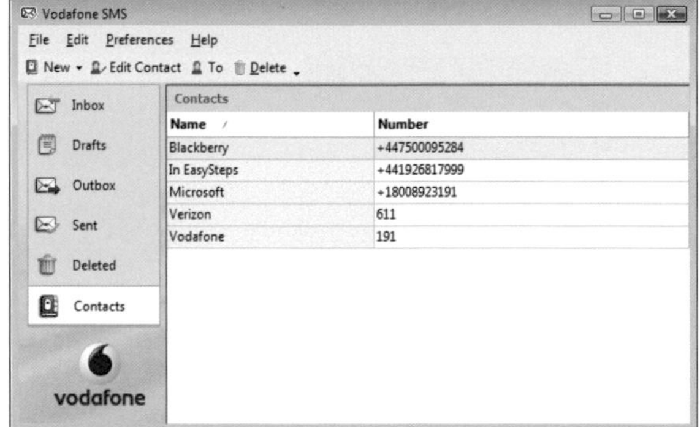

Don't forget

Select a contact and click To, to create a new message for that contact.

2. Select a contact and click Edit Contact to change that specific contact, or press Delete to remove it immediately.

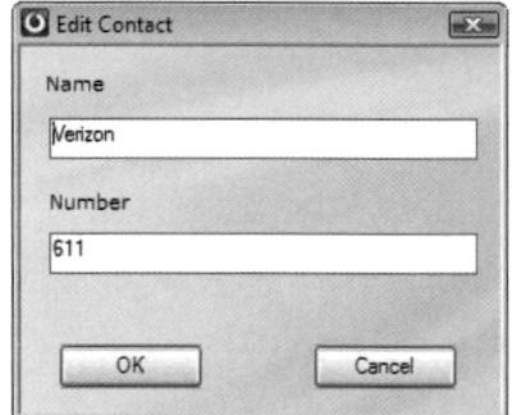

You can save your address book as a backup or to share it with another system.

3. Select File, Export Contacts

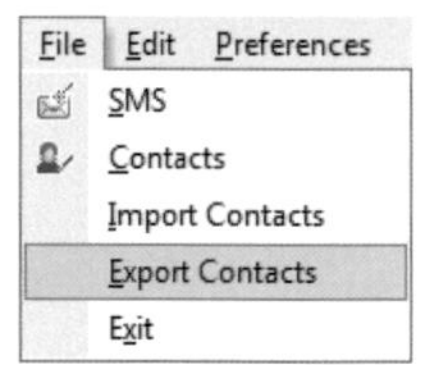

4. Select comma separated values (.csv)

5. Specify the file name and click Save, and the contacts will be exported to the specified file

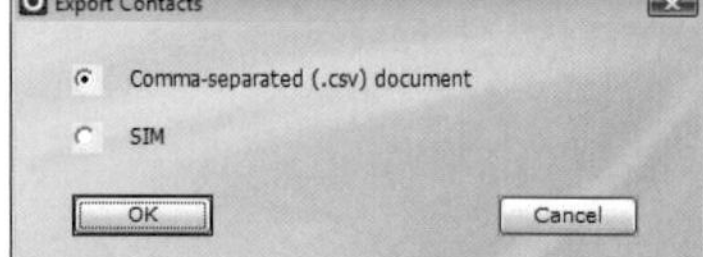

Hot tip

You can also export your contacts to your phone's SIM, if your phone supports this. See page 140 to attach your phone to the computer.

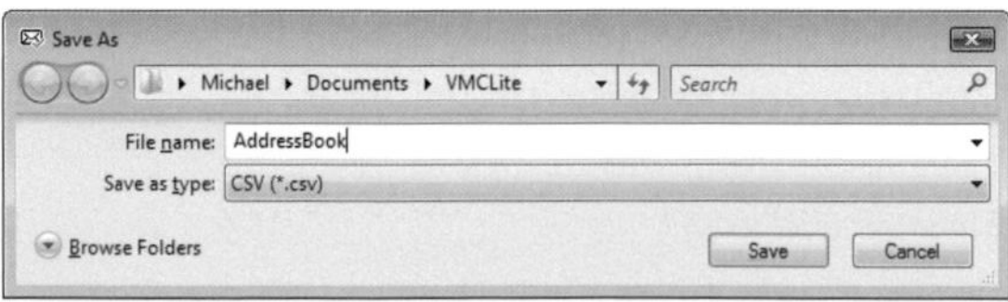

3 Mobile and 3 Like Home

3 Mobile is the brand name under which Hutchinson operates cell phone networks in Australia, Austria, Denmark, Hong Kong and Macau, Indonesia, Ireland, Italy, Sweden, and the United Kingdom. It includes mobile broadband servers, and is of particular interest to travelers since it offers a "3 Like Home" network, available to both Pay Monthly and Pay As You Go customers. This means you can obtain your cell phone or modem in one country and use it in other countries with sister networks, taking advantage of the home country rates and allowances.

Hot tip

If you are spending an extended period in countries with a 3 Network, this may be an economical choice for mobile broadband access.

3 Mobile Broadband

USB modems with a 3 Mobile SIM card provide access to the Internet at home or while you are away. For example, there's the Huawei E160G modem which supports maximum speeds of 3.6 Mbps for download and 384 Kbps for upload.

Don't forget

You can connect the USB modem directly to your laptop or computer, or attach it using the cable supplied.

To set this up:

1. Remove the cap on the end of the USB modem
2. Pull out SIM holder and insert the SIM card
3. Slide the holder back into the USB modem
4. Plug the modem into your laptop or desktop computer

Once you're connected the light under the 3 logo will change from green to blue.

On the first connection, the device drivers are installed from the data storage part of the modem, then the modem software loads. On subsequent connects, the modem software will load straight away.

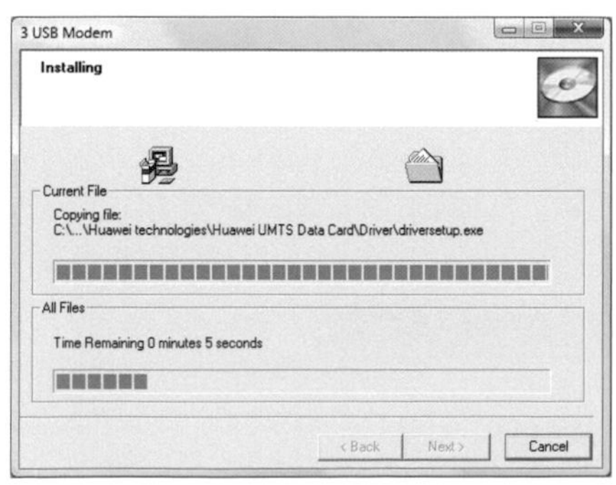

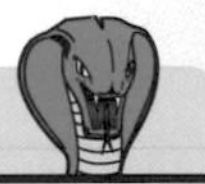

Beware

As always, if you have AutoPlay disabled, you'll need to choose to run the program, in this case AutoRun.exe.

Using the Modem

An icon is added to the system tray, when the 3 USB Modem software starts up.

Don't forget

You may be asked to permit access through the firewall.

1. To begin an Internet session, click the Connect button

2. Use your email client and your Internet browser as normal

3. Click the Message button to send an SMS text message

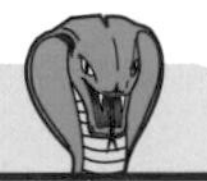

Don't forget

You may be able to purchase a 3 Mobile SIM card and use this in your existing USB modem, to gain the advantage of 3 Mobile roaming rates.

4. Click the Phone Book button to make changes to your contacts list

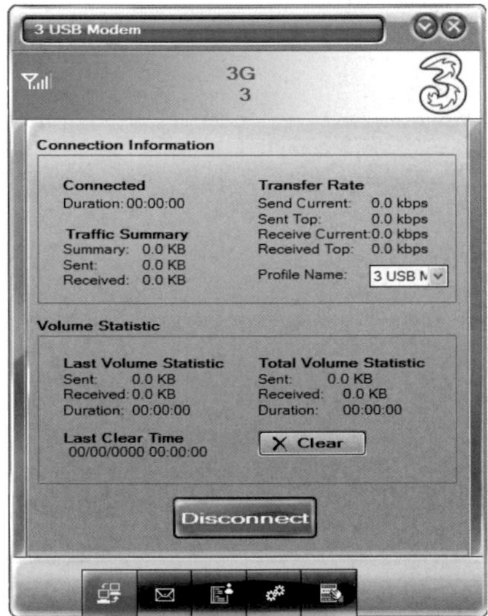

5. Click Disconnect to end the Internet session

6. Click the Main Menu button and select Exit to finish with the modem

Beware

The modem contains storage, so it is best to Safely Remove Hardware (see page 81) before removing the modem.

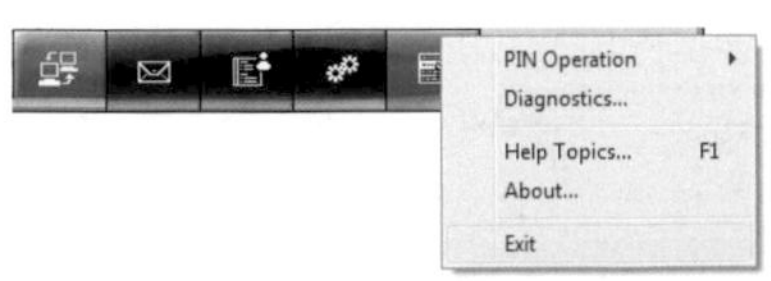

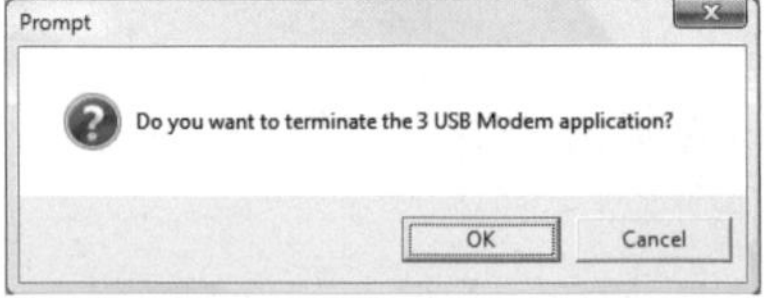

6 Networking with Vista

Windows Vista helps you manage and maintain your wireless network. It provides the Network Icon for status reports. The Network Folder gives access to workgroup computers and their shared resources. The Network and Sharing Center consolidates network facilities and makes it easier to securely share your files, folders and printers. Finally, the command line offers specialized tools.

Vista Networking Tools

Hot tip

Windows Vista provides a powerful yet easy to access set of tools to help you configure and manage your network.

When you have planned, configured and installed your network, you can use the networking tools and functions provided in your operating system to control and manage the network thereafter.

You can access these facilities in Windows Vista in various ways:

- Network Icon in notification area, for common commands
- Start Menu, with the Network and Connect To commands
- Connect To a Network dialog box, to connect and disconnect
- Network folder, with access to computers and devices
- Network and Internet, the Control Panel section
- Network and Sharing Center, the main networking resource
- Command Prompt, for powerful, last-resort networking tools

Don't forget

The Notification Area at the right hand end of the Taskbar, also known as the System Tray, holds icons for active programs and devices.

We'll start off by exploring the capabilities associated with the network icon that Vista places in the notification area whenever there's a network card of any type installed in your computer.

If the icon isn't displayed, even though you have a network card fitted, then it may be hidden. To reveal the network icon:

Hot tip

If you can't locate an empty section on the taskbar, right click the Start button and select Properties (see page 99).

1. Right-click an empty section of the taskbar, and then click Properties

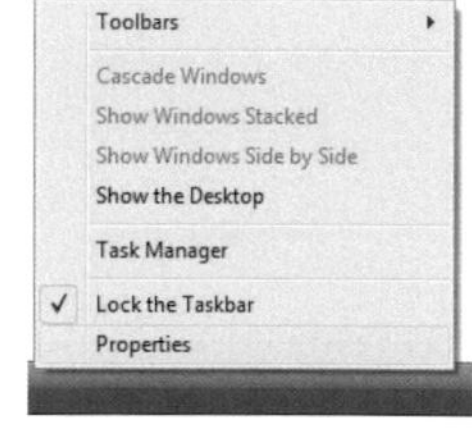

2. On the Taskbar and Start Menu Properties, click the Notification Area tab

3. Click in the Network box to add a check mark, as shown, then click OK

Network Icon and Status

The network icon changes to indicate the current connection status of the wireless (or wired) network.

 Connected and with Internet access

 Disconnected from the network

Connected but with no Internet access

 Network error condition detected

1. Move the mouse pointer over the network icon, to get a more detailed report, including wireless signal strength

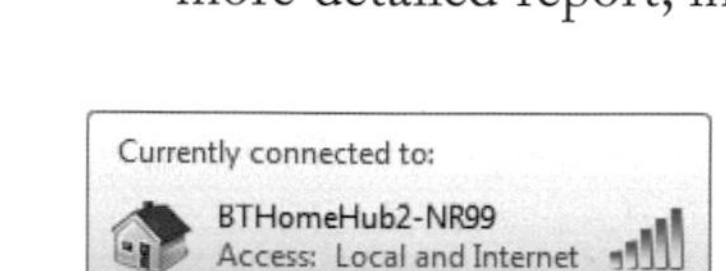

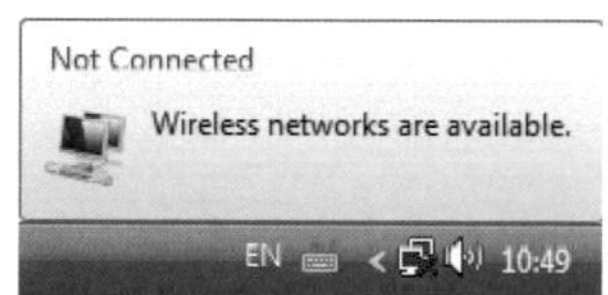

2. Left click the network icon to display commands that are specifically related to the current status e.g.

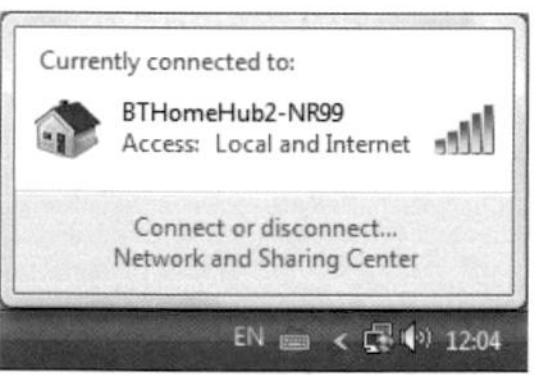

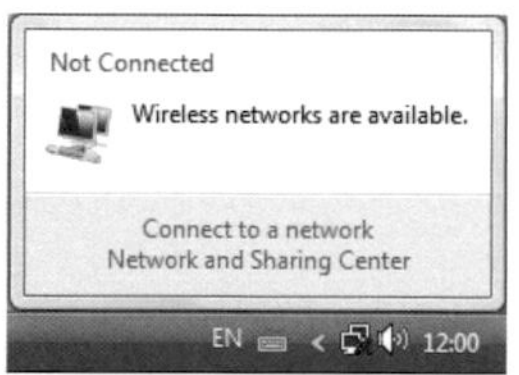

3. For additional commands, again tailored to the current status, right click the network icon

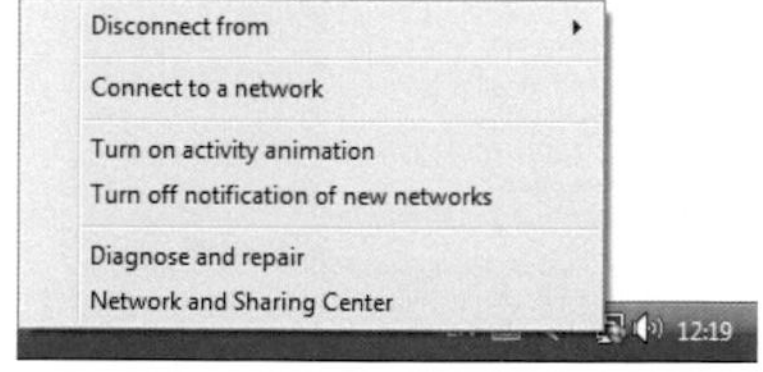

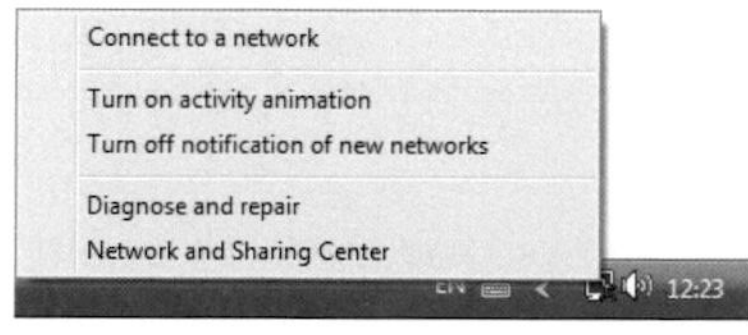

The network icon can also show you when data is being transferred across the network, if you have enabled Activity Animation.

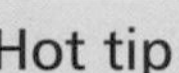

Hot tip

The same network icon is displayed for wireless or for wired networks.

Don't forget

There's also a desktop network icon, but this will simply open the network folder.

Don't forget

Right click the network icon and select Turn on activity animation to have the network icon show when data is being transferred.

Start Menu for Networking

The Start Menu includes two commands specific to networking:

1. Click Start and then Connect To, to open the Connect to a Network dialog box

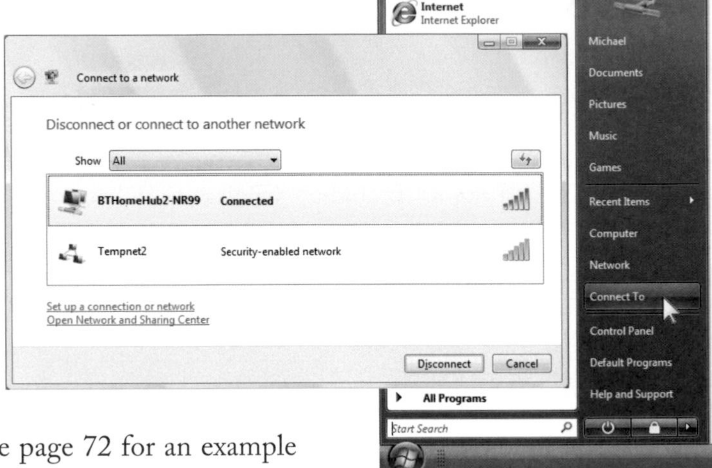

See page 72 for an example of connecting to a security-enabled wireless network.

2. Click Start, Network to view the computers and devices on your network

This shows that there are seven computers and devices currently attached to the network. There are four computers (named Diamond, Opal, Pearl and Peridot), a wireless network printer (All-in-one), a router/modem (BT Home Hub) and a shared media file stream, provided by one of the computers (Diamond). See page 113 for details of media file sharing.

Hot tip

You can also open Connect to a Network from the Network icon menus or the Network and Sharing Center.

Don't forget

You can also open the network folder by double clicking the Network icon on the desktop, or from the Network and Sharing Center.

Beware

The computers and devices shown will vary, since those that are currently switched off or in power-save mode will not be detected.

If the Network and Connect To entries do not appear on your Start Menu, you can restore them:

1. Right click the Start button and select Properties

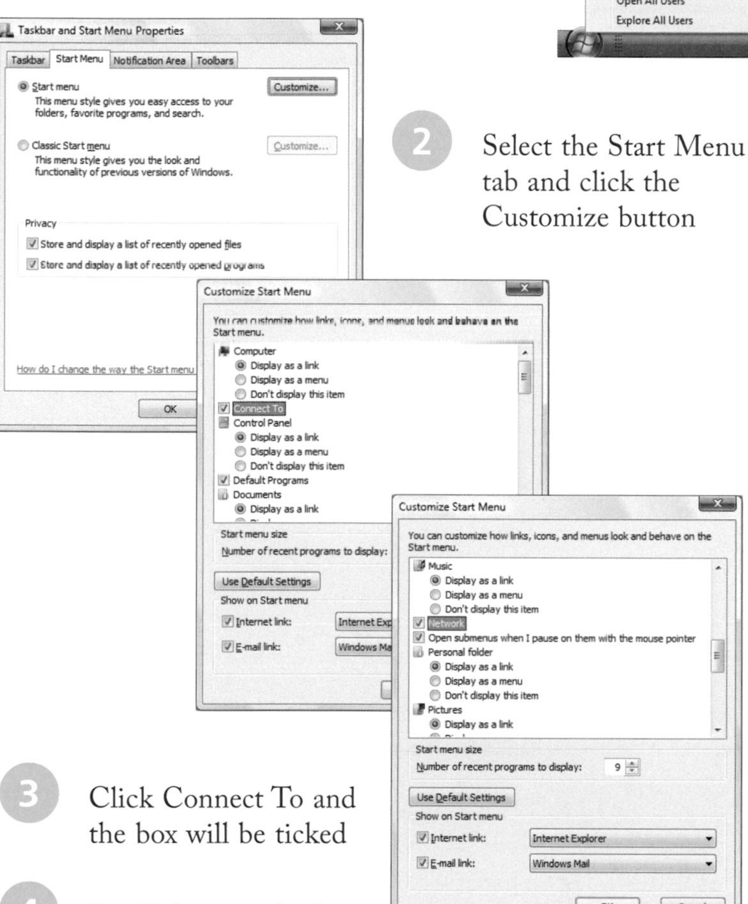

2. Select the Start Menu tab and click the Customize button

3. Click Connect To and the box will be ticked

4. Scroll down and select Network and that box will be ticked

5. Click OK and then OK again to apply the changes and save the new Start Menu settings

The Connect To and the Network buttons will now be displayed on the right hand pane of the Start Menu.

Hot tip

You could right click an empty part of the taskbar to select Properties.

Hot tip

Alternatively, click the Use Default Settings button, and show both Connect To and Network on the Start Menu.

Don't forget

Connect To and Network are both toggles – so clicking again will clear the ticks.

Network and Internet

You can Connect to a Network, and View computers and devices, as well as other networking functions from the Control Panel:

1 Click Start and select Control Panel

Hot tip

If Control Panel does not display on your Start Menu, you can select it on Customize Start Menu.

2 Click the Network and Internet option

Don't forget

View network status and tasks, and Set up file sharing are both links to Network and Sharing Center.

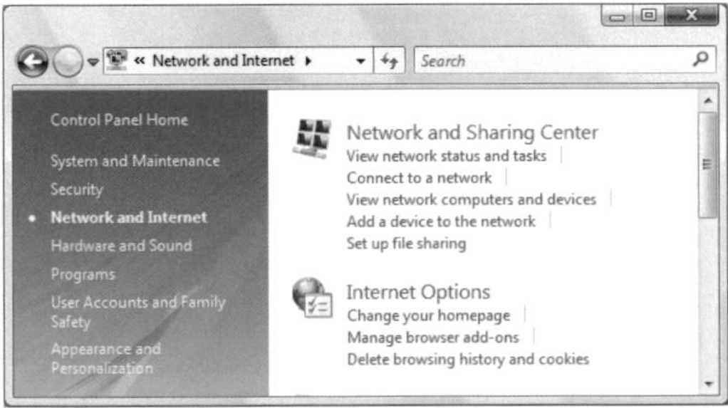

This provides no less than three links to the main networking resource in Windows Vista, the Network and Sharing Center:

- Network and Sharing Center
- View network status and tasks
- Set up file sharing

There are also three other links provided:

- Connect to a network
- View network computers and devices
- Add a device to the network

Hot tip

Multiple links to the same place is a reminder that once separate Network functions have now been consolidated to the Network and Sharing Center.

You can use Add a device to the network to set up a USB Flash Drive with your network settings, and use this to add new computers to the network (see pages 70 and 72).

1. Select Add a device to the network then click the link I want to add a device or computer that is not on the list

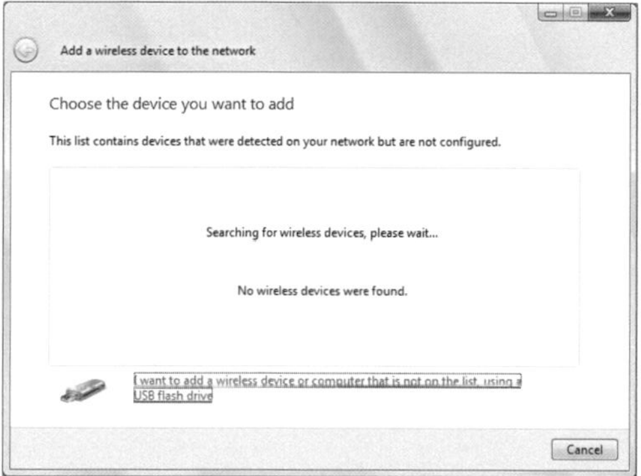

2. Select Add the device or computer using a USB flash drive, and follow the prompts to transfer network settings

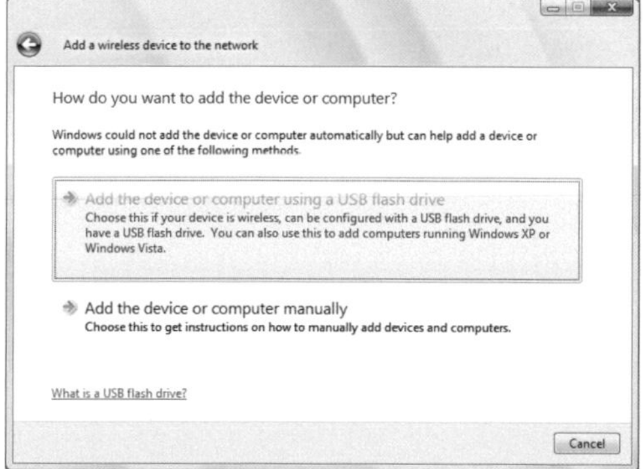

3. The Wireless Network Setup Wizard and the network security credentials will be added to the USB flash drive, for use when adding new computers to the network

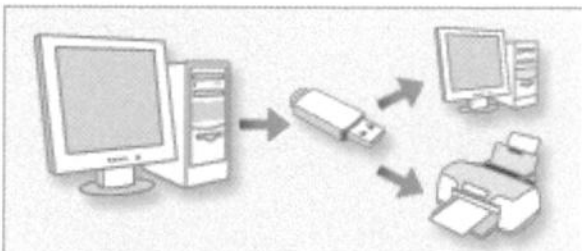

Hot tip

You can also click the button Add a wireless device, on the toolbar in the Network folder.

Add a wireless device

Don't forget

Windows will first of all search for any wireless devices that may be detected on your network but not yet configured.

Hot tip

The network setup files will be added to the USB flash drive in the AutoPlay format.

Network and Sharing Center

This is the main networking resource in Windows Vista and it consolidates the functions needed to manage your network. You can access the center from several places, including:

- Network icon menus
- Network folder toolbar button
- Connect to a Network window link
- Control Panel, Network and Internet links
- Press Start, type network, and select Network and Sharing Center

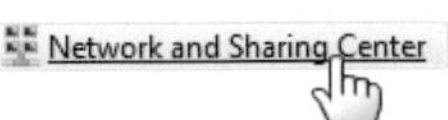

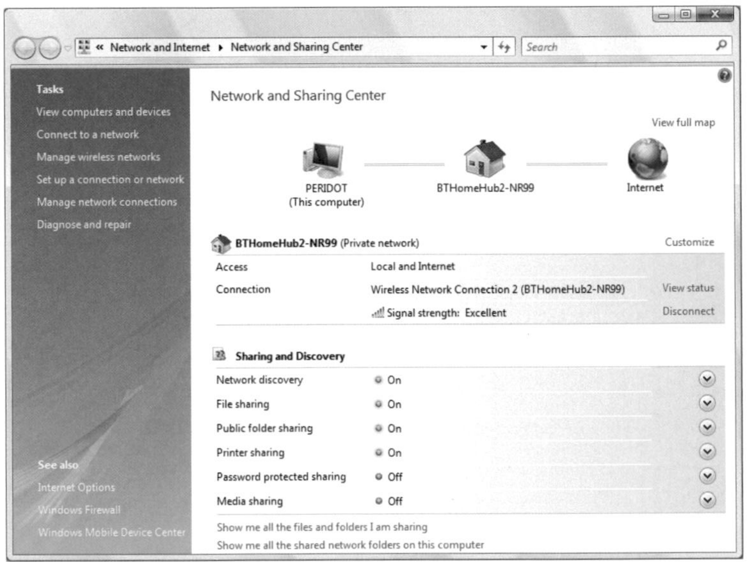

There are four main parts to the Network and Sharing Center:

1. Graphical Display – a miniature network map, giving a visual display of the current connection
2. Network Details – name, category (private/public), access (local/Internet) and connection (wired or wireless)
3. Sharing and Discovery – the current network detection and sharing settings
4. Tasks – a list of key networking tasks

Hot tip

Network and Internet provides five different links that display the Network and Sharing Center.

Don't forget

The Tasks pane also provides a See Also section with links to network related tasks.

Don't forget

If you are connected to more than one network, or you have multiple connections to the same network, network details are provided for each of your network connections.

The graphical display area shows the current network status, e.g.

1. There is no connection, local or Internet

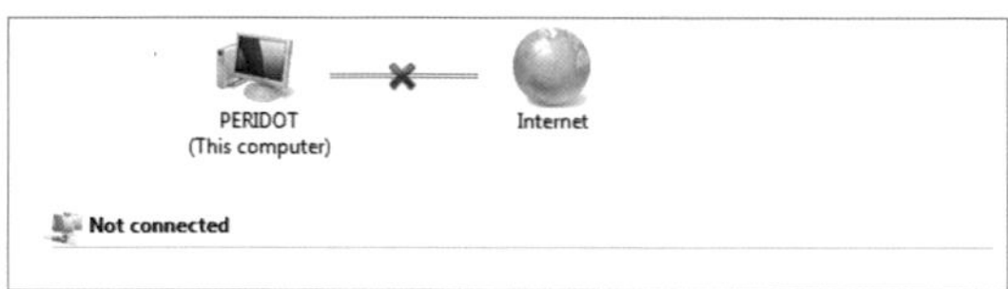

2. There is a local network connection, but no Internet

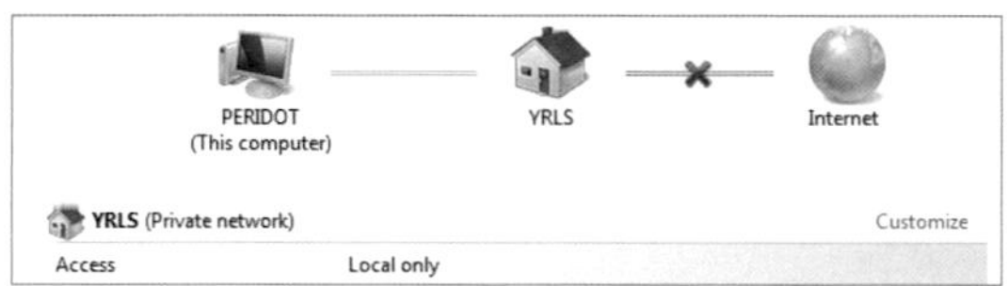

3. There is a problem with your network connection

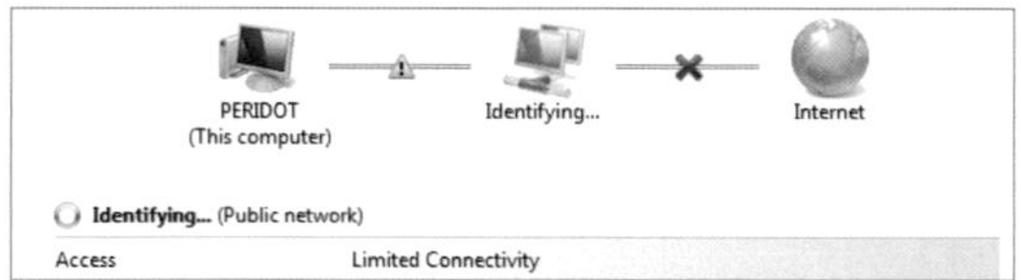

4. For further details of the problem, click on the error icon

Windows runs the network diagnostics to identify the possible causes of the problem.

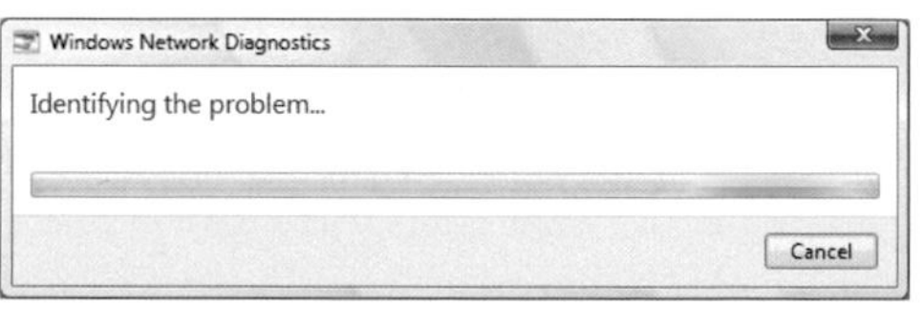

When the diagnostics complete, the potential solutions are displayed, and links are provided for further information that may help you in resolving the problem.

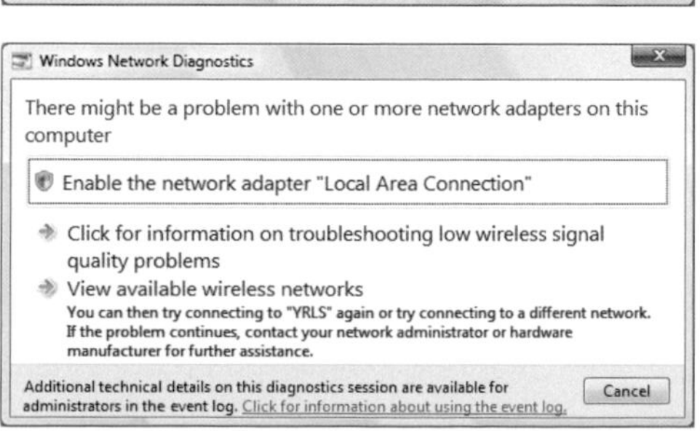

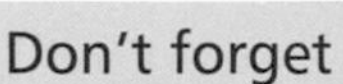

These illustrate some of the situations that may arise, when you are using a wireless network.

Beware

These suggestions are just best guesses. For example, here Windows detects that the wired network adapter is disabled and suggests enabling it. This wouldn't be appropriate for a wireless only network. The correct action is to try connecting again.

Change Network Settings

In the network details area, the Customize link allows you to make changes to the network location and settings:

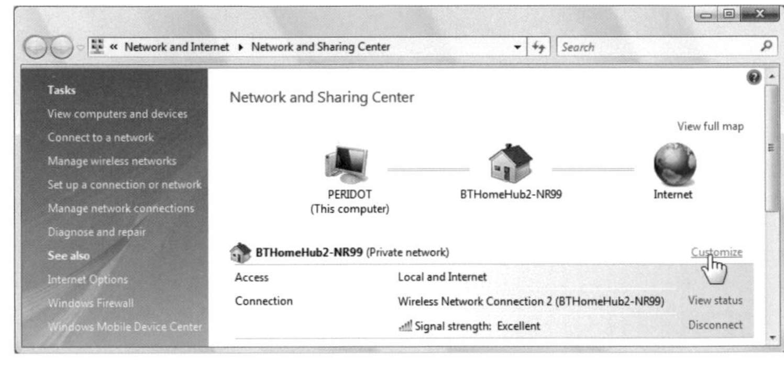
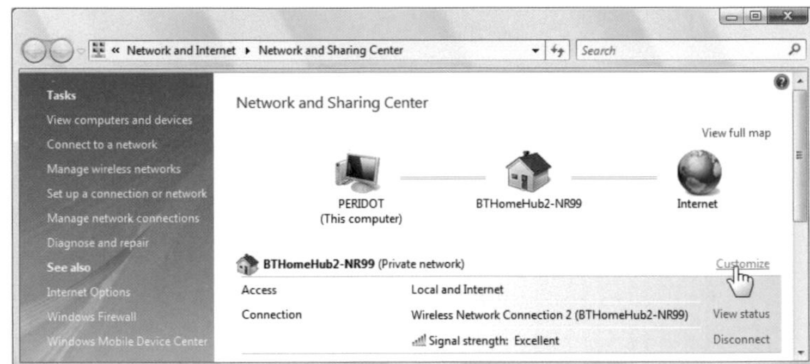

Don't forget

This might be required when you are sharing access to a wireless network with unknown users.

1. Click Customize to change network location to Public

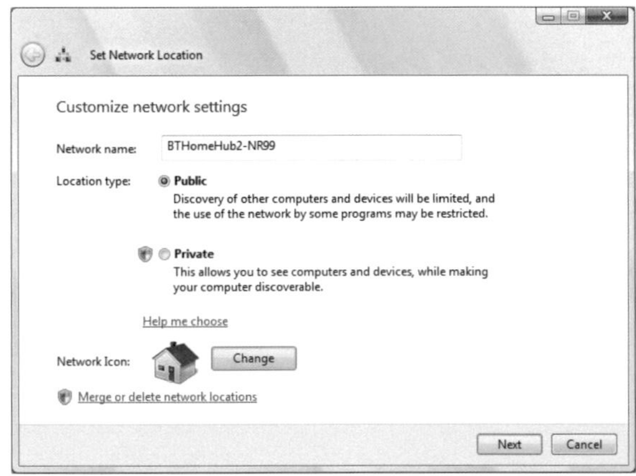

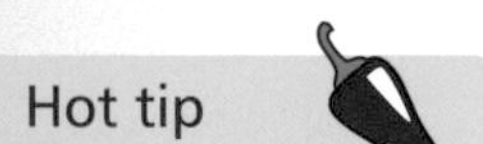

The changes to the network location and other settings will apply only to the particular computer.

2. Revise the network name if desired, then click the Change button and select a different icon for the network

3. Click OK to apply the change of icon, then click Next to make the network category Public

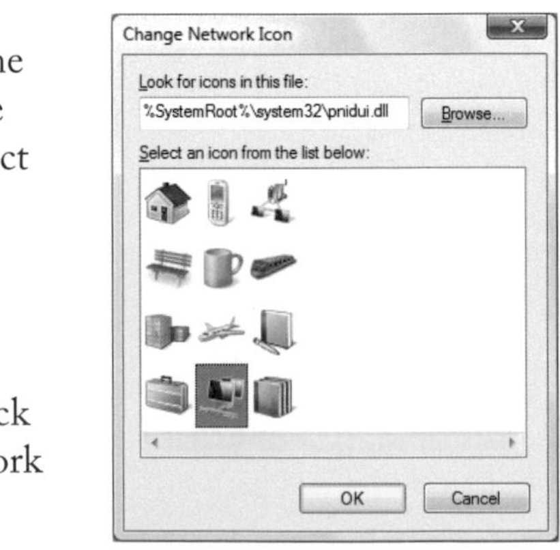

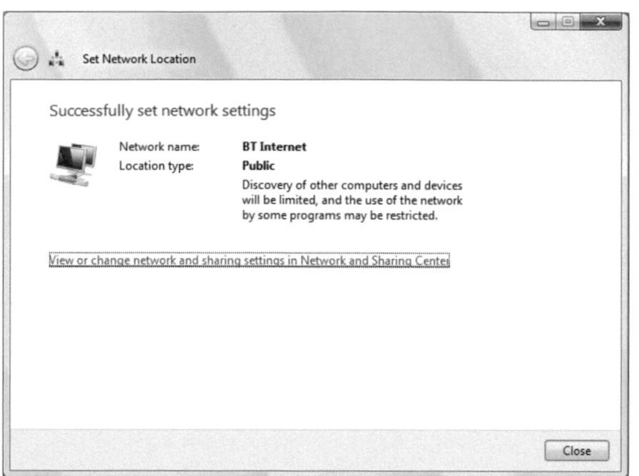

Hot tip

When you make a network Public, the computers and devices that it contains are no longer as readily accessible, thus increasing your security on a shared network.

4. Click View or Change network settings to amend the changes, or click Close to redisplay the network center

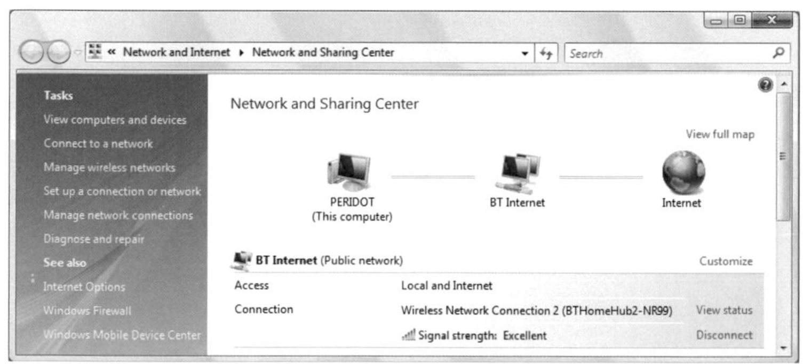

Don't forget

Click Customize again to restore the network location to Private.

5. To remove redundant networks, select Customize then click the link to Merge or delete network locations

6. Select the network or networks that are no longer required and click Delete

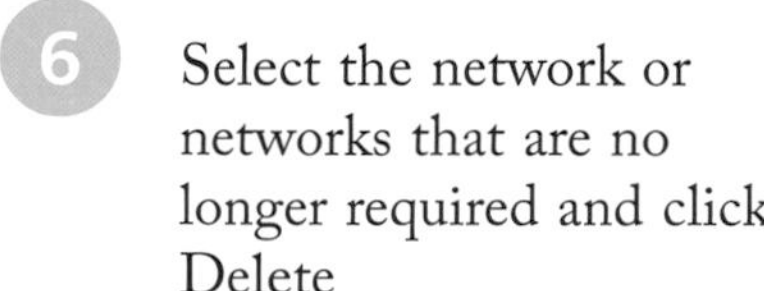

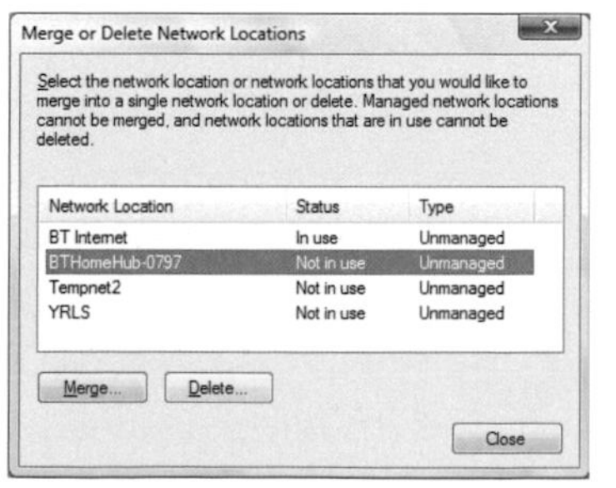

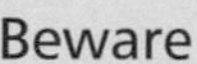

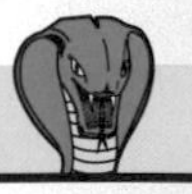

Beware

Only delete a network when you are sure it is no longer required, for example when you update to a new network router.

Network Map

Hot tip

The map shows devices and computers that are currently active on the network. Devices that are in sleep mode cannot be identified so will not be displayed.

You can view a full map of the network from the network center:

1. Click the link to View full map

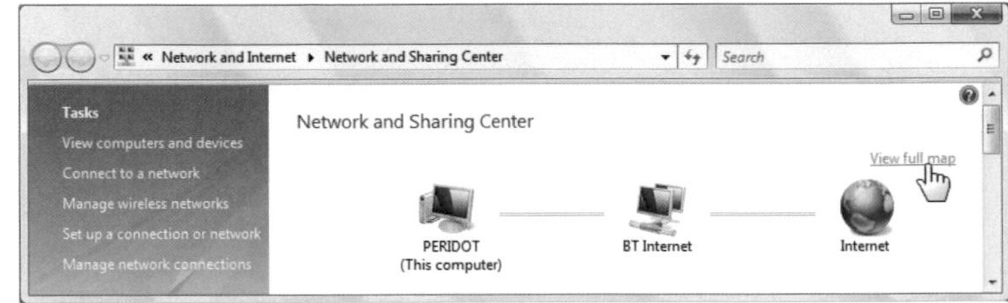

2. Windows searches for computers and devices on the network, then displays them in a map format

Don't forget

The network router is shown as three separate devices – wireless hub, gateway to the Internet and switch for wired Ethernet connections (see page 15).

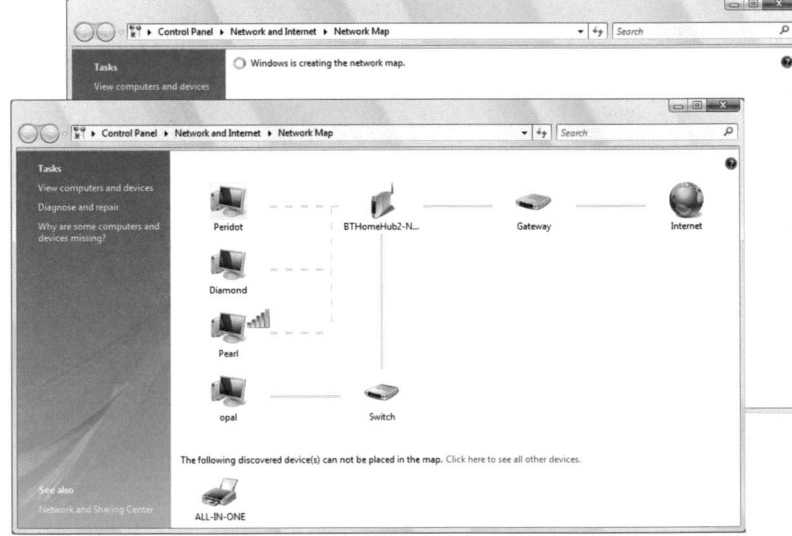

Beware

Some devices cannot be placed in the map so are shown separately, for example the wireless printer.

3. Move the mouse pointer over a computer icon on the map for details, in particular the IP (Internet Protocol) address assigned to that device

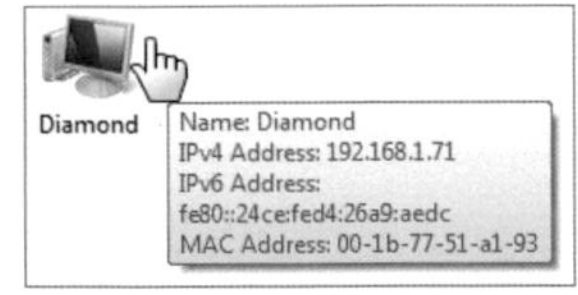

Don't forget

IP addresses are allocated by the DHCP server, a function of the wireless router.

4. The router gateway also has an IP address assigned to it

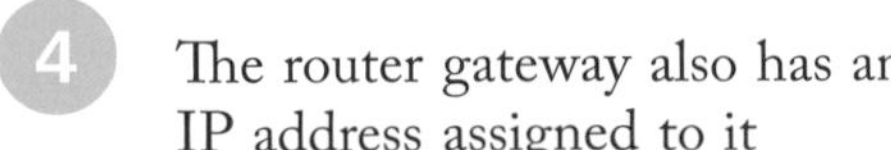

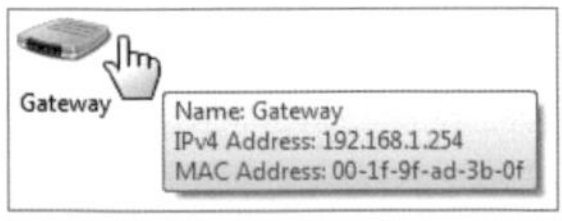

Network Connection Status

1. Open the Network and Sharing Center and click the View Status link for the network connection

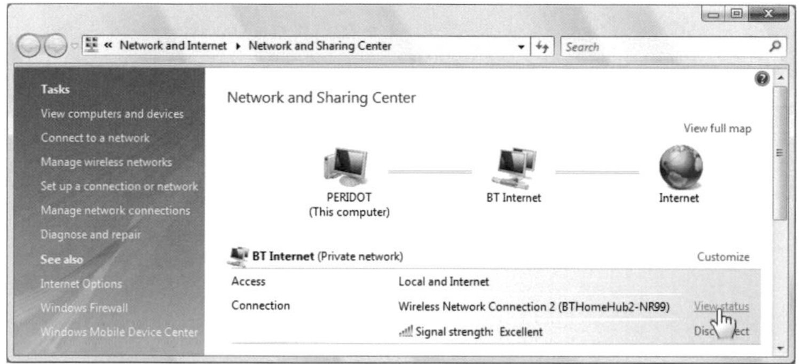

2. General information about the wireless network connection is given, including the SSID, the duration, the speed, the signal strength and the level of activity in terms of data transferred

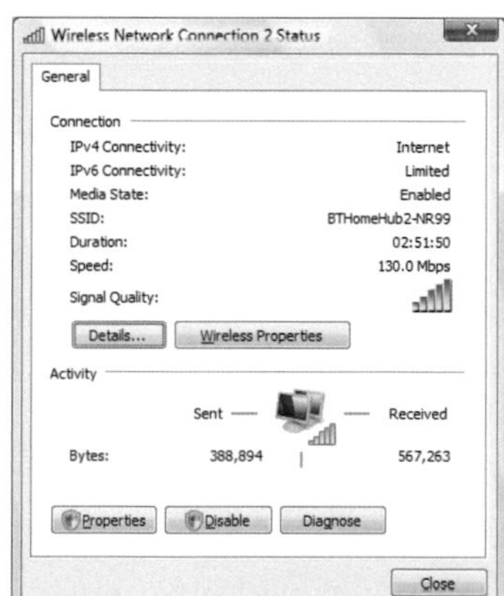

3. Click the Details button for more information

4. The key items here are the IP addresses for the computer, and the gateway server device, plus other technical details that may be required for network problem investigations

5. Click Close then Close again to exit the status information

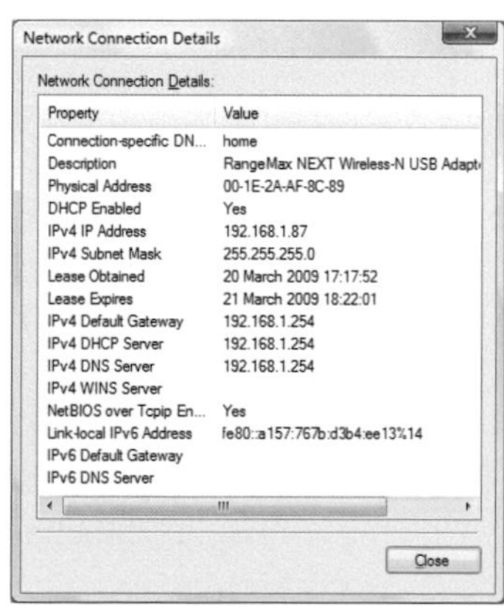

The Wireless Properties button gives details of the wireless connection. The Properties button displays details for the network adapter.

Network Discovery

Vista uses the network discovery feature to control whether other computers on the network can locate and access files and printers on your computer (and vice versa). In a private home or office network, it is usual to have network discovery turned on. In a public network, such as a wireless hotspot, network discovery should normally be turned off. To turn network discovery on:

1. Open the network center and click the down arrow next to Network Discovery

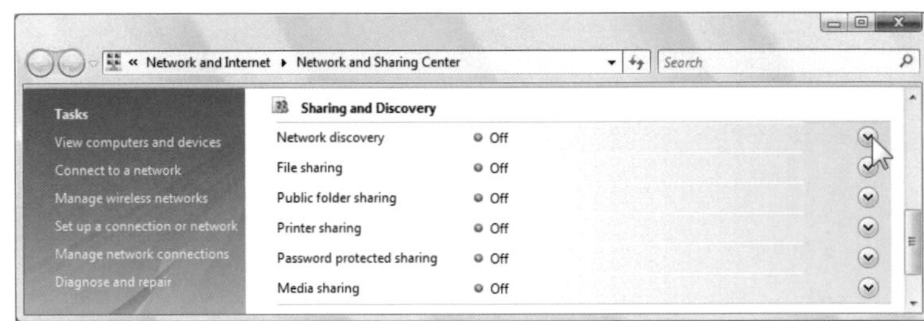

2. Click Turn on network discovery, then click Change Settings if you want to amend the workgroup name

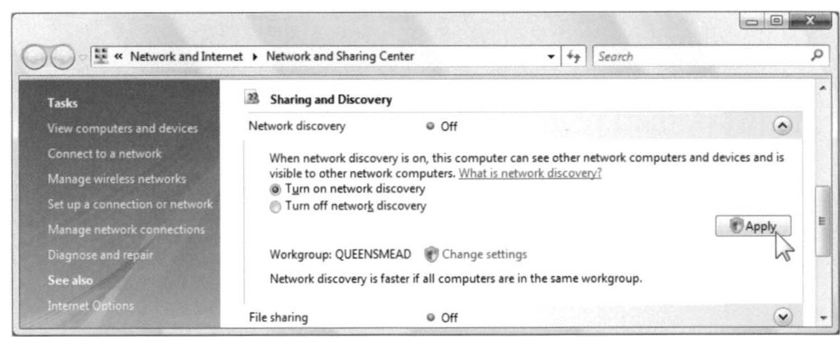

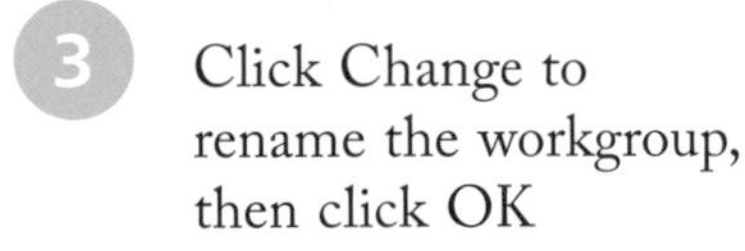

3. Click Change to rename the workgroup, then click OK

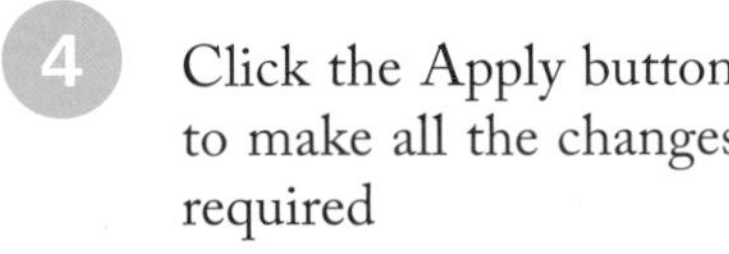

4. Click the Apply button to make all the changes required

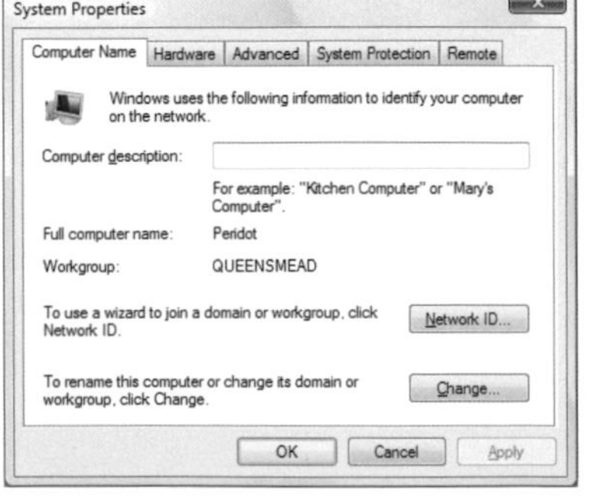

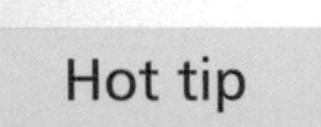

Hot tip

Use the same method to turn off network discovery, for example on a computer that contains particularly sensitive or confidential information.

Don't forget

Network discovery works faster if all the computers on the network are in the same workgroup.

File Sharing

The file sharing option is a general control for file and printer sharing. If this is turned off, it overrides the settings for the other sharing options, so these will all be turned off.

To turn on file sharing:

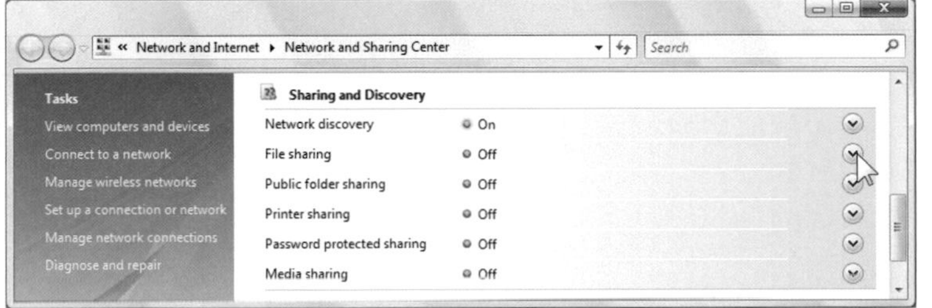

1. In the network and sharing center, click the down arrow next to File Sharing

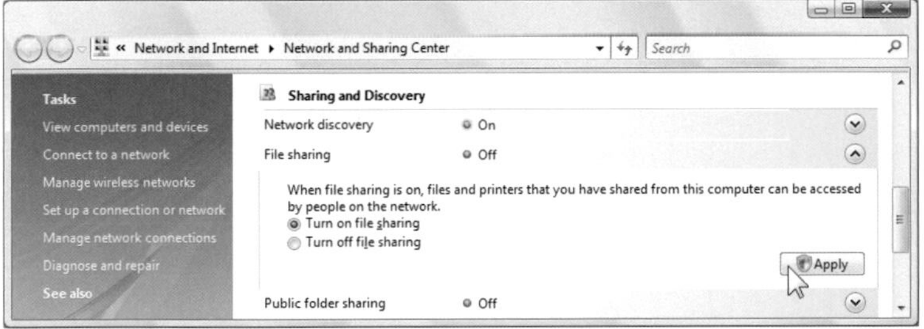

2. Click Turn on file sharing, then click Apply

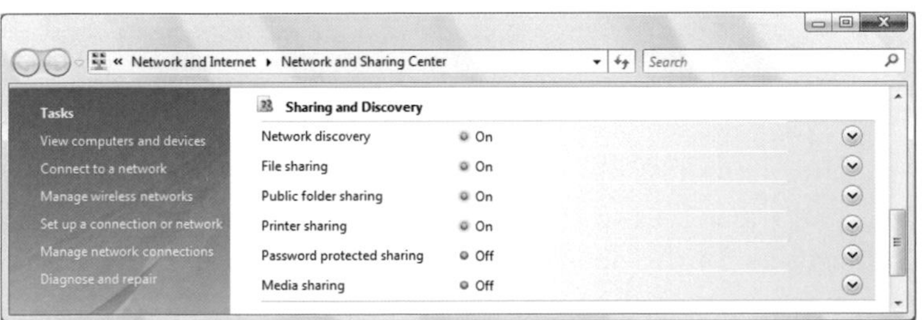

3. Note that the settings for the other sharing options may also change when you reset the file sharing option

Turning on file sharing will allow you to enable sharing for public folders, printers and media files.

It will also allow you to share selected files and folders, using the File Sharing Wizard (see pages 114-115).

When you choose to turn off file sharing on a computer, this will also turn off any other file sharing options that have previously been enabled.

Public Folder Sharing

Don't forget

Other users on the same computer will be able to access public folders, whether or not public folder sharing is turned on. The sharing option applies only to networked users.

The Public folder provides a place to store documents and other files that are needed by other users on the computer. You can also make them available to other users on the network.

To change the settings:

1. Click the down arrow next to Public folder sharing

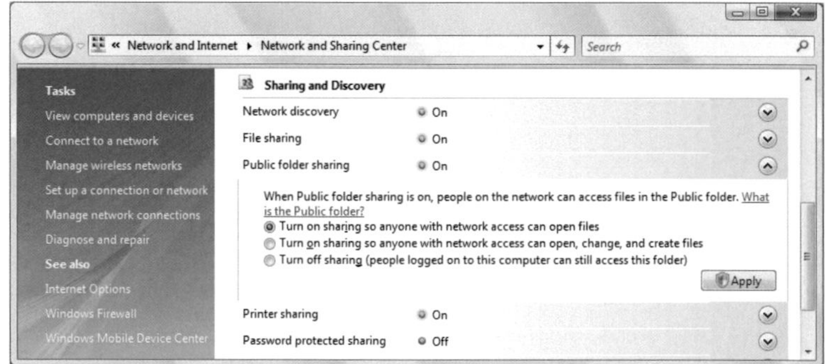

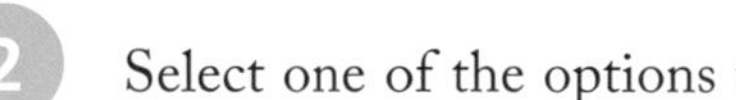

2. Select one of the options then click Apply

- Turn on sharing so anyone with network access can open files **read-only access**
- Turn on sharing so anyone with network access can open, change, and create files **full access**
- Turn off sharing (people logged on to this computer can still access this folder) **no network access**

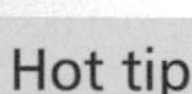

Hot tip

Allow full access if you want other users to be able to make changes, or to deposit files into your public folder for your review.

With this method of file sharing, you'd copy or move documents, pictures or other files to the public folder to make them available to other users on the network. This is the safest approach, since it minimizes the level of access.

However, you can allow users to access the files directly in their current locations, using the File Sharing Wizard to specify the files, folders and drives that you want to share.

Printer Sharing

The printer sharing option controls sharing the contents of the Printers folder. To turn the setting on or off:

1. Click the down arrow next to Printer sharing

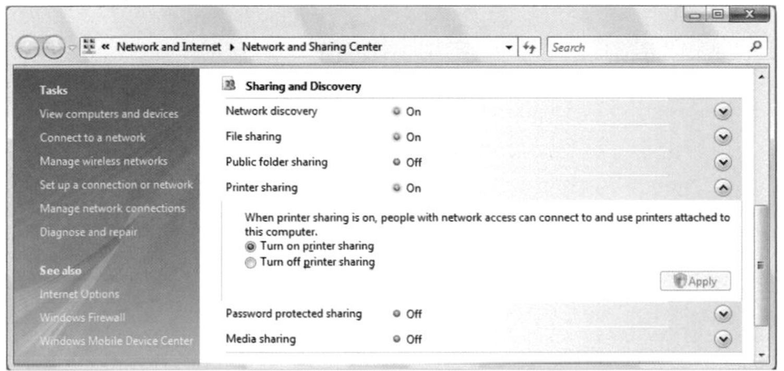

2. Select the required option to change the setting, and then click Apply

This will allow other people on the network to access the printers defined in your Printers folder.

To view your Printers folder:

1. Select Start, Control Panel, then click the Printers entry in Hardware and Sound

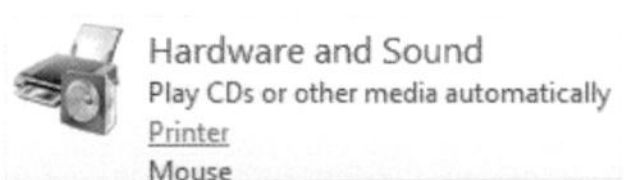

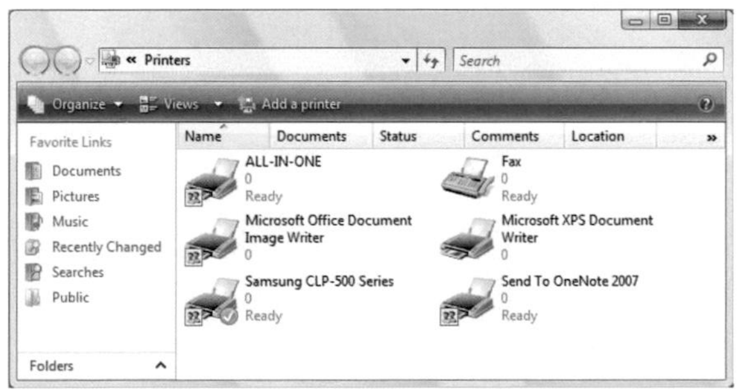

When you enable printer sharing, the devices in your Printers folder will immediately be flagged with the Sharing indicator. Similarly, when you disable sharing, the indicators are removed.

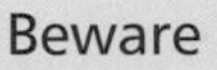

Beware

The Printer Sharing option is disabled when there are no printers attached to the computer.

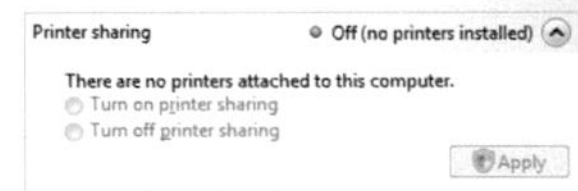

Don't forget

Some of the devices defined in the Printers folder are not able to be shared, for example the Microsoft XPS Document Writer and the Microsoft Fax printer (software defined devices).

Password Protected Sharing

Hot tip

When you turn on password protected sharing, only people who have the username and password for an account on your computer will be able to access your shared resources.

Beware

Windows Vista does not allow users without passwords to access network resources, so the accounts used for shared access must be set up with passwords.

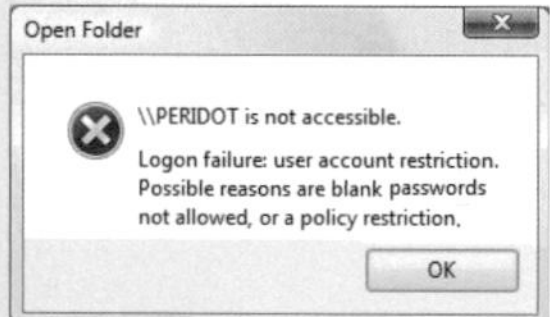

Don't forget

If you click the box to Remember my password, then the next time you want to access that computer, you'll just have to open it.

1. Click the down arrow next to Password protected sharing

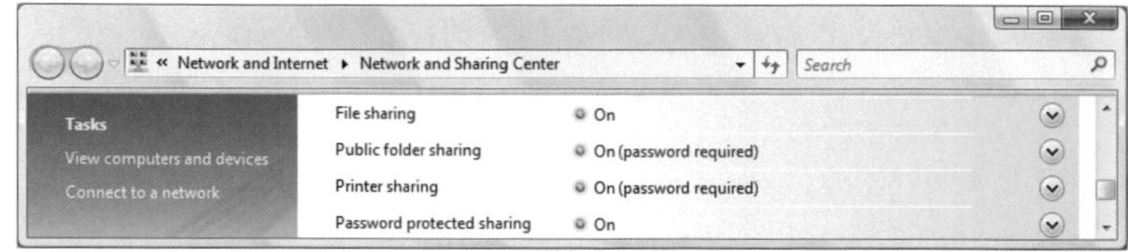

2. Select Turn on password protected sharing and Apply

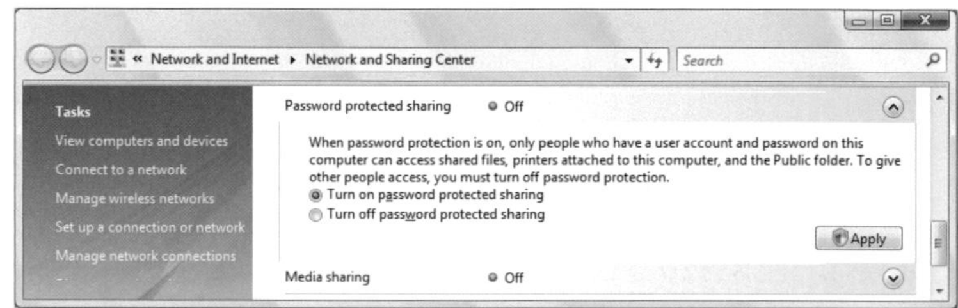

Public folder sharing and Printer sharing are now flagged as Password required. To access a computer requiring a password:

3. Select Start, Network and double click a computer icon

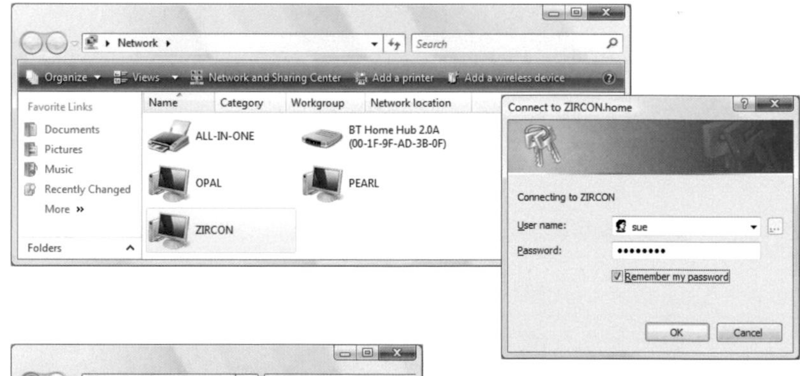

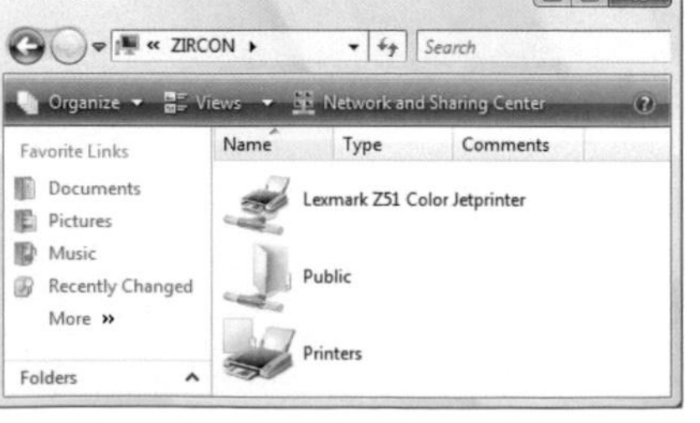

4. Enter a username and password for that computer and click OK to display the shared items available

Media Sharing

The final entry in the sharing and discovery portion of the Network and Sharing Center is media sharing. To turn this on:

1. Click the down arrow next to Media sharing and select the Change button to display the Media Sharing dialog

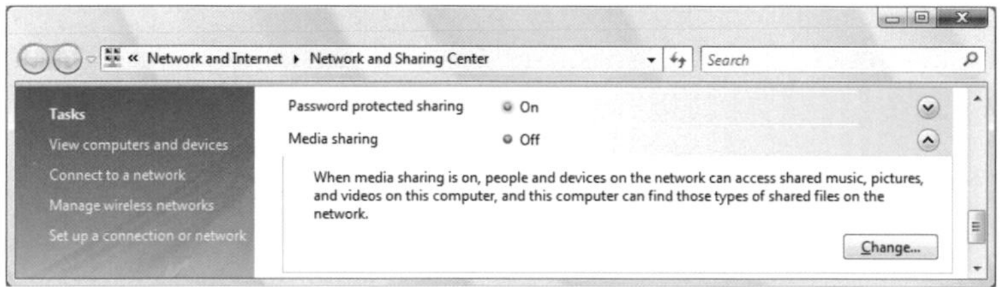

2. Click the box to Share my media, then click OK

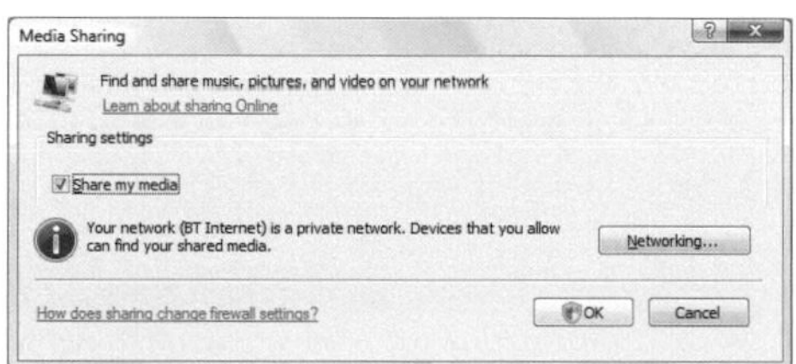

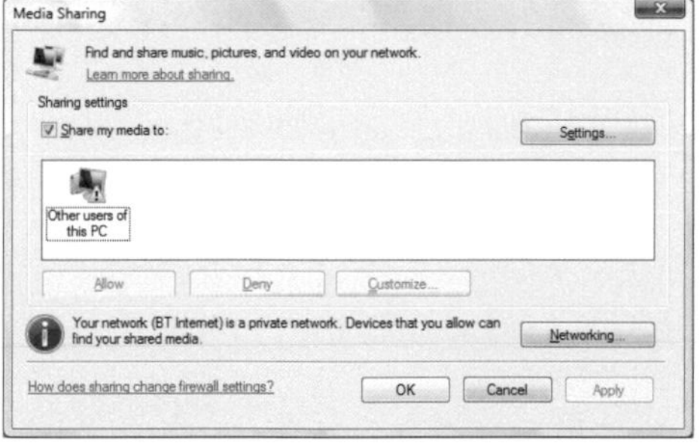

3. Click OK to confirm and Media sharing will be enabled

4. Open the Network folder, and you'll see additional entries for computers that offer shared media

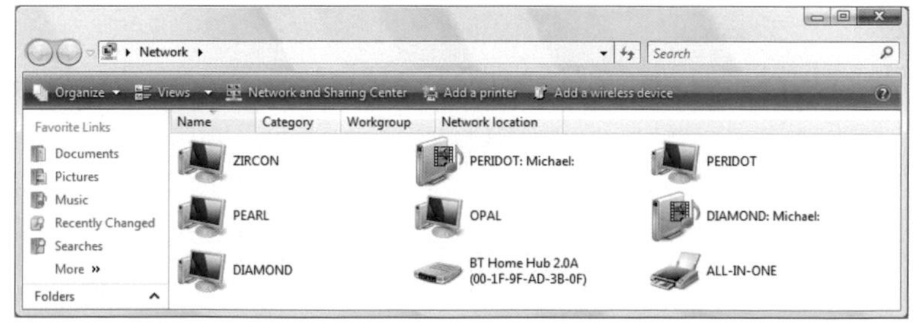

Hot tip

This is part of Windows Media Player, and you could start the program, display the Library tab menu and select Media Sharing from there.

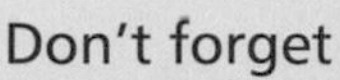

Don't forget

Click Settings to select the media types, star ratings and parental ratings for the media files you want to share.

Hot tip

The media files that you share can be used by other computers on the network or by networked devices such as digital media receivers.

File Sharing Wizard

If you want to share folders or files that are not in the Public folder, you can use the File Sharing Wizard:

1. Locate the folder to share, for example select Start, Computer, and double click the C: drive icon

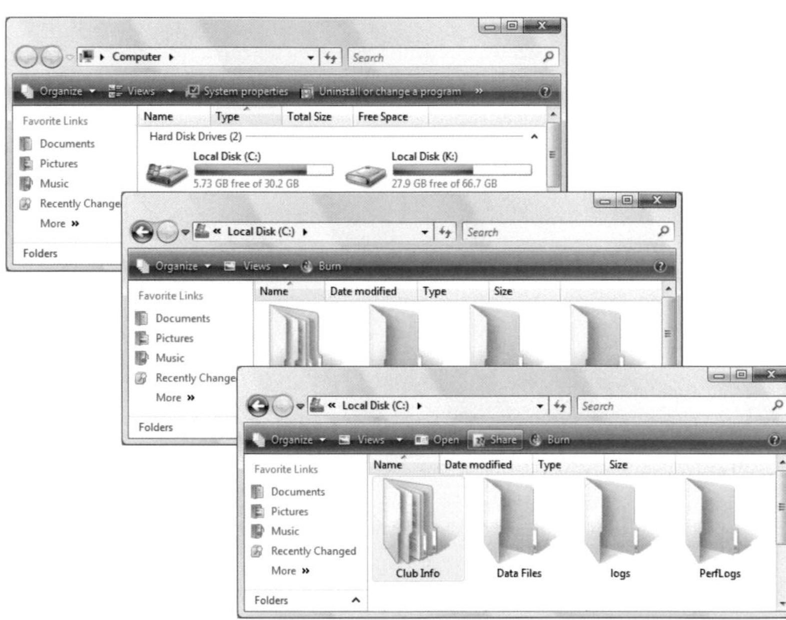

2. Select the folder you want to share, e.g. Club Info and click the Share button that appears on the toolbar

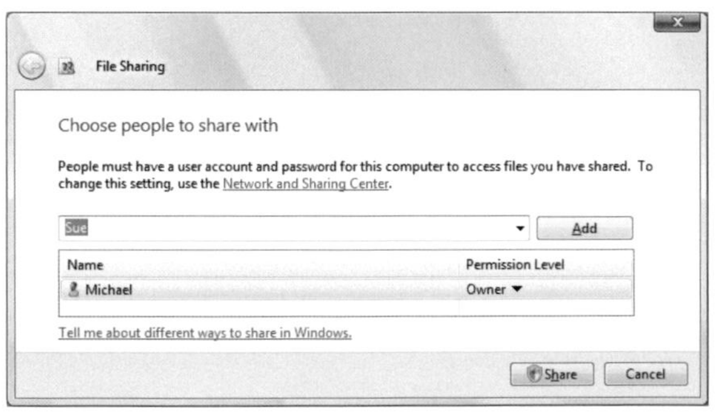

3. In the File Sharing Wizard, type or select the required username (defined on this computer) and click Add

Hot tip

If you want to share a subfolder or file, open the folder, and then select the subfolder or file required.

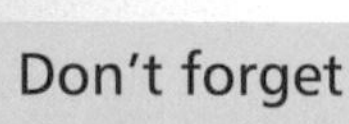

Don't forget

Click the down arrow to select a user from the list, to add all users on the list, or to create a new user name.

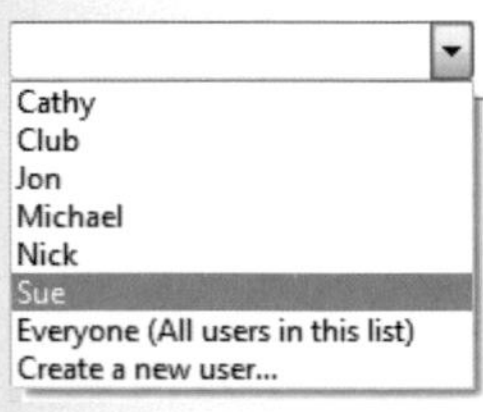

4. Check the permission level assigned, and click the down arrow to change the selection

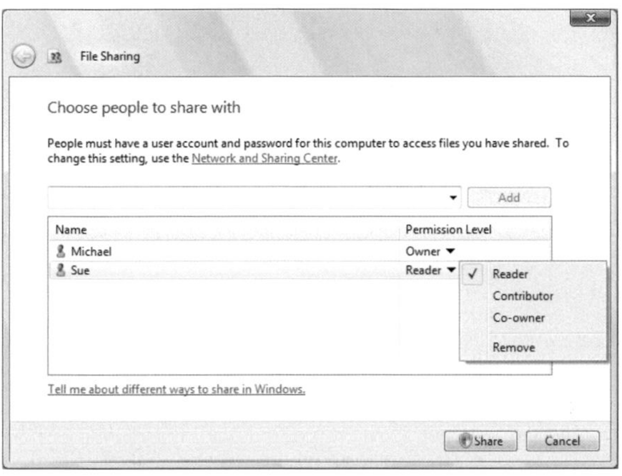

There are four permission levels offered:

- Reader, the default level, where users can view only
- Contributor, where the user can add new files to the shared folder, and change or delete any file that user has added
- Co-owner, where the user can create new items, and make changes to or delete any item
- Remove, to withdraw permission for that user

5. Click the Share button when the required users are added

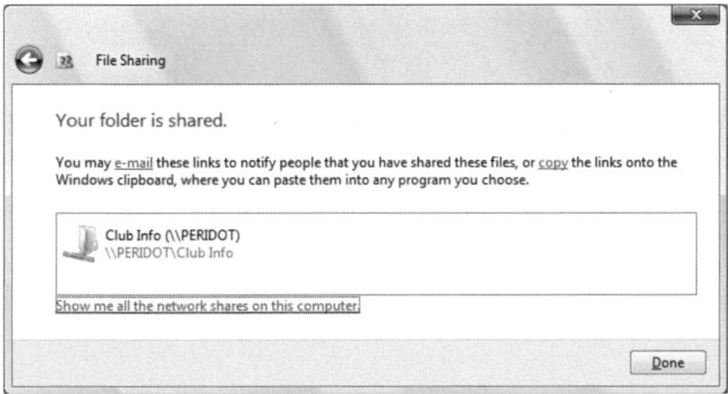

6. Click Done to finish with the File Sharing Wizard

Hot tip

Repeat steps 3 and 4 to add additional users to share the selected folder or file.

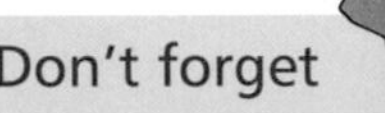

Don't forget

To send an email to the users to let them know the folder or file is being shared, click the email link. If there are matching nicknames in your Address Book, the email addresses will be entered automatically.

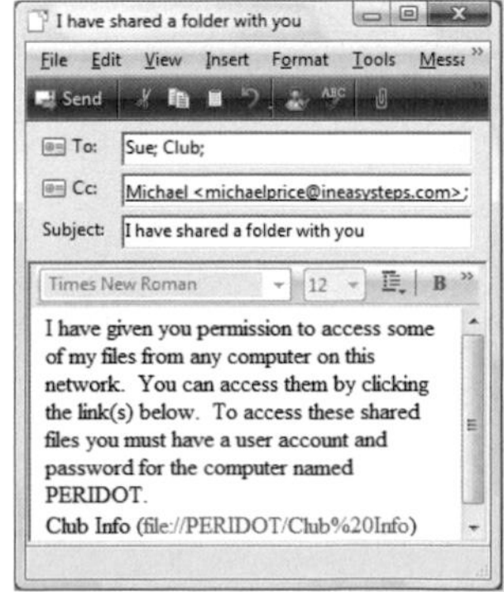

Command Line Tools

Beware

Note that to use their full function, the tools may need to be run with elevation, i.e. as an administrator level user.

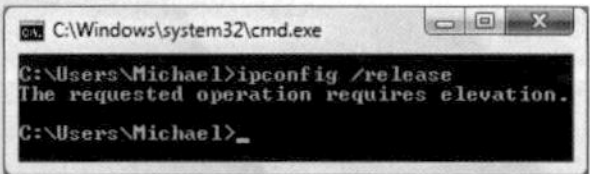

You can access Windows Vista networking tools from the command prompt. These can be used to monitor networking activity and to repair network connections. Some are best left to the networking specialists, but there are a couple that can be very useful in helping you to investigate and resolve network problems.

IPconfig

This displays the IP address, subnet mask and gateway for each network adapter on your computer.

1. Click Start, type cmd and press Enter to display the command prompt

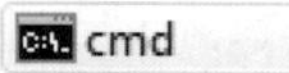

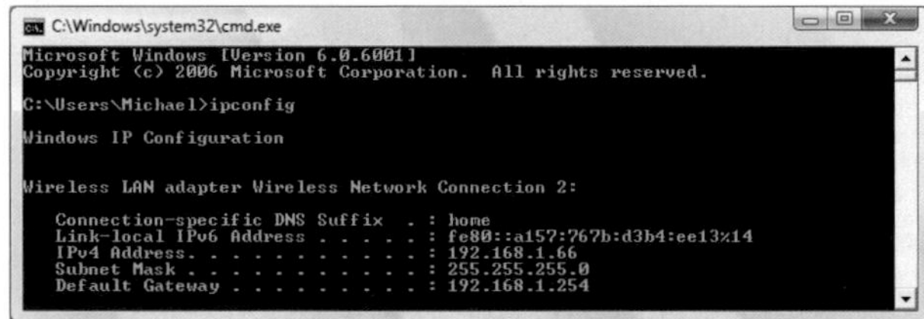

2. Type ipconfig and press Enter

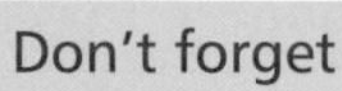

Don't forget

Ping sends echo request messages to the target and listens for echo response replies. It measures the round-trip time and records any data loss.

Ping

This is used to test whether a particular computer or device is reachable across the network and to check computer names or IPs

1. Display the command prompt and type ping diamond

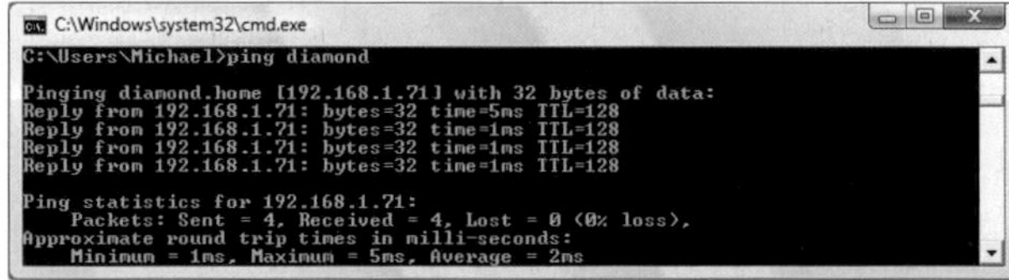

Hot tip

If you know the name, you can find the IP. If you know the IP, you can find the name.

2. Type ping -a 192.168.1.71 to find the computer name

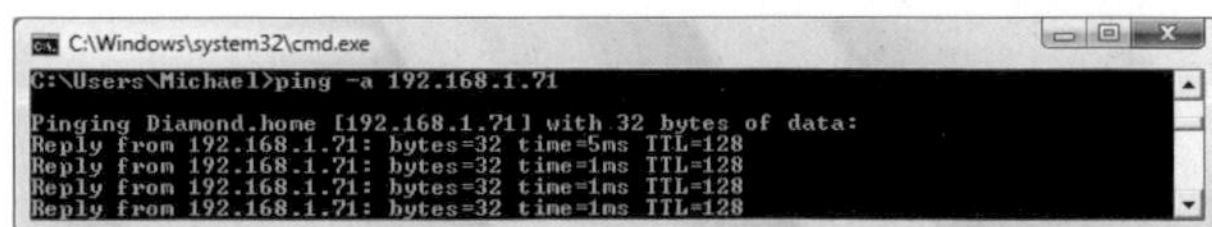

7 Other Networking Environments

You (or your visitors) may have computers with other operating systems, such as XP, Apple Mac or Linux. You can allow these to participate in your wireless network. We also look at Windows 7, the follow on to Windows Vista, and at the Windows Home Server.

Non-Vista Computers

Hot tip

Although Windows Vista may be your primary operating system, your wireless network is not just for Vista.

You may use a Windows Vista computer to set up your wireless router, for example the Netgear DGN2000 (see page 60). However, when the configuration is completed, the router operates independently of Windows Vista, and any computer will be able to connect to the wireless network it creates, whatever operating system that computer may be running. All that's necessary is a compatible wireless adapter in the computer and the appropriate security information for connecting to the network.

Don't forget

You can provide a guest ID on your computers, to give visitors controlled access to the resources on your system, for example to offer printing capability without making your private data accessible.

This will allow you to attach an older non-Vista computer to your network. It also makes it easier for you to invite visitors to access your home network, whatever type of computer or operating system they may be using.

To help make the connection with your wireless network, you should make the necessary network details available, e.g.

- The SSID or network name you have set up
- The type of encryption you are using, WEP or WPA
- The required passkey or security code
- User name and password if sharing network resources

You should also make sure that the computers are set up and ready to make the connection, with:

- Wireless adapter inserted and turned on
- TCP/IP settings set to DHCP
- DNS settings, if required, set to DHCP
- Antivirus software installed and up to date

Windows XP Computers

There are some important differences in the way Windows XP and Windows Vista operate, which you need to be aware of when you mix these systems on your wireless network.

Shared folders

In Vista the shared folders are stored in the Public folder, which contains Public Documents, Public Pictures etc.

In XP the equivalent is Shared Documents, which contains shared document files plus shared folders My Pictures, My Music etc.

Workgroup name

An XP computer can only detect and access computers that are in the same workgroup as itself. To check the workgroup name:

1. Click Start, right-click My Computer, and then click Properties, and select the Computer Name tab

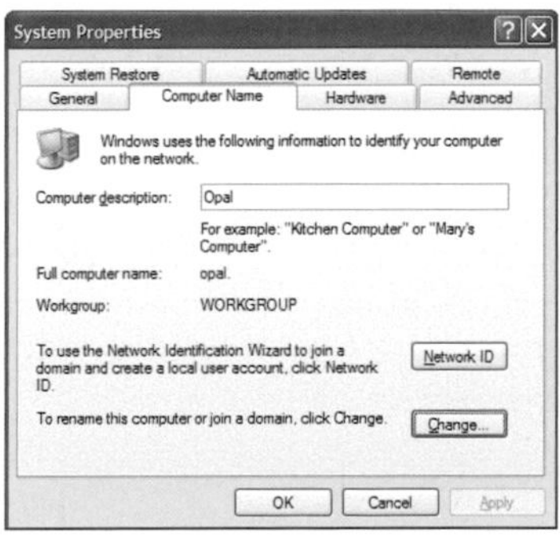

2. To change the name, click Change, type the new name in Workgroup, and click OK, then OK again

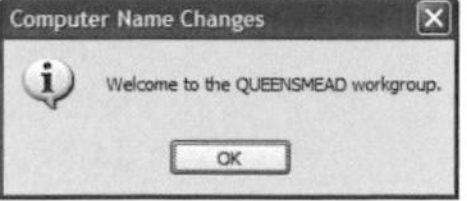

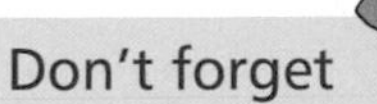

Don't forget

Vista normally requires a user name and password for access to shared folders. In XP, the default is to allow simple file sharing, so there is less protection for your data.

Hot tip

In Vista the default name is Workgroup, as it is in most editions of XP except in XP Home Edition, where the default is Mshome. However, in each case, you could have changed the name.

Beware

You must restart the computer for this change to take effect.

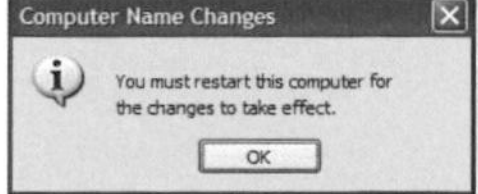

Connect an XP Computer

Hot tip

Make sure that there is a wireless adapter installed and active, and check that you have assigned the same workgroup name as the existing computers use.

To connect an XP computer to your wireless network:

1. Select Start, Connect To, and then click Wireless Network Connection

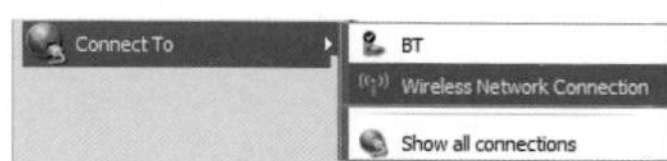

2. Select the wireless network you want, and click Connect

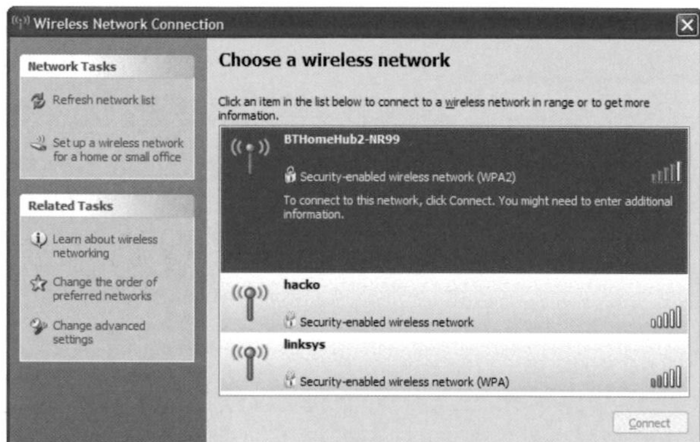

3. Type the network key, confirm the key, then click Connect

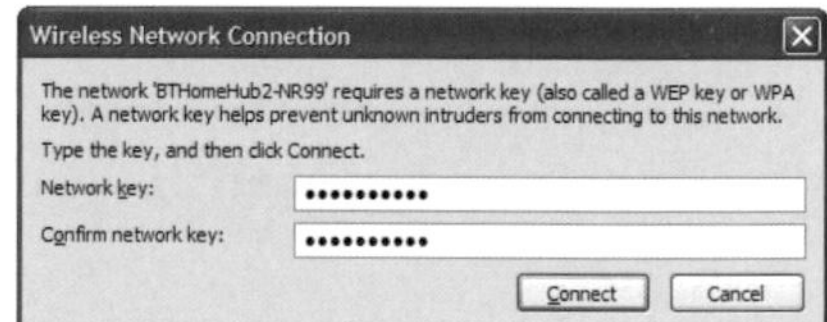

4. Windows locates and acquires the selected wireless network and marks it as Connected

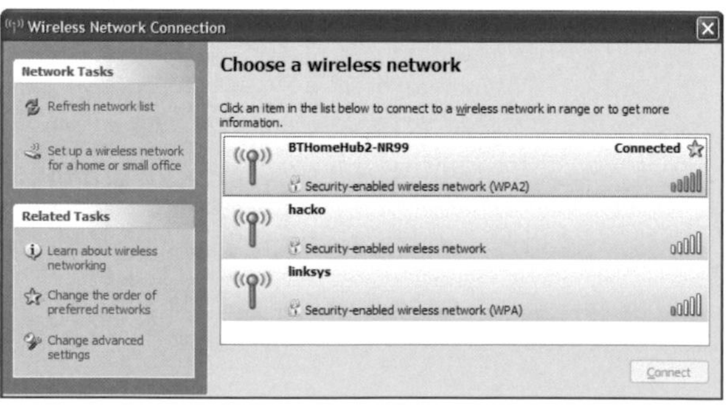

5. The Windows XP computer is now be part of the wireless network and able to take advantage of shared resources

Mapping XP Computers

1. Open the Network and Sharing Center and click View full map to see the XP computer on your network

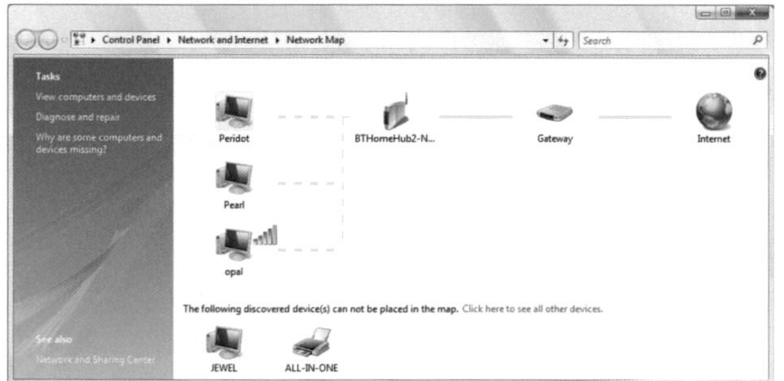

To make the computer Jewel fully detectable:

2. At the Windows Download Center www.microsoft.com/downloads, search for Link Layer Topology Discovery

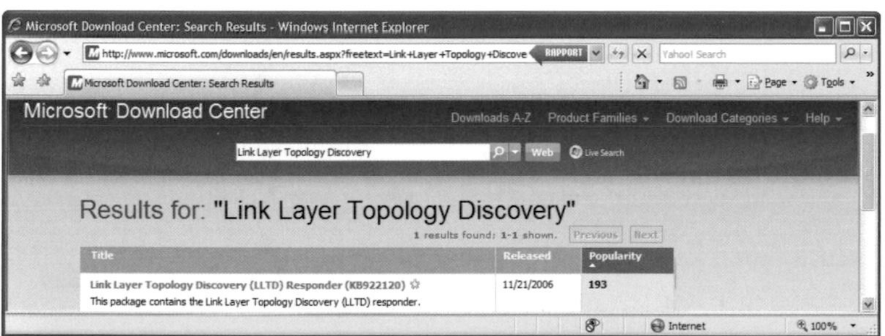

3. Select the resulting document, and then download and install the file WindowsXP-KB922120-v5-x86-ENU.exe

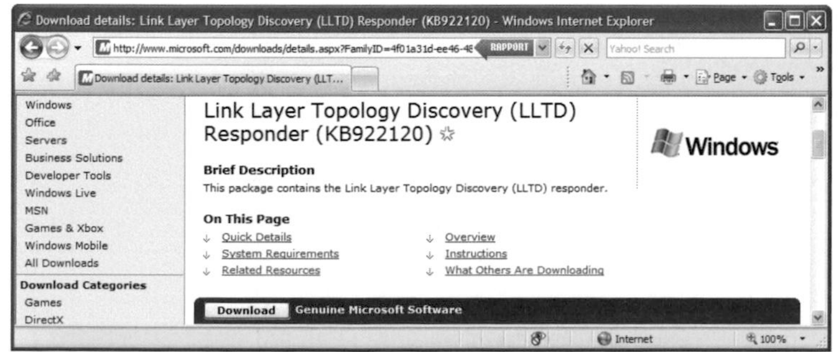

Hot tip

Before an XP computer can be detected for the Vista network map in the Network and Sharing Center, it needs the Link-Layer Topology Discovery (LLTD) protocol so it can respond to scans.

Don't forget

The XP computer Opal appears on the main map. However, Jewel, another XP computer is not properly detected.

Beware

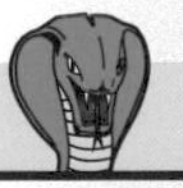

The LLTD responder is already incorporated into the system for computers with the updated SP3 version of Windows XP.

Apple Mac Computers

The required support is already included in the OS X operating system. However, there are several items you may need to check:

Don't forget

Most Apple Mac computers have a wireless network adapter built in, or else you can install an Airport card to add this function.

Enable Windows Sharing

Open System Preferences, select Sharing from the Internet & Network section then click Windows Sharing

Hot tip

Windows Sharing must be enabled on the Apple Mac, otherwise, Windows systems will be unable to access its resources.

Check Workgroup Name

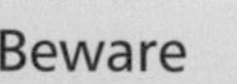

Beware

Both Apple and Vista use the name Workgroup as the default, but this could be changed on either system.

1 Select Applications, Utilities, Directory Access and check that SMB/CIFS is selected, then click Configure

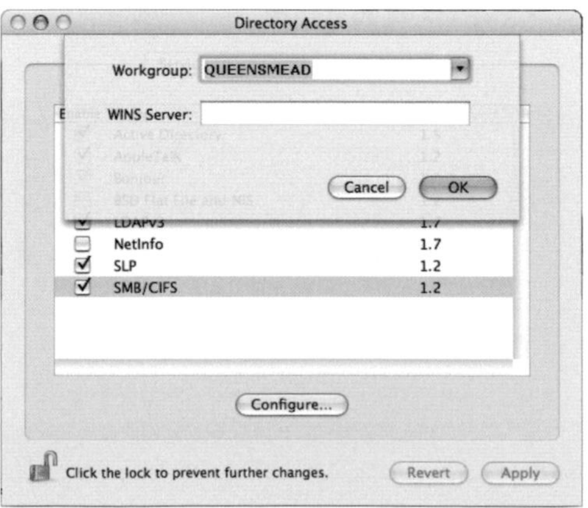

2. Check the workgroup name and if needed, change the workgroup name to that used by the Windows Vista computers on your wireless network

User Accounts

User accounts must be created on the Apple computer, to allow Windows users to access the shared resources on that machine.

1. Open System Preferences, select Accounts from within the System section and click the plus sign to create new user accounts

2. Windows users must enter the appropriate usernames and passwords to access resources on the Apple computer

Connect to the Wireless Network

To connect to the wireless network, you'll need to know the SSID network name and the security password.

1. Click on the Airport icon on the top right of the desktop to display networks within range

2. Click on the required network and the sign on screen will appear

3. Select the Wireless Security type, enter the password, and click Join to connect

You will now be able to open your web browser and surf the Internet, or access resources on the other computers, or make resources on your computer available to others on the network.

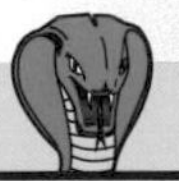

Beware

Depending on the type of security and the software level you are using, you may be required to enter security keys as hexadecimal numbers.

Linux Computers

Hot tip

This particular laptop had no built in wireless adapter, so a D-Link USB wireless adapter was inserted. This was recognized by Ubuntu without requiring any installation CD or software download.

You may have visitors who would like to connect to your network, using a laptop running a version of Linux. This is increasingly likely since many of the small, light weight netbook computers use Linux as their operating system.

For example, to connect to the wireless network using a laptop with Ubuntu installed:

1. To start with, the network status indicator icon shows that there is no connection established

2. Left click the status icon to display the drop down menu

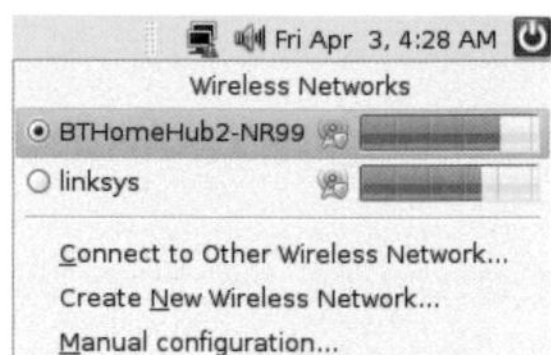

3. Ubuntu locates available networks, in this case the wireless home network router and extender

4. Click the required network name and you'll be prompted for the wireless network key

5. Confirm the wireless security and type, then enter the security key and click Login to Network

6. After a short wait the network connection should be activated

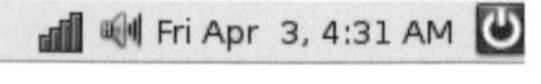

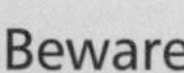

Beware

When you have roaming mode enabled, Ubuntu will automatically locate an open network (one with no encryption set up) or a network for which it already has the security key, and then connect to it.

With the connection made, you can make use of the network, e.g.

1. Click the Browser button to surf the Internet

To open the Network folder, select Places and then click Network.

2. In the Network folder, double click Windows Network, then double click the workgroup to display the computers

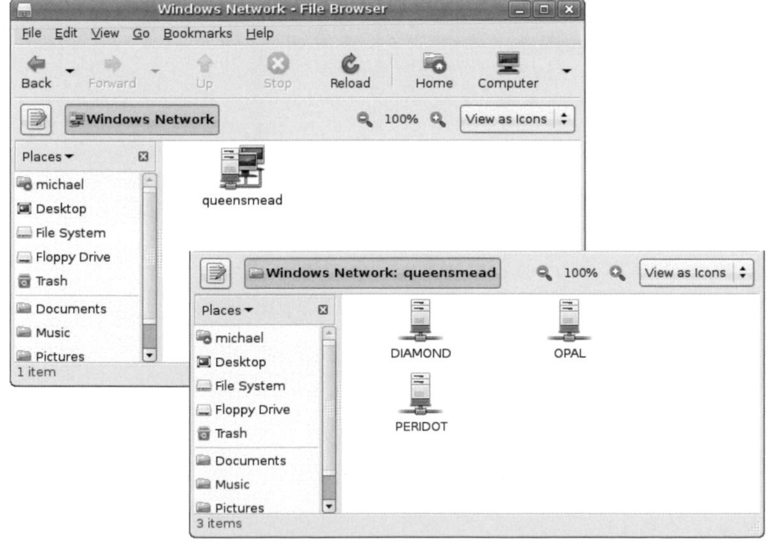

Double click the computer icon to display its components e.g. drives and public folder. Note that you'll need a user name and password to access their contents.

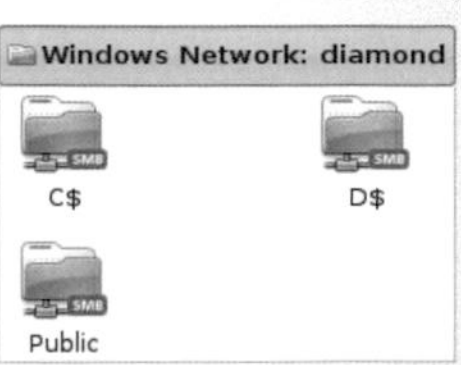

Windows 7 Computers

Hot tip

Note that these screen images are from the early release version. The appearance and other details may vary in the final release.

This version of Windows is the follow on to Windows Vista, and it retains and improves on the Vista networking capabilities.

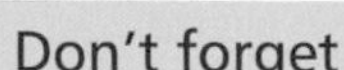

Don't forget

Initially the Network Status icon indicates that you are not connected but connections are available.

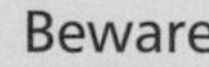

Beware

By default, Windows saves the security details and connects automatically the next time your computer is in range with the selected network.

If the wireless adapter is already installed, adding a Windows 7 computer to an existing wireless network is quite straight forward.

When your computer is in range of the required network:

1. Left click the Network Status icon in the notification area and the available wireless networks will be displayed

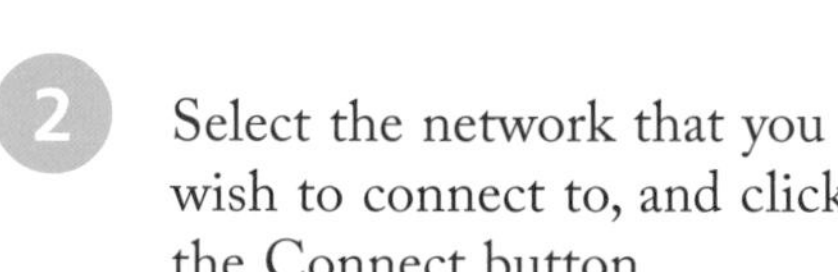

2. Select the network that you wish to connect to, and click the Connect button

3. Windows interrogates to the network and determines the type of network security that is in operation

To log in to a secure wireless network:

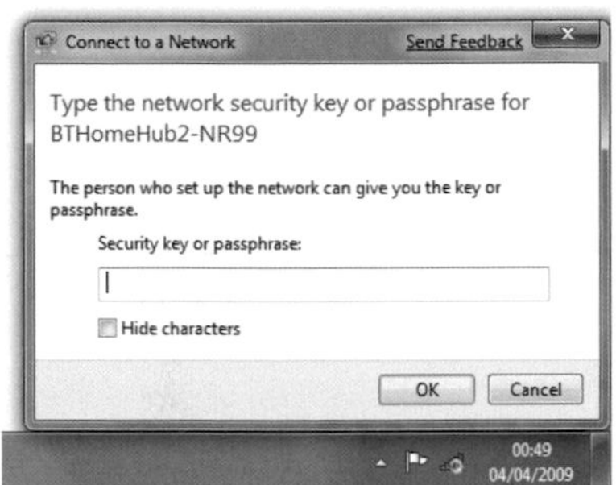

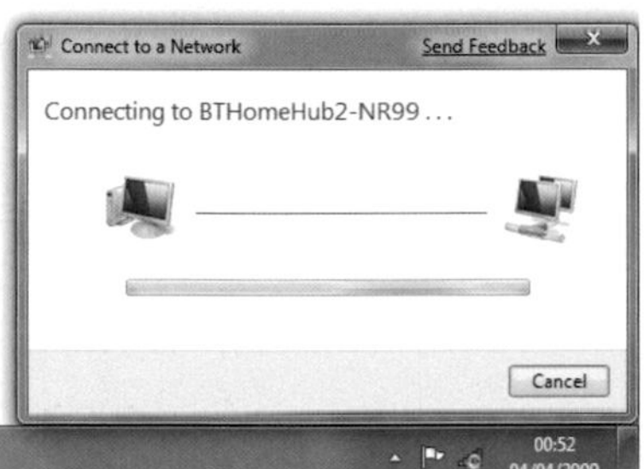

1. Click the box to Hide characters, type the password and click OK

2. Windows connects to the network which by default is Public, and the display is updated to show the new status

3. Left click the Network Status icon if necessary, then right click the network name to disconnect, to display detailed status information or connection properties, and to diagnose any network problems you may have

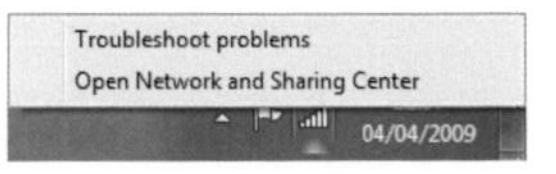

4. Right click the Network Status icon to run the diagnostics to Troubleshoot problems

Hot tip

It is best to hide the characters you type, especially if you are in a public location.

Beware

In Windows 7, the connection activity is at the Network Status icon rather than in the Network and Sharing Center.

Don't forget

The right click menu and the left click menu both provide a link to the Network and Sharing Center.

Windows 7 Network Center

1. Left click the Network Status icon if necessary, then select Open Network and Sharing Center

This provides the basic network information and allows you to view or change the networking settings, or to display the full network map.

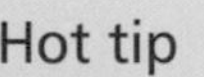

Hot tip

The Advanced sharing settings provides access to the network discovery, file and printer sharing, media sharing and password protected sharing options featured in the Windows Vista Network and Sharing Center (see page 102).

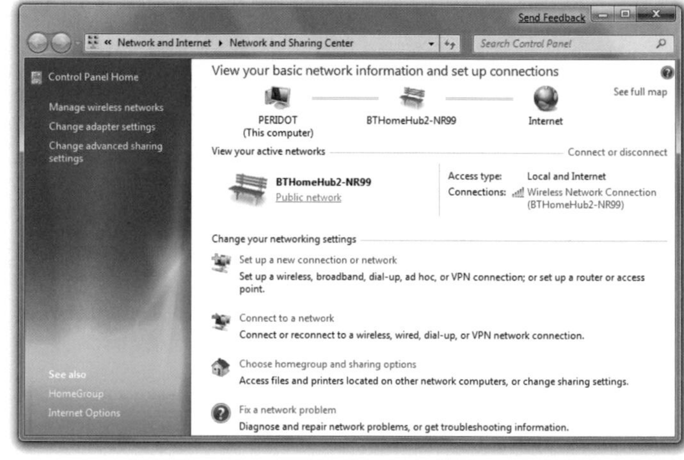

2. Click the current network location (e.g. Public network)

Don't forget

In Windows 7, there are different network settings for each of these three network locations.

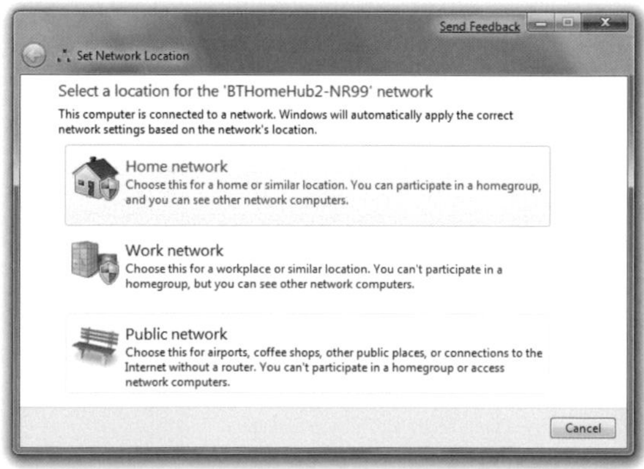

3. Select the appropriate location (e.g. Home network)

When you select the Home network location, you are offered the opportunity to create a homegroup to share libraries and devices.

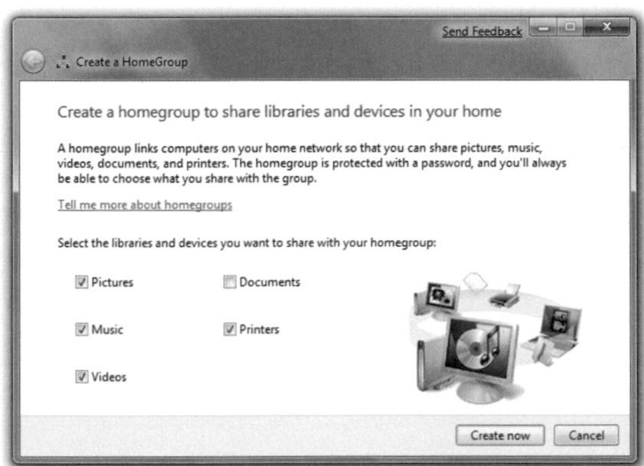

Using a homegroup is one of the easiest ways to share files and folders on a wireless home network. However, homegroups are not available on work or public networks, and computers must be running Windows 7 to participate in a homegroup.

For a Windows 7 computer connected to an existing network with Windows Vista computers:

1. Click Cancel to postpone creating a homegroup

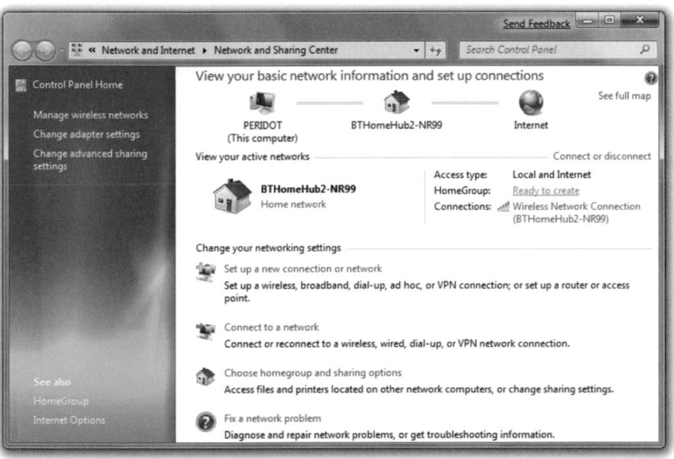

If you decide to try a homegroup, open the Network and Sharing Center and select Ready to create

Only computers running Windows 7 can create and join homegroups.

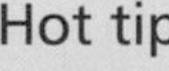

When you do create a homegroup, you can require a password so only authorised users can join and access the resources.

Windows Home Server

Your wireless home network provides an easy way to share data on your computers, whether it is through the Windows Vista file, folder and media sharing or via the Windows 7 homegroups. However, there is one major drawback – the resources are only available while the host computer is active on the network. Sharing your media files, for example, could mean having all your computers up and running, even when there's no users logged on.

The business environment would use a dedicated file server to resolve this problem. For the home environment, there's a halfway house – the Windows Home Server (WHS). This allows you to:

- Back up and restore files and computers
- Access your data from home, office or on the road
- Store and share digital media files
- Provide additional storage capacity for your computers

Windows Home Server-based computers are available in a number of configurations and designs from a broad range of manufacturers, though availability varies by country. For example, HP offers the MediaSmart Server which provides 500GB or 1 TB capacity, plus room for massive expansion.

You don't have to go for a ready-made solution. You can download Windows Home Server and try it out for yourself, with the free 120 day evaluation edition. For details see **http://www.microsoft.com/windows/products/winfamily/windowshomeserver/eval.mspx**.

You'll need a computer with at least:

1 GHz Pentium III (or equivalent) processor
512 MB RAM
70 GB hard drive as primary hard drive
Bootable DVD drive
VGA or higher-resolution monitor
keyboard and mouse or pointing device
100 Mbps or faster Ethernet adapter

Hot tip

With Windows Home Server, you can back up all of your family's PCs automatically. Plus you can connect, organize, and share your photos, videos, music, and other files with friends and family.

Beware

The home network must include a broadband router with a 100 Mbps or faster wired Ethernet connection for your home server. All other computers can connect wirelessly.

Don't forget

The download size is about 875MB, so you may prefer to order the evaluation kit and receive the evaluation software on DVD (NB: shipping and handling charges may apply).

The following discs are included with Windows Home Server:

- WHS Installation DVD, used to install the server software on your home server
- WHS Connector Software CD, to install the connector software on your home computers
- WHS Home Computer Restore CD, to restore a home computer from a backup located on your home server

To install Windows Home Server

1. Use a wired connection to connect your home server to your broadband router then power up the computer

2. Insert the Setup DVD, restart the computer and boot from the DVD. When prompted, enter your region, language, product key and home server name

3. Setup will proceed and may take several hours, but no additional input will be required until it completes

4. When the Welcome page appears, you'll be asked for a password and to allow automatic Windows Updates to keep the software up to date

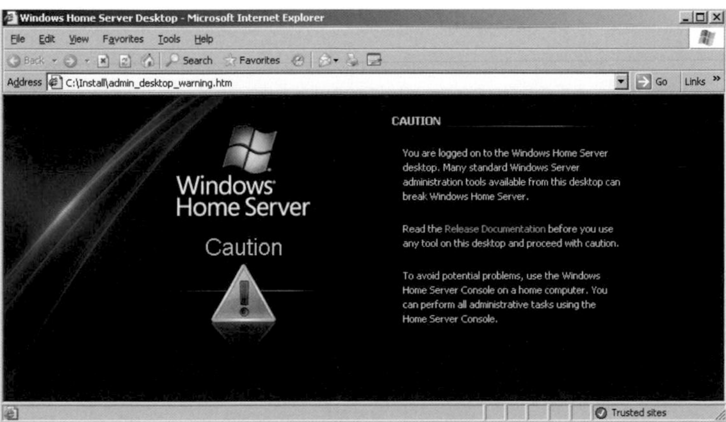

5. Finally, log off and shut down, then disconnect keyboard, mouse and monitor, and restart the computer

Hot tip

When the software is installed, you no longer need a keyboard, mouse, or monitor attached to your home server. You can install and use the WHS Console on your home computers to configure the server.

Don't forget

Disconnect any external USB or FireWire hard drives, otherwise Setup won't proceed. You can add external hard drives to your home server after Setup is complete.

Beware

The hard drives on your computer will be formatted and all existing data will be lost.

Don't forget

Windows Home Server is meant to be a remotely administered device, and should be configured from a home computer after installation.

WHS Connector

The Windows Home Server Connector software will:

- Connect your home computer to Windows Home Server
- Automatically back up your home computer nightly
- Monitor the health of your home computer
- Enable you to configure and remotely administer Windows Home Server from your home computer

To install the Windows Home Server Connector software

1. Insert the Windows Home Server Connector CD into a computer that is connected to your home network

2. The Connector Wizard installs to your computer then finds your home server on the network

3. Enter the Administrator password for the server

Don't forget

You can install Connector software from the shared Software folder in the server which you'll find in the Network folder. You must sign on as Administrator using the server password.

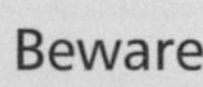
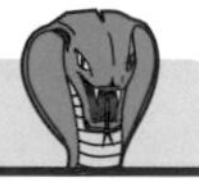

Beware

If you have an advanced network setup, you may be asked to provide the home server name to assist the Connector in locating the server.

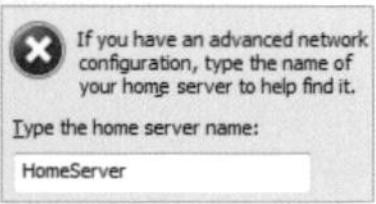

The Connector joins your computer to the server and configures the computer backup.

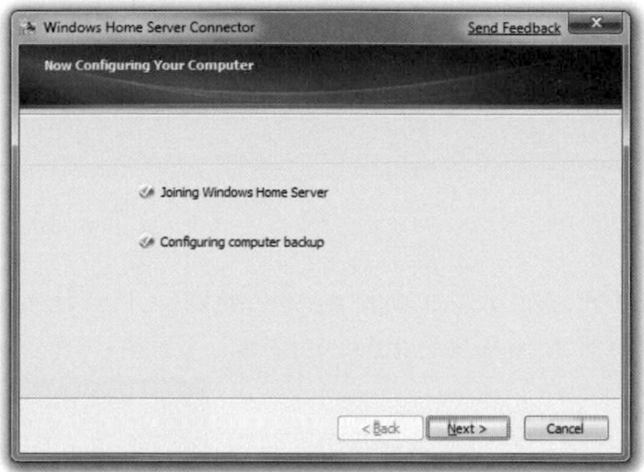

When the configuration is completed, the Connector Wizard reports the results. It tells you that the computer will be backed up between midnight and 6 am each day.

Note that in this example the Connector has found a volume on the hard disk that cannot be backed up because it is not NTFS. This is in fact a hidden FAT32 partition on the second hard drive.

You can make changes to the backup configuration, shared folders and other Windows Home Server settings:

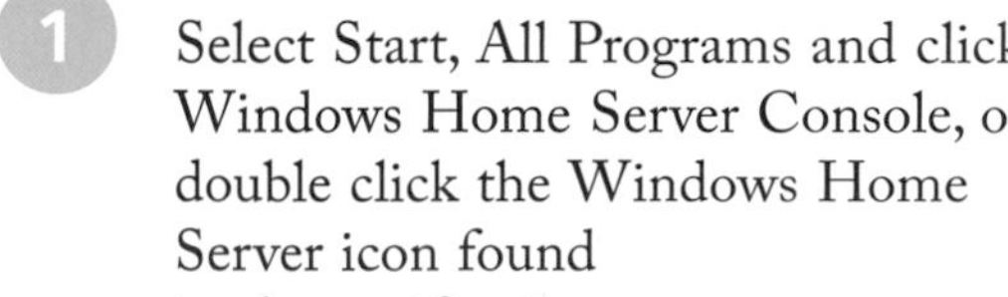

1. Select Start, All Programs and click Windows Home Server Console, or double click the Windows Home Server icon found in the notification area

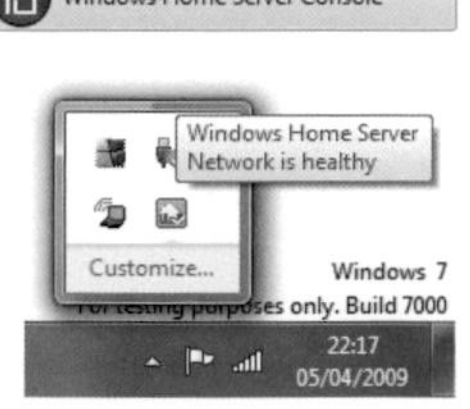

Hot tip

Run the Windows Home Server Connector Wizard on all of the home computers to connect them to Windows Home Server. Be sure to run the wizard on one computer at a time.

Don't forget

The server selects all NTFS partitions on the installed hard drives, whether they are visible or hidden.

Hot tip

The Windows Home Server icon displays a status message when you move the mouse pointer over the icon.

WHS Console

Hot tip

Click the Options button to get a hint if you've forgotten the password. In a secure environment, you could ask Windows to remember the WHS password for you.

1. Type the administrator password for the home server and click the arrow (or press Enter)

2. Your home computer will connect to the Windows Home Server

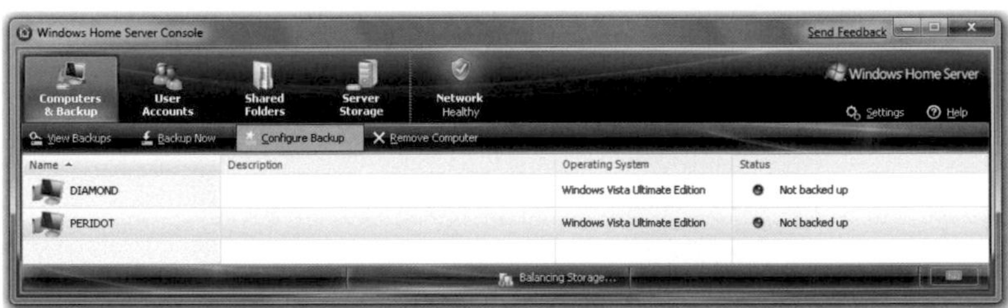

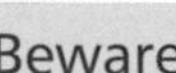

Beware

You can run the Backup Configuration Wizard to change the backup configuration for any of the computers on your home network.

3. Click Computers & Backup, select your computer from the list and click Configure Backup to start the Wizard

4. Click Next to continue running the Wizard

5. Clear the box for any drive that you do not want to backup

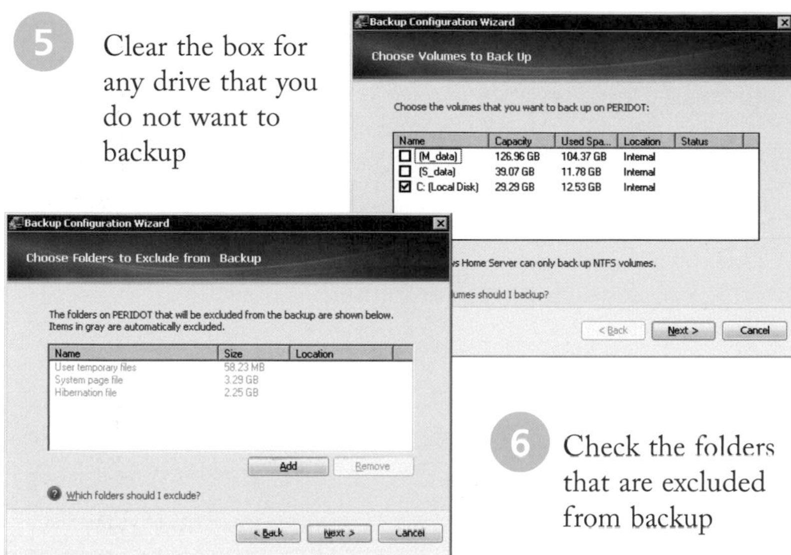

6. Check the folders that are excluded from backup

7. The Wizard summarizes the revised configuration for the automatic backup of your computer

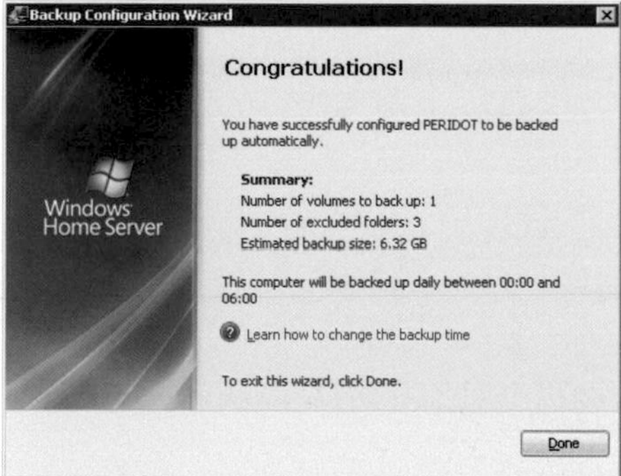

8. When you sign on later, you'll find the backup completed

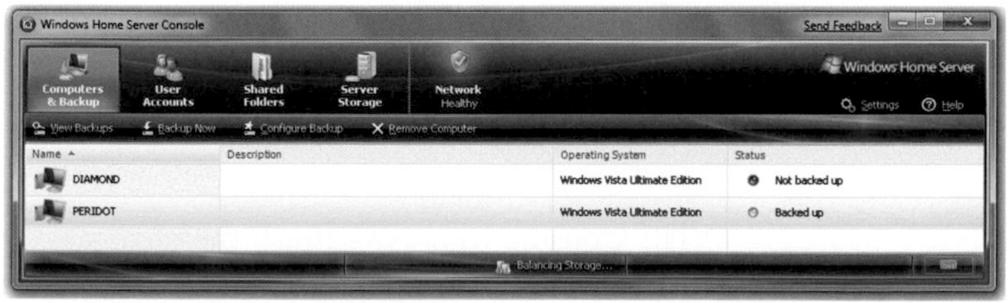

Hot tip

In this example, the server has selected the partitions on the second drive, but these do not need backup, so they can be deselected.

Don't forget

The server does not backup temporary files or working files such as the page file and the hibernation file. Add any other folders that you don't want to backup.

Configuring the Server

When Windows Home Server has been set up and all your home computers connected, you can use the Windows Home Server Console to configure various items on the home server, including:

- User accounts
- Shared folders
- Computer backups
- Server storage
- Windows Home Server Settings

1. Open WHS Console and click the Server Storage button

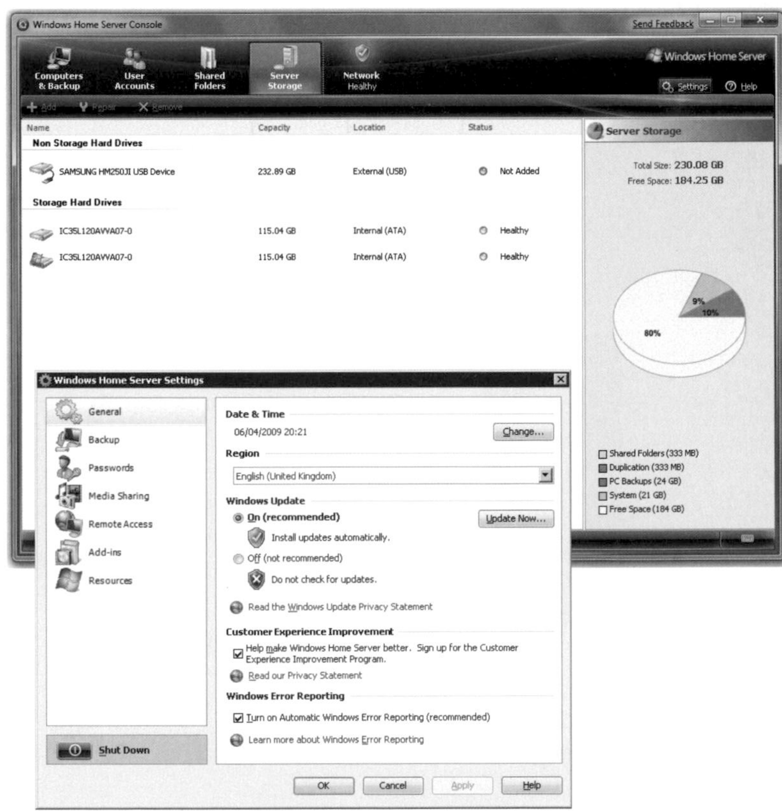

2. Click the Settings command and select the category (e.g. General) to adjust the associated WHS options

3. Close the WHS Console when you finish the changes

Hot tip

Only one home computer at a time can be logged on to the WHS Console.

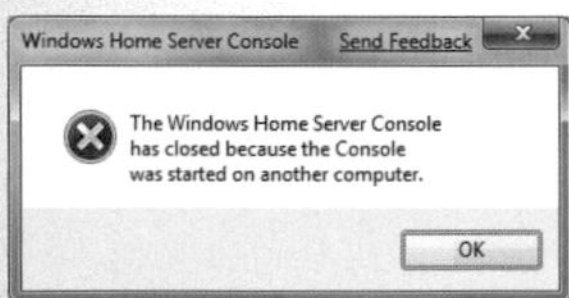

Don't forget

If you need more server storage, you can add external USB 2.0 hard drives, external FireWire (IEEE 1394) hard drives, or internal hard drives.

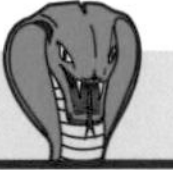

Beware

Your hard drive will be formatted when it is added to your server storage, so make sure there's no required data on the disk.

8 Expanding your Wireless Network

Expand your wireless network by adding devices such as cell phones. These can be connected by USB cable, by Bluetooth or using Wi-Fi if supported. You can also connect cell phones such as the Skypephone directly to the Internet. You can attach a wireless printer. You can also extend the range of the wireless network with a repeater or second router.

Cell Phone to Computer

Hot tip

Your cell phone may offer other methods of attachment, such as Infrared or Wi-Fi.

Don't forget

The installation CD for your device may include other options such as the user guide or an introductory tutorial.

You can connect your cell phone to your computer, by cable or wireless. For example, the BlackBerry Pearl Smartphone offers USB or Bluetooth. It also provides BlackBerry Desktop Software to help manage the interaction.

1. Ensure that the BlackBerry device is not attached to your computer, then insert the BlackBerry User Tools CD

2. If the program doesn't start automatically, select Run Start.exe

3. Choose your language and click Begin

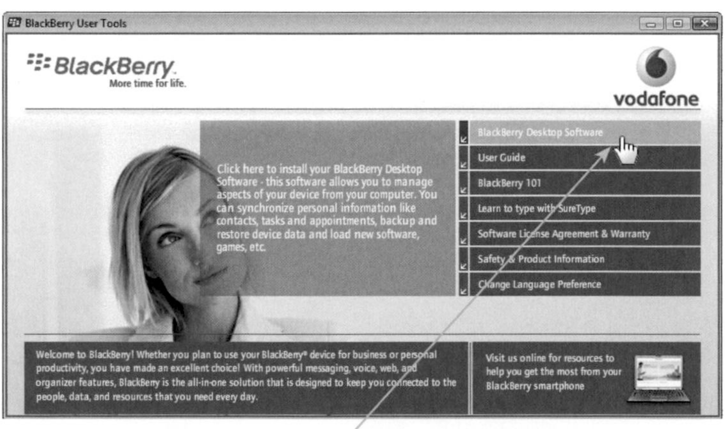

4. Click the links to Install BlackBerry Desktop Software

5 When the InstallShield Wizard starts, follow the prompts to select your location, accept terms and conditions etc

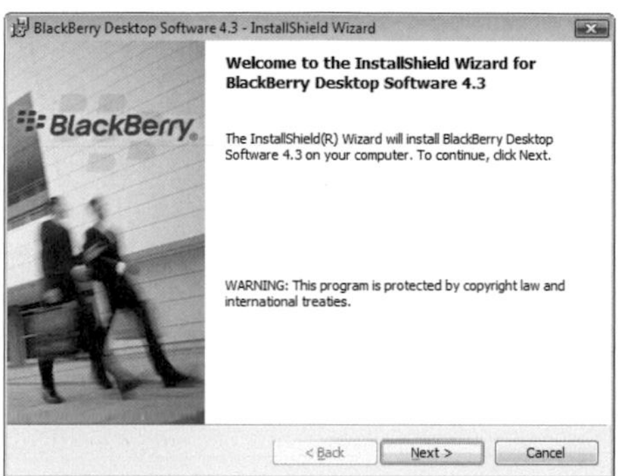

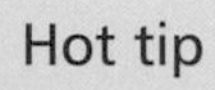

Hot tip

You'll also be asked to confirm the suggested destination folder, setup type (typical or custom) and startup options.

6 For a business account, choose BlackBerry Enterprise Server, otherwise select BlackBerry Internet Service

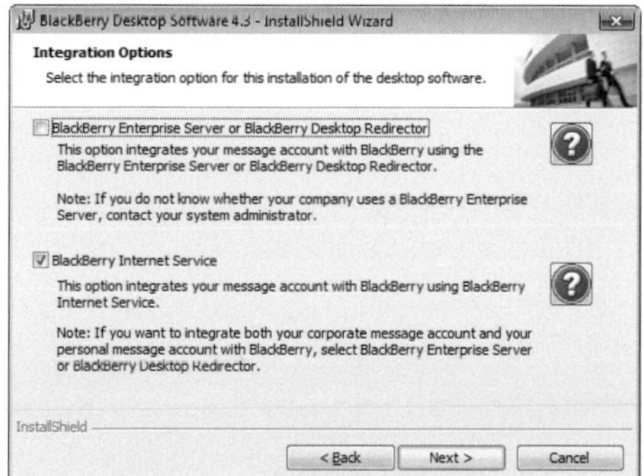

7 Continue the process to install the components of the software

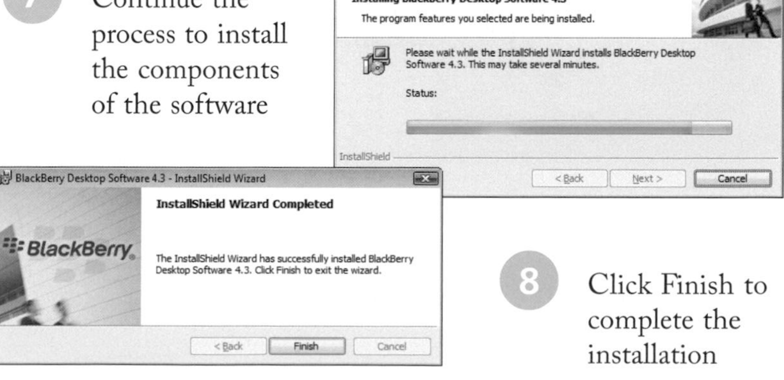

8 Click Finish to complete the installation

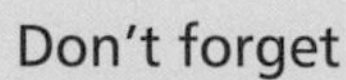

Don't forget

You must restart your system for the configuration changes to take effect.

Attach your Cell Phone

With the default installation, the BlackBerry Desktop Software is loaded when you restart Windows.

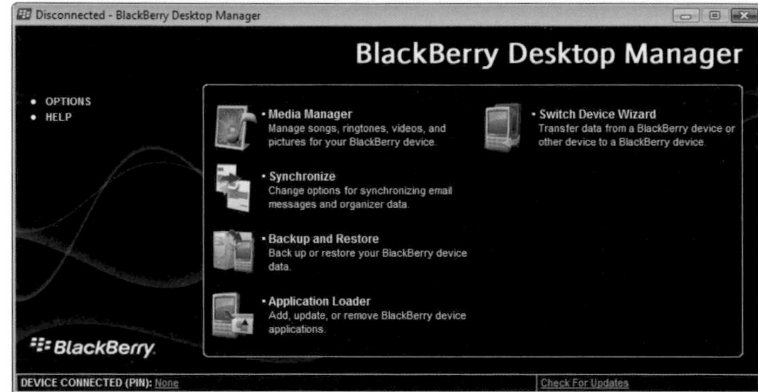

1. Connect the large end of the USB cable to an available USB port on your computer

2. Connect the small end of the USB cable to the micro USB port on the side of your BlackBerry

3. The device is detected, the device driver software is enabled and the device shows as Connected

4. Click Help and then BlackBerry Desktop Manager Help

Hot tip

The BlackBerry, like most modern cell phones, uses the mini-USB connector for the power supply and for computer connection.

Beware

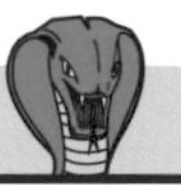

Try to avoid using a USB port on a hub or on a keyboard, because these can have power supply problems.

Don't forget

Click Help and then Device Properties for device information, including the amount of free application space and the battery level.

When you attach your BlackBerry to your computer, you can:

- Synchronize data such as contacts, calendar entries, tasks and memos between your device and your computer
- Back up and restore device data
- Transfer files between your device and your computer
- Add applications to your device
- Set up and manage email message forwarding or wireless calendar synchronization
- Charge your device

Hot tip

The functions offered by your cell phone or PDA may be different, but this list is typical of the functions made available.

Bluetooth Connection

You can connect your BlackBerry to your computer using the Bluetooth facility. This uses radio transmissions to enable devices to connect over short distances. To make the connection in this case requires you to pair the computer and the cell phone device.

To initiate this process:

1. Open the Network and Sharing Center and select the Bluetooth Devices entry

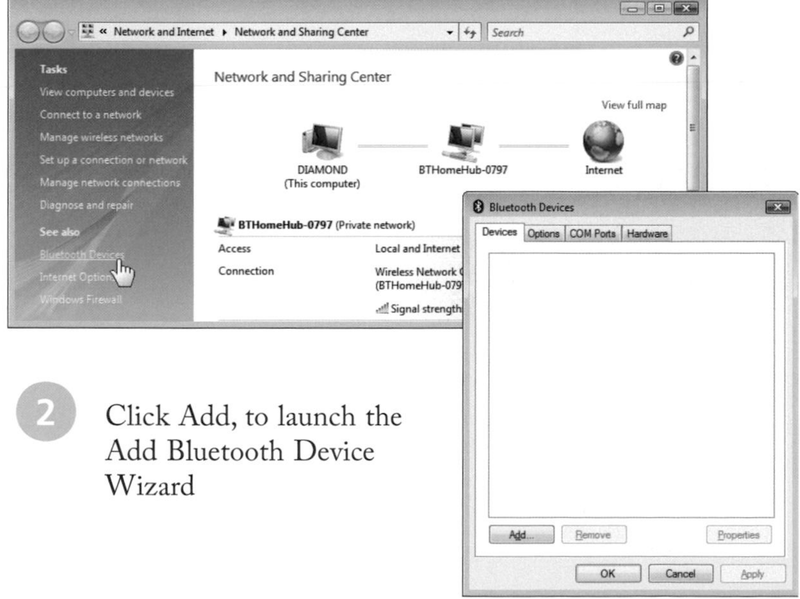

2. Click Add, to launch the Add Bluetooth Device Wizard

Don't forget

You could open the Control Panel and select Network and Internet (or select Hardware and Sound) and then select Bluetooth Devices.

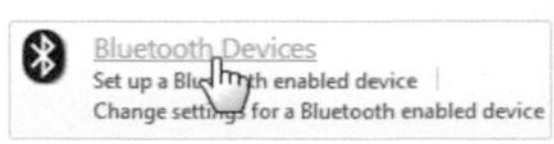

Add Bluetooth Device

Before letting the wizard proceed, you need to set up your device so that the computer can find it.

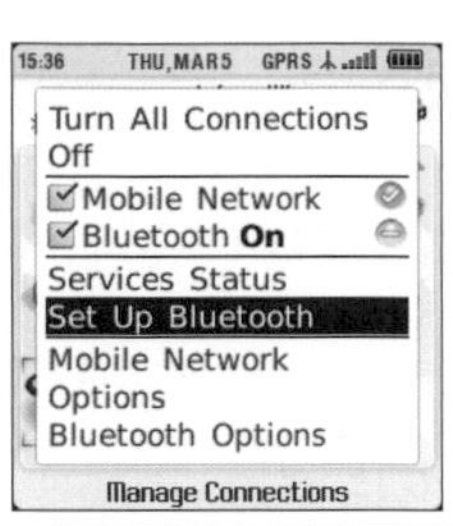

1. Turn on your device and choose Manage Connections

2. Make sure that Bluetooth is set On, then select Set Up Bluetooth

3. Under Add Device, choose Allow Another device to find me, and click OK

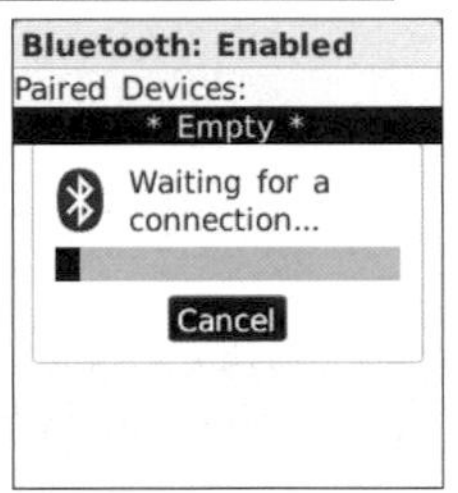

4. The device will be Waiting for a connection.

Now you can switch to the computer to complete the process.

1. Start the Add Bluetooth Device Wizard and click the box to indicate your device is set up and ready to be found

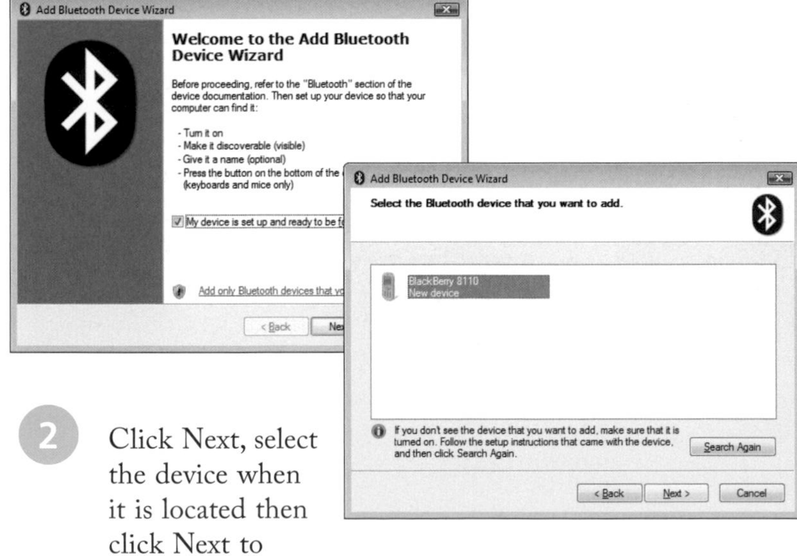

2. Click Next, select the device when it is located then click Next to continue

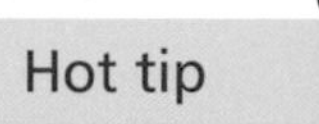

You can search for other Bluetooth devices from the cell phone, but for connecting to a computer it's best to wait to be found.

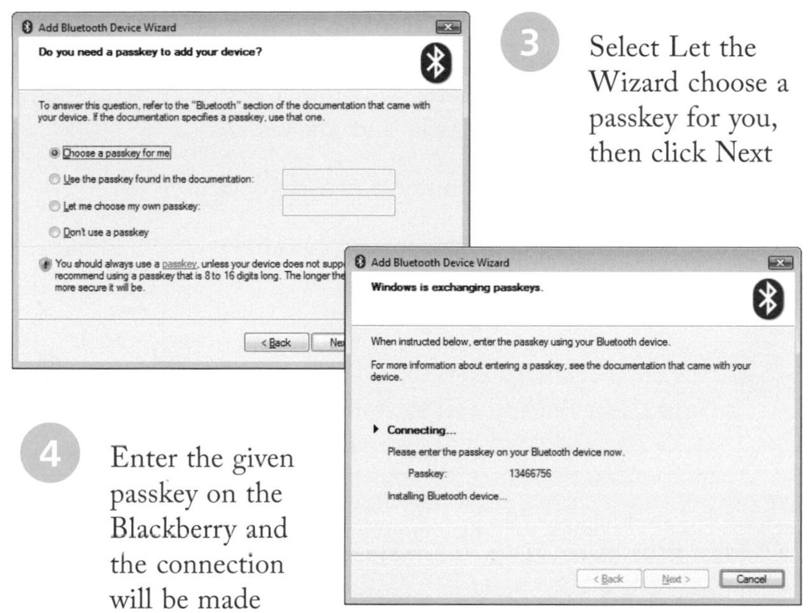

3. Select Let the Wizard choose a passkey for you, then click Next

4. Enter the given passkey on the Blackberry and the connection will be made

When you've entered the passkey on the cell phone, you must confirm that you want to allow the connection request.

Completing the Connection

When the computer and Blackberry have been paired, you can tell the Desktop Manager to use Bluetooth for connection.

1. Click Options and select Connection Settings

2. Enable Bluetooth support and set to switch to USB as the preferred option when that is connected

When the computer detects the cell phone, you'll be asked to confirm that you want it to make the connection.

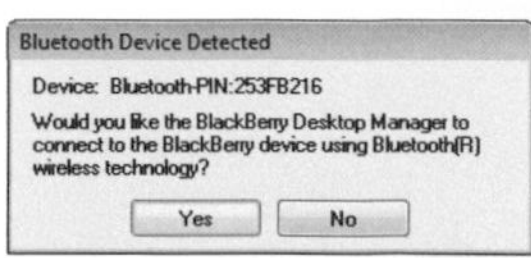

Managing the Cell Phone

Hot tip

You can connect by USB cable or Bluetooth. However, the cable connection is the most certain for data integrity purposes.

With the cell phone connected to the computer, you can use the functions of the BlackBerry Desktop Manager to add or update applications, backup and restore, synchronize organizer data such as contacts, calendar entries, tasks and memos.

For example, to backup the contents of your device:

1. Connect the BlackBerry to your computer

2. Open Blackberry Desktop Manager and select Backup and Restore

3. Select Backup, amend the suggested file name if desired and click Save

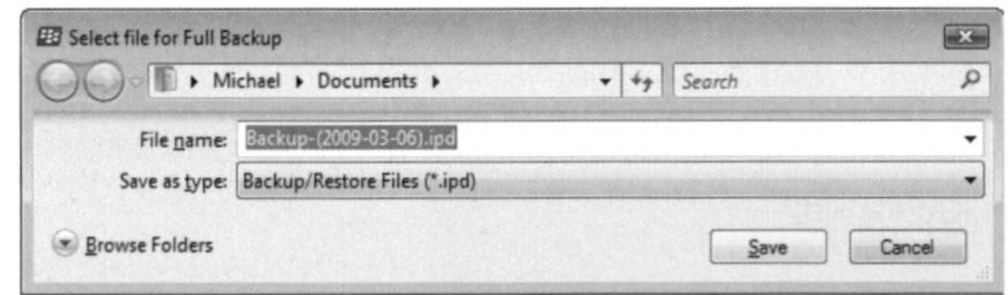

Don't forget

To restore specific sets of device data from the backup file, click the Advanced button and choose the items that you require.

4. The various data items on the BlackBerry device are transferred to the computer and stored in the backup file, ready for future restore if required

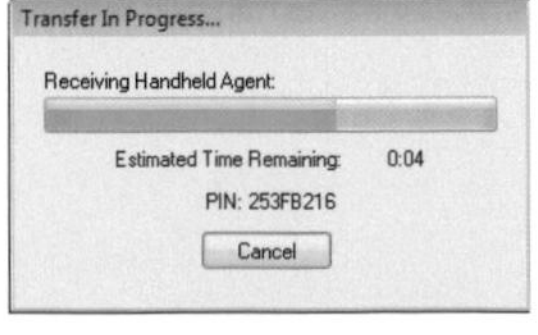

Wi-Fi Connection

Some smartphones are Wi-Fi capable. This feature allows you to access the Internet when you are in range of an accessible Wi-Fi network, either commercial (such as a coffee shop), public (e.g. municipal), or private (home or office).

To scan for available Wi-Fi networks and make a connection you need to carry out the following actions on your smartphone:

1. Click the Menu button and select the Manage Connections option

2. Select to Set Up Wi-Fi Network

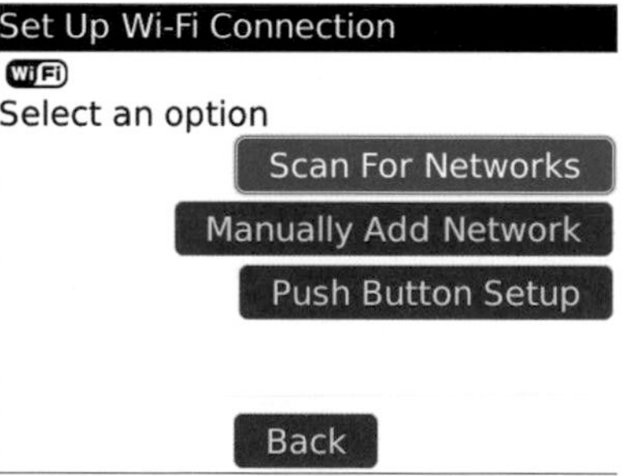

3. Select the option to Scan for Networks

4. If requested, select the option Turn Wi-Fi on

5. Your smartphone will scan to search for available Wi-Fi networks

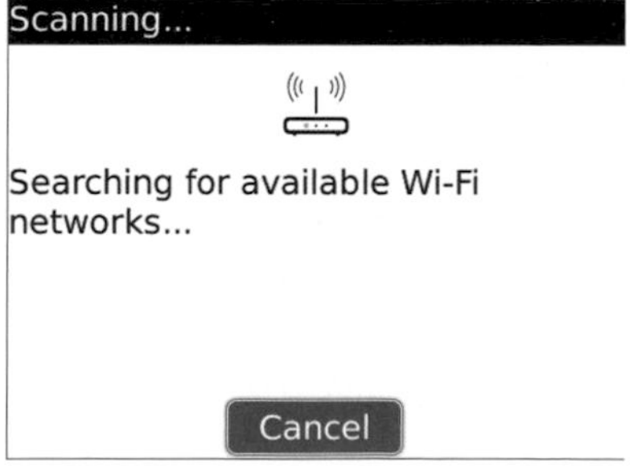

Hot tip

BlackBerry models that support Wi-Fi include the Bold 9000, the Pearl Flip 8220, and the Curve 8900 illustrated below.

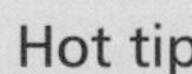

Hot tip

Only the Wi-Fi option needs to be turned on. You won't be using the Mobile Network.

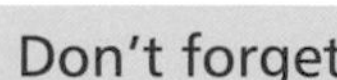

Don't forget

The scan will locate all types of Wi-Fi network that are detectable in the immediate locality.

Wi-Fi Profiles

Hot tip

Using VoIP over the Wi-Fi network may be preferable to using the regular mobile network, especially for international calling.

Don't forget

By default, the selected network will be saved in a profile with the same name as the network SSID. This means you can connect the next time without having to scan.

Hot tip

You can prioritize the profiles so that the appropriate network is selected whenever you move into range.

1. From the list of available Wi-Fi networks, select the one you require

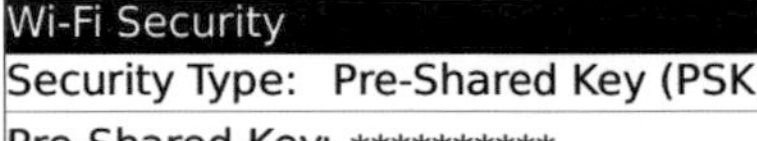

Pre-Shared Key: **********

Back Save

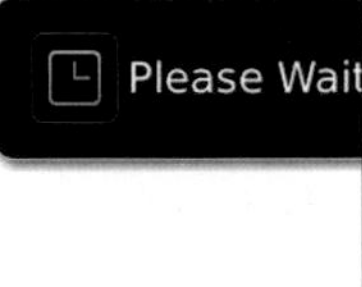

Set Up Wi-Fi

Connecting to BTHomeHub2-NR99 ...

Cancel

2. Specify the required security credentials and click Connect

3. Leave as Yes to Save this Wi-Fi network as a profile

4. Accept or amend the suggested profile name and click Next

Connection Successful!

Save this Wi-Fi Network as a Profile? Yes

Profile Name: BTHomeHub2-NR99

(Home, Work, etc...)

Back Next

Wi-Fi Setup Complete

Success!

BTHomeHub2-NR99 has been added to your list of Saved Profiles.

Prioritize Wi-Fi Profiles

Many Wi-Fi "hotspots" require registration (e.g. credit card).

Wi-Fi Hotspot Login

Finish

5. If required, log in to the Wi-Fi hotspot

6. Click Finish and you'll be able to start using the Wi-Fi network

Wireless Phone Calls

You can use the Internet to make telephone calls. You may already be familiar with Skype, which uses a microphone/headset or web camera on the computer to set up voice or video calls to other Skype users on the Internet. This gives you effectively free calls, whether local, long distance or international. You may also be able to call users on their ordinary telephones, for the price of a local call in the destination country.

The early implementations used wired components that would keep you in your place in front of the computer. However, you can use a wireless headset such as the Freetalk wireless stereo headset. This consists of two components – the headset itself and the transmitter/receiver puck which connects to your computer via USB.

It is stereo and has CD quality sound, and with it you have the freedom to walk about while you talk.

Another option is to use a Bluetooth headset such as the Plantronics Audio 910 Bluetooth Headset. This is Skype certified, and designed to interact well with Skype.

The sound quality won't be as good, and it is a mono device. However, it features Multipoint Versatility, which means you can have the Audio 910 paired to both your computer and your cell phone at the same time, so whether you get a Skype call or a mobile call, you can answer it by pressing the call control button.

While working at home with your computer and your wireless network, you may want the option to receive landline calls. For this, you may want an option that uses the VoIP facility in conjunction with the normal PSTN telephone system.

Hot tip

Skype is based on Voice over Internet Protocol (VoIP). Note that Skype is not a replacement for your ordinary telephone and can't be used for emergency calling.

Hot tip

This hub features a master USB port that can be used to attach a device such as a USB printer or USB flash drive, making that device available over the network.

Some wireless Internet routers include the option to add a telephone. The BT Home Hub for example supports VoIP Internet calls via a wireless handset. This could be the BT Hub Phone, an optional handset that is designed to work in conjunction with the Home Hub.

Don't forget

Depending on the calling plan you sign up for, some calls may be free, for example evening and weekend calls to UK numbers.

However, a normal wireless telephone which supports DECT can be attached to the hub. This phone will use the BT Broadband Talk service to make calls. Broadband Talk is like an extra phone line with its own phone number. It sends calls using your BT Broadband connection instead of your existing phone line. You can call numbers such as:

- Other Broadband Talk customers
- Any person in the UK
- Specified international destinations (52 regions)
- The rest of the World (at reduced rates)
- Any UK mobile number

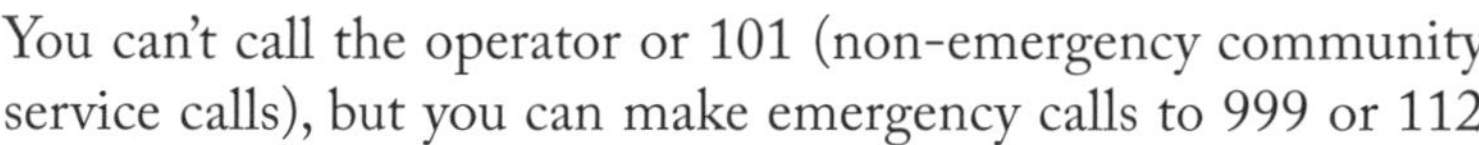

You can't call the operator or 101 (non-emergency community service calls), but you can make emergency calls to 999 or 112.

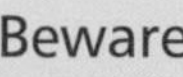

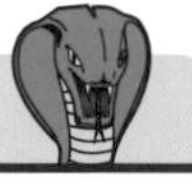

Beware

You are advised to have a standard phone attached to your landline, since emergency calls may not work in the event of power or broadband connection failure.

You receive the calls for the Internet service number on this handset, but it can also receive calls meant for the landline number that is associated with the Broadband service.

This method allows you to make calls over your Internet connection without having to use your computer. You are free to move around within a reasonable distance of the wireless router, but you have no call facility when you are away from home. For that you need a VoIP solution based on the cell phone network.

Skypephone

You can also use Voice over Internet Protocol (VoIP) with a cell phone that's designed to use the Internet to make free calls to other Skype users and even send text messages, whether you are at home or on the move.

Skype can be used on cell phones from e.g. Nokia, Sony Ericsson, and LG. However, the most well integrated is perhaps the 3 Mobile Skypephone, either the original S1 or the new and improved S2. This phone can use standard GSM for its Skype functionality and all calls between Skype users are free. With the Skype enabled cell phone, you can also make non-Skype calls using the preferential Skype rates or make calls via the cell phone network, which will be charged at normal cell phone rates.

Hot tip

Although Skype is the featured service on this phone, it also comes preconfigured to provide access to Facebook, MSN Messenger, and Google (search, map and mail).

Set Up Skype

If you have a Skype account:

1. From the Start screen, scroll to Skype and press the central Select button
2. Select Sign in for existing users, then enter your username and password
3. Scroll to Sign me in and set it as Automatically or Manually

If you don't have a Skype account:

1. From the Start screen, select Skype and then select Create account for new users
2. Accept Terms & Conditions and enter your name, amend the suggested Skype name if desired, enter your password and email address, then press the Select button
3. The account will be created. Issue a Skype test call to check the account and confirm your setup

Don't forget

If you select Automatic, you'll automatically sign into Skype each time you turn on your mobile.

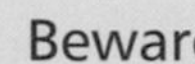

Beware

A Skype name based on your name is suggested. If this is already in use, you'll be prompted to provide an alternative.

...cont'd

The Skypephone will operate only in those countries where there is a 3 Network. These include Austria, Italy, Sweden, Denmark, Australia, Hong Kong, Ireland and UK. If you are visiting one of those countries for an extended stay, it could be well worth considering the Pay As You Go option. You'd purchase the Skypephone for a one-time charge and this would give you worldwide access to Skype subscribers at no additional cost.

Hot tip

You need to check the details of the contracts available at the website www.three.com or your country's equivalent.

Skypephone Modem

You can also use your Skypephone as a modem, to connect your laptop to the Internet when there's no accessible Wi-Fi network available for it to use.

1. Plug your mobile into your laptop and select Run Autoinstall.exe

Don't forget

The program runs automatically if you have enabled AutoPlay.

2. The Mobile Modem software will install and then start up on your laptop. Click the Connect button to get online

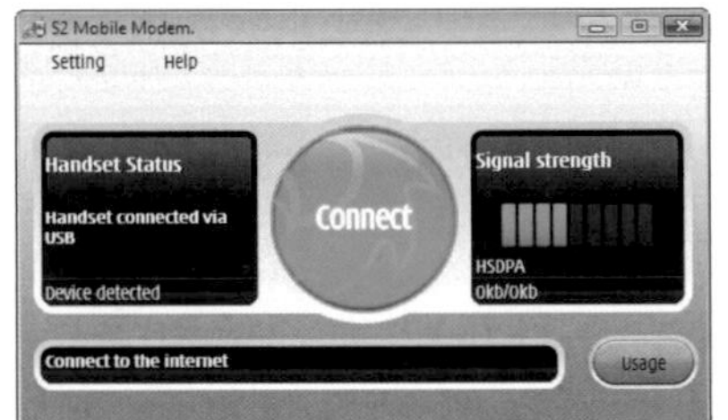

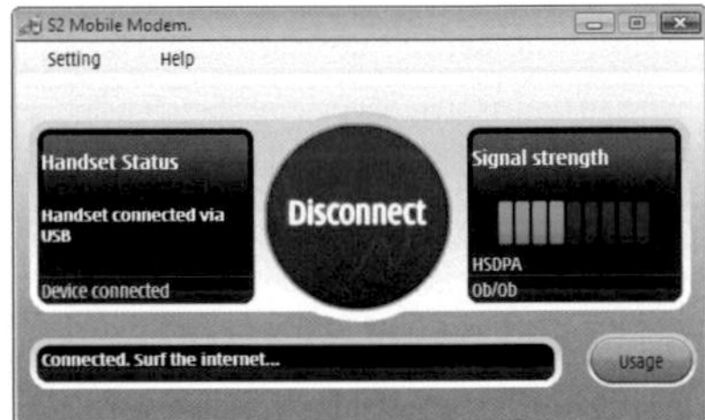

Don't forget

The icon added to the system tray indicates the status of the connection.

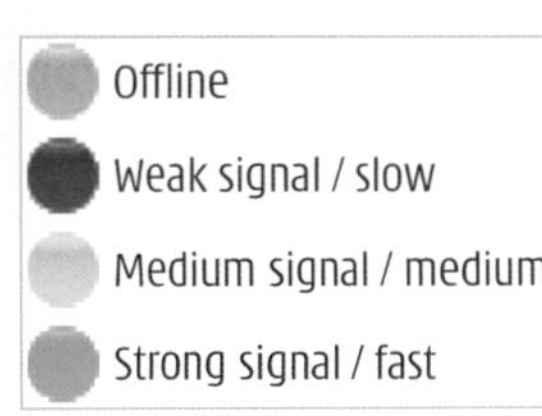

The Mobile Modem software also shows you the strength of your mobile signal and how fast an Internet connection you have.

With the modem connected, you can now surf the Internet via the handset. Click the Disconnect button when you have finished.

Add a Wireless Printer

You can add a Wi-Fi capable printer to your network and use it from any computer on the network, without it being directly connected to any particular computer.

The Lexmark X7675 for example, has an 802.11g wireless print server which is compatible with 802.11 b/g/n routers that are Wi-Fi certified. To install the printer on your wireless network, you must first install the printer software on one of your computers. Choose a computer that has a spare USB port since the printer will use an installation cable for a temporary connection to set up the wireless settings of the printer:

1. Insert the installation software CD and select Run Setup.exe (if AutoPlay is not activated)

2. Click Install to begin the printer setup

3. Follow the prompts i.e. accept the terms of the license agreement

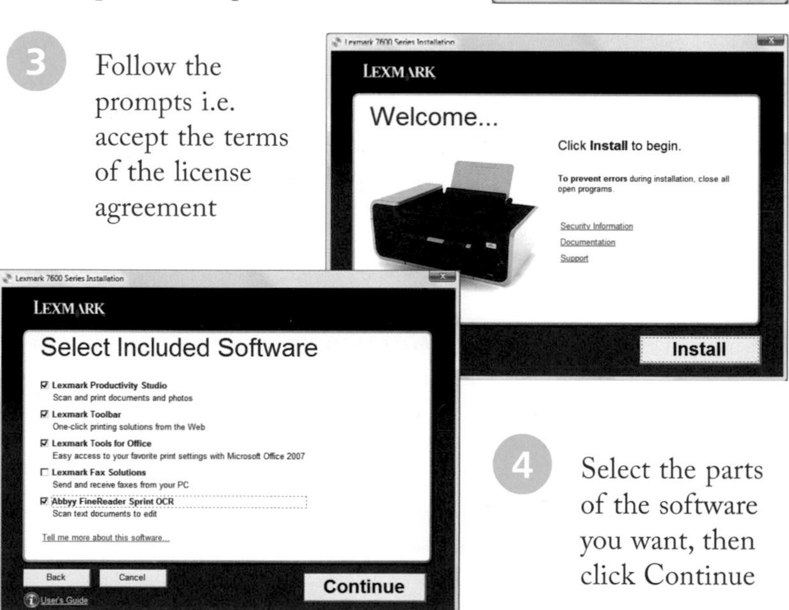

4. Select the parts of the software you want, then click Continue

5. You may be offered the option to check for software updates on the Internet, but you can skip this if you already know you have the latest version

Skip Update

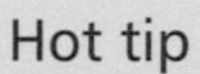

Hot tip

Check that the wireless network that the printer will use is set up and working properly.

Hot tip

In this case, the fax facility isn't being used, so that part of the software package will be skipped.

...cont'd

Don't forget

You only configure the printer once, but you need to tell each computer individually about the new printer.

Once the software has been selected, you'll be asked if you are setting up the printer for the first time

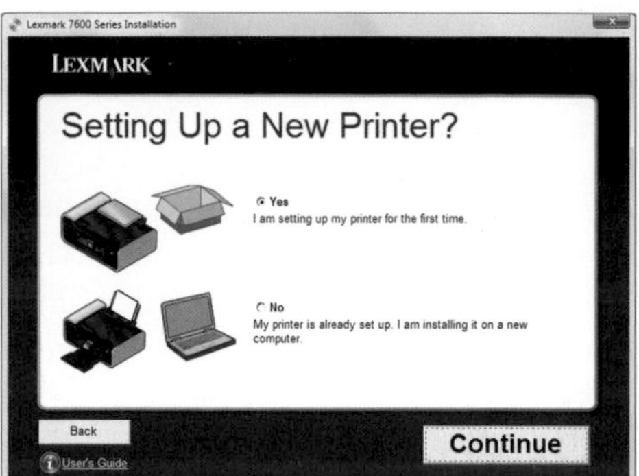

1. Click Yes, when you add the printer to your wireless network

In the background the files for the printer software are transferred to the computer. While this is happening, the setup program takes you through physical set up for the printer. For example:

Beware

Do not attach the USB installation cable until you are instructed.

- Remove adhesive tape and packing material
- Install the printer control panel for your language
- Adjust the paper guides and load paper into the printer
- Connect the power cord and turn on the printer
- Set language and country/region if prompted
- Enter the settings for the fax, if you want to use this
- Insert the color and black print cartridges and close printer
- Print an alignment page (adjustments will be applied automatically)

Don't forget

The actions required to set up the printer are explained in clear, pictorial terms, with moving images where appropriate.

Lexmark 7600 Series Installation
LEXMARK
Discard or recycle the alignment page
Notes:
- Streaks on the alignment page are normal and not an indication of a problem.
- The alignment page that prints may differ from the one shown.

< Back
User's Guide
Continue >

- Press Continue to go forward and set up the wireless network connection

Connect to the Network

1. Choose the connection type, for example wireless network

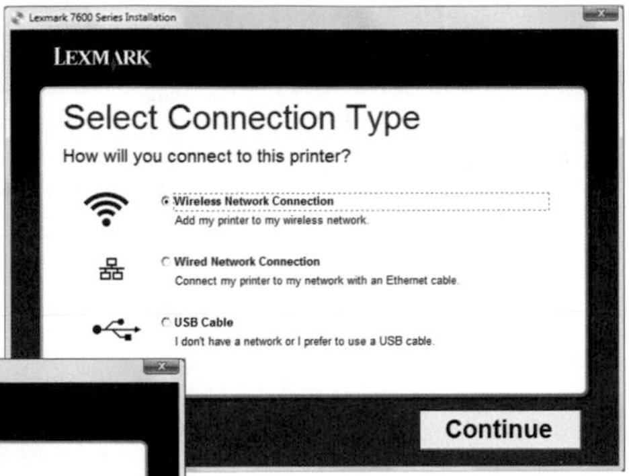

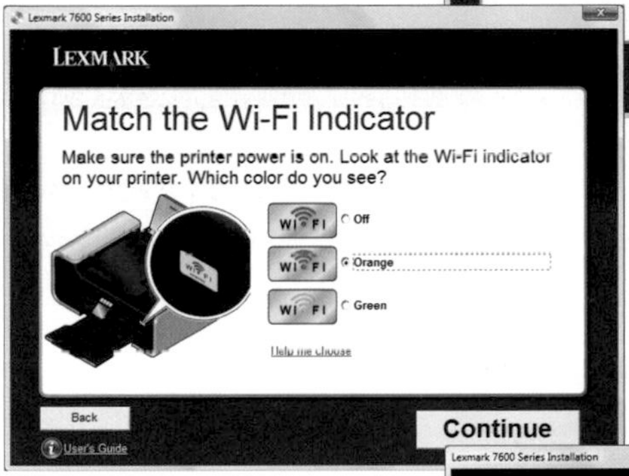

2. Indicate the type of Wi-Fi indicator shown on the printer

3. You need the network SSID and the WEP or WPA security key

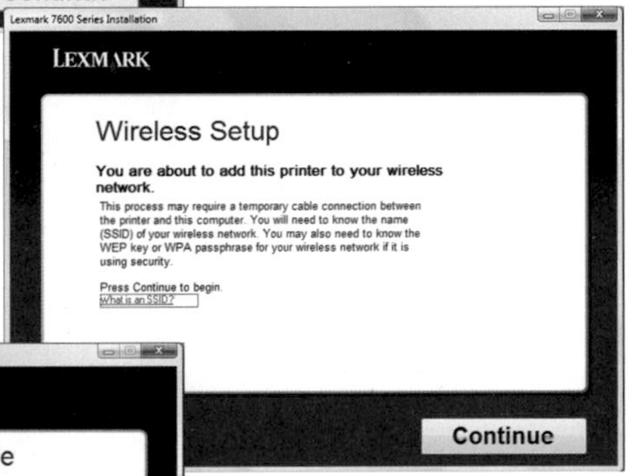

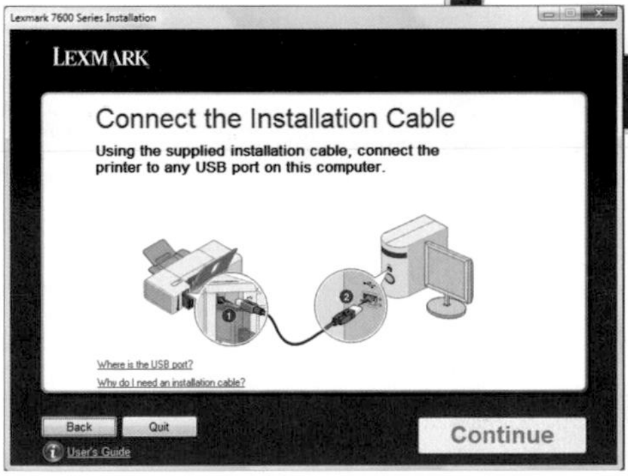

4. Now you can connect to a USB port, using the installation cable

The printer will search for all the wireless networks that it can detect within the locality.

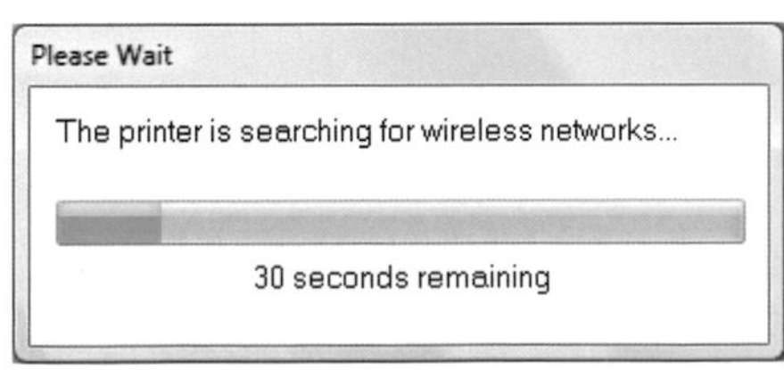

Hot tip

Orange means the printer is not yet set up. Green means the printer is connected to a wireless network and ready to use.

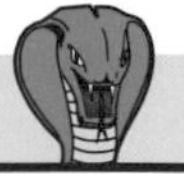

Beware

It may detect other networks to which you do not have access. These should simply be ignored.

...cont'd

Hot tip

The computer that you are using to setup the printer must be on the same network.

5. Select the network, using the SSID to identify the correct one, and click Continue

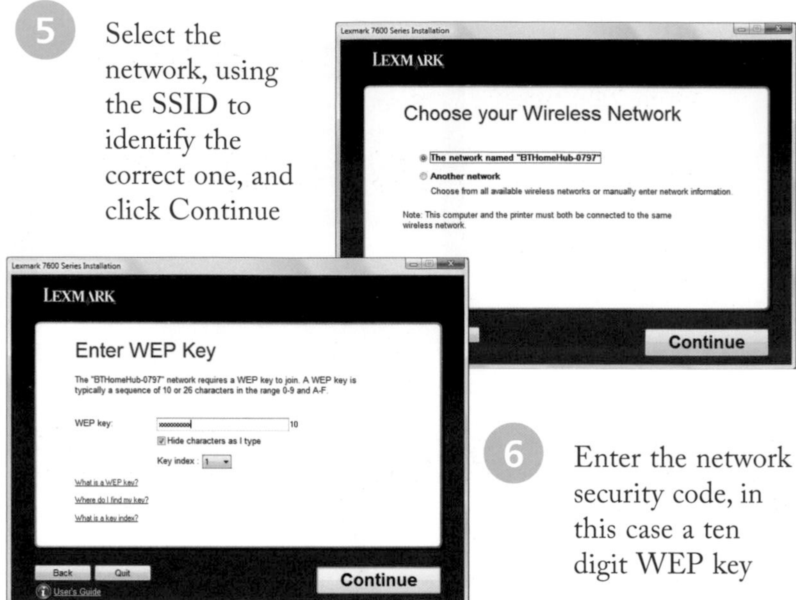

6. Enter the network security code, in this case a ten digit WEP key

Don't forget

The printer will be assigned an IP address automatically through DHCP on most wireless networks. You can find this on the network map (see page 106).

7. When the link with the network is set up, remove the USB cable

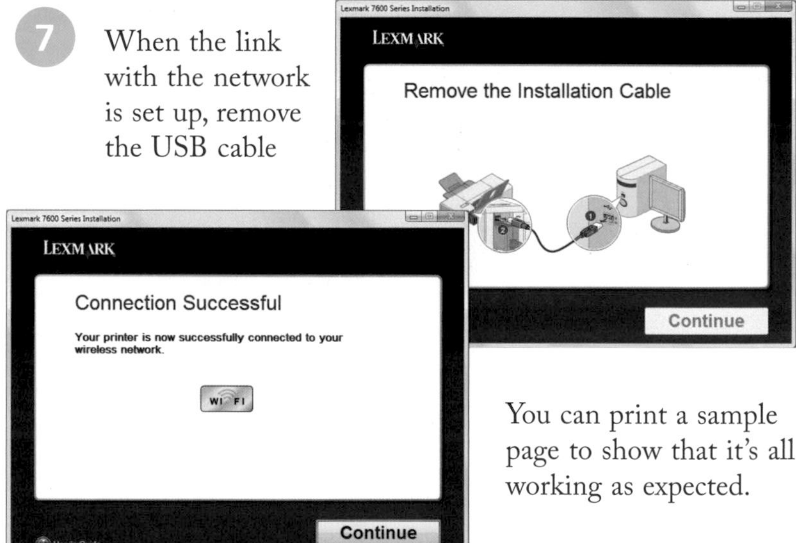

You can print a sample page to show that it's all working as expected.

You'll be prompted to provide a nickname for your printer (the setup program suggests "Lexmark 7600 Series" but you can choose something simpler, for example "All-in-one".

Finally, you'll be offered the opportunity to enter your personal and products details to register your wireless printer on the Lexmark website.

Access the Wireless Printer

1. Insert the installation software CD to run Setup.exe and select the software required

2. Specify that the printer is set up, but you want to install it on a new computer

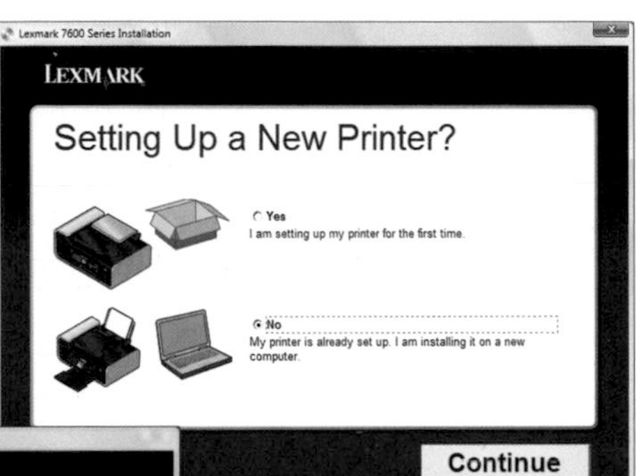

3. Choose Wireless (connection type) and Green (Wi-Fi indicator)

4. Select your printer by name, i.e. All-in-one

Once the printer has been set up on the new computer, you can print a test page to try it out.

Note that it will have been set up as the new default printer. To change this, open the Printers folder, right click the preferred printer and select Set as Default Printer.

Hot tip

You can access the printer from other computers on the network, but the printer must be defined on each one in turn.

Don't forget

The software is added as before, but this time the printer itself does not need to be worked on.

Hot tip

If the Printers folder is not listed on the Start menu, click the Start button, type Printers and press Enter to select the Printer's program.

Extend Network Range

If there's a location in your house where wireless reception is poor, try these options to improve the situation:

- Re-position your wireless router
- If your router must be against an outside wall, replace the standard antenna with a hi-gain directional antenna
- Change your wireless channel
- Add a wireless range extender (also known as a repeater)
- Use a second router or wireless access point

Changing Wireless Channels

To change channels on the LinkSys Wireless-N WAG160G:

1. Go to the configuration page for the router, the IP address for the device, for example 192.168.1.1

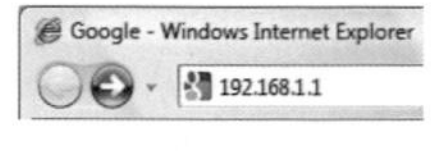

2. Log in as administrator, then select Wireless, Basic Settings

3. Select a different channel and click Save Settings to try out the new channel

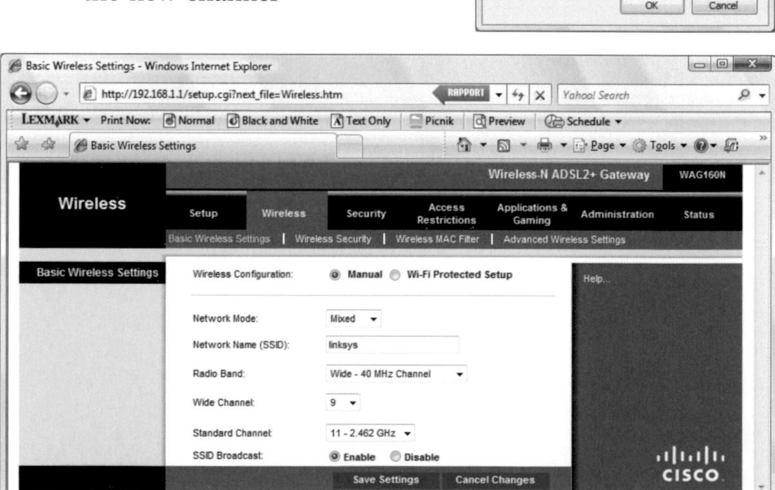

4. Try another channel if the signal doesn't improve, until you've identified the best channel in your situation

Hot tip

Standard antennas are omnidirectional, but hi-gain antennas focus the signals in a particular direction.

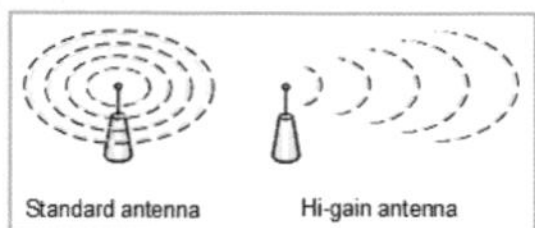

Don't forget

The exact procedure will vary, depending on the particular model of wireless router that you have installed.

Beware

Click on the down arrow to select from the choices offered. The channels that are allowed are country dependent.

Add a Range Extender

A range extender can effectively double the operating distance of your wireless network. It takes the signal from your wireless access point or router and retransmits it. Place it halfway between your wireless access point and the wireless trouble spot.

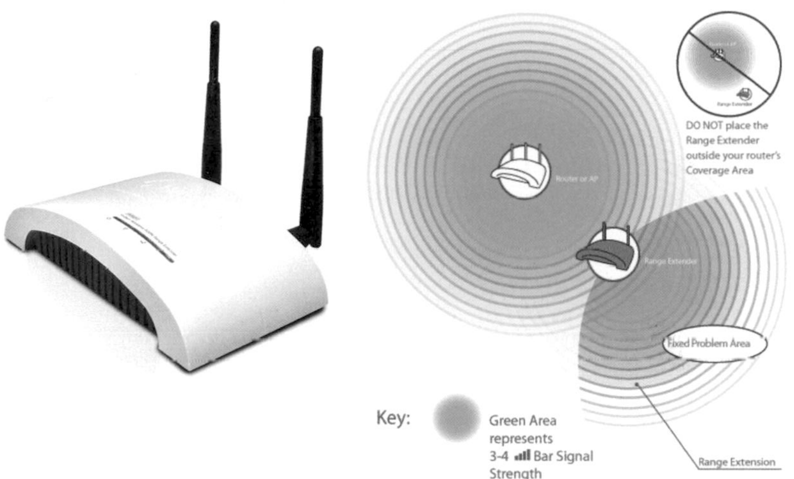

The Hawkin Hi-Gain HWREN1 Wireless-300N supports most wireless 802.11b/g/n networks and devices, and includes a software setup wizard that will scan for a network to extend.

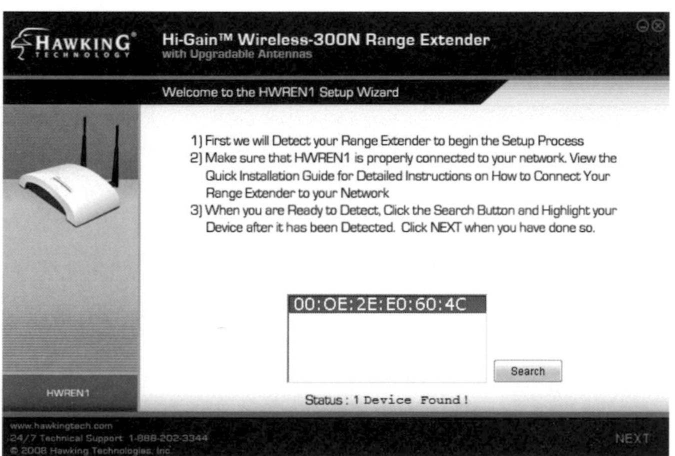

Use your laptop to map your wireless network and identify dead spots or areas of weak reception, then place the range extender to fill in the gap in the network coverage.

Hot tip

If possible, choose a range extender from the same manufacturer as your wireless router. However, for wireless-N, there are as yet few such devices, so you may need a specialized device such as the Hawkin Hi-Gain range extender.

Beware

The ranger extender is a directional device, so it must be carefully positioned and oriented for best coverage.

Don't forget

If you have a spare wireless router, you may be able to use the extra router as a range extender. Your routers must support repeater mode of operation.

Using a Spare Router

Don't forget

Only one DHCP server is allowed on the network, so you must switch this function off for the spare router.

You may be able to configure a spare router as a range extender. Alternatively, you could connect two routers using an Ethernet cable, and establish a second wireless access point.

In either case, you'll need to turn off the DHCP server on the second router when you add a link between the two routers.

1. Open the router configuration and select Basic Setup

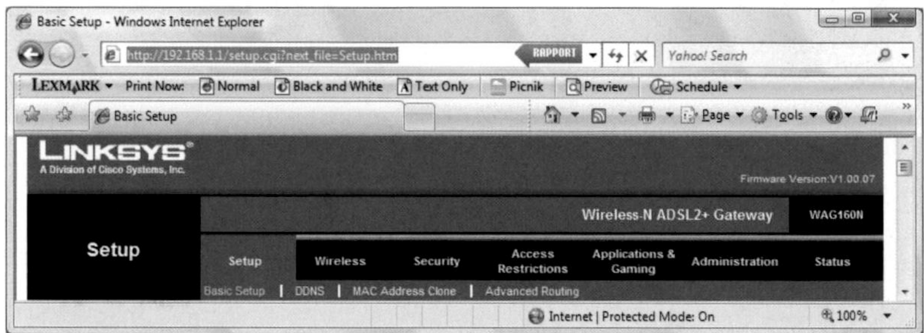

2. Scroll down to DHCP server settings and select Disable

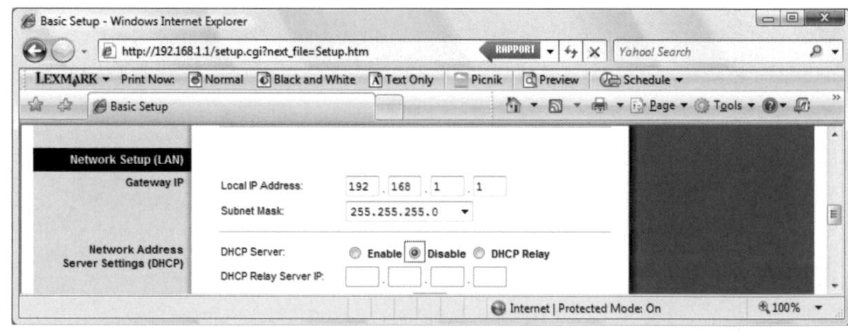

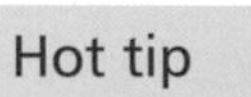

Beware

If the two routers use the same configuration page IP address, you'll also need to specify an alternative IP address for the second router.

3. In the Network and Sharing Center, select View full map

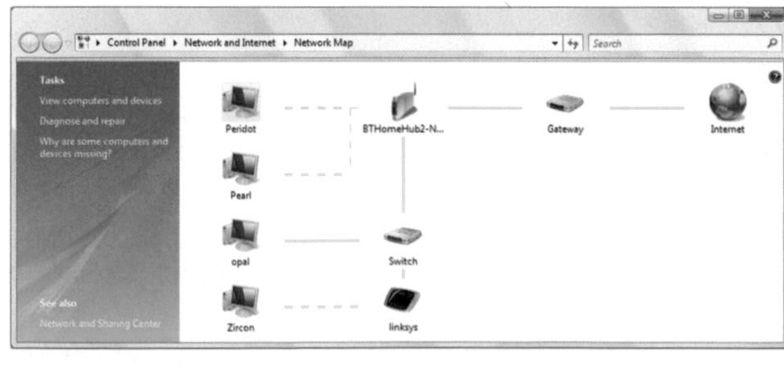

Hot tip

This shows the two routers connected by Ethernet cable, with each router providing a wireless access point.

9 Public Wi-Fi and Remote Networking

You can go online while you are away, via mobile broadband or using a wireless hotspot. These can be located in many public locations. They let you access email, Internet and even the files, folders and programs on your own home network.

Home and Away

When you are away from home, you can go online to the Internet and using that connection you can not only surf the web, but also access your email, your home computers and your home network. There are several ways to get online when traveling. You can connect your laptop to the Internet via mobile broadband or a cell phone modem or go back to basics and use a landline and a dialup modem. However, perhaps the simplest method is using your wireless adapter to connect via a Wi-Fi hotspot.

A Wi-Fi hotspot provides public access to a wireless network. The usage may be free, it may depend on purchases e.g. a meal or a flight or it may be for a fee. You can find Wi-Fi hotspots at many types of location, including:

- Airplanes and cruise ships
- Airports and bus or train stations
- Bookstores and libraries
- Coffee shops and restaurants
- Hotels, motels, shopping centers and malls

The scope of hotspots will vary, depending on the type of wireless network and the antenna that is being used. Standard devices may permit distances of typically 100 to 300 feet, but special purpose devices can increase this significantly.

It is also possible for a number of wireless hotspots in close proximity to be grouped together to provide access over a wider area, such as a college campus or a municipal area, or even whole counties and some small countries. These are often referred to as hot zones, but in practise they are just another form of hotspot.

Don't forget 

The hotspots are not just for laptop computers. You should also be able to connect your PDA, cell phone or other Internet enabled device.

Hot tip 

Hotspots don't have to be commercial – you could set up your own hotspot if you wish. All it needs is a router or wireless access point that you open to the public.

Beware 

By its very nature, the hotspot is insecure, so you will need to take the appropriate precautions (see page 179).

Wi-Fi Hotspot Facilities

Once you've made up your mind to take advantage of Wi-Fi hotspots, you may be surprised at the number of establishments that have such facilities available, starting with the ubiquitous Starbucks, in association with AT&T and T-Mobile. See the website **http://www.starbucks.com/retail/wireless.asp** for details.

Hot tip

When you register your Starbucks Card and use it at least once a month, you'll receive two consecutive hours a day of complimentary Wi-Fi, courtesy of AT&T.

You'll also find wireless facilities at many McDonald's restaurants worldwide. See **http://www.mcdonalds.com/wireless.html** for details. In some countries the service is free, e.g. McDonald's UK.

Don't forget

Connectivity and/or usage fees may apply. However, sometimes promotional coupons may be offered.

Visit Barnes & Noble at **http://www.barnesandnoble.com/**

Click the Stores & Events button and AT&T Wi-Fi to get information on their wireless services. They also have Starbucks coffee!

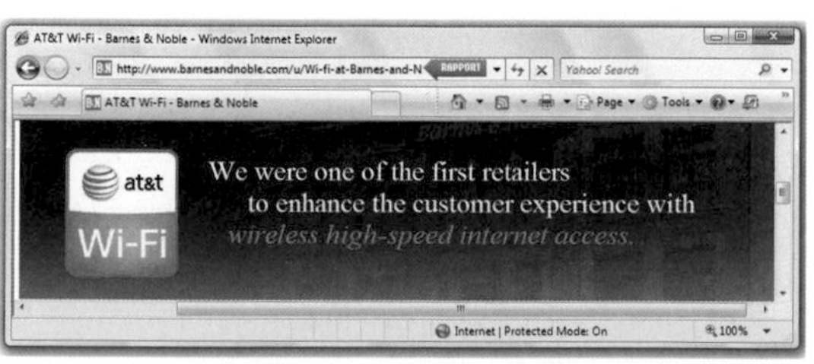

Don't forget

Libraries and book stores often feature Wi-Fi services, and are good places to start your search for wireless facilities away from home.

Hotspot Directories

You can find out where wireless hotspots are located, using one of the many online directories to be found on the Internet, e.g.:

Hot tip

Wi-FiHotSpotList.com is intended as a resource for people seeking Wi-Fi public network nodes. It is not to be used for commercial purpose without prior authorization.

Wi-FiHotSpotList.com

To find hotspots near a location, enter a complete or partial address. By default, all hotspots within 1 mile of the location will be shown.

Click Browse by Region to see hotspots organized by city within country and state or province.

Maps of the location are provided for hotspots within the U.S. and Europe.

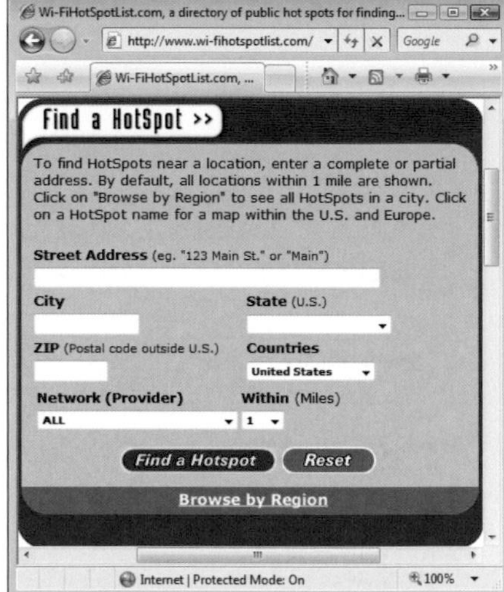

Don't forget

You can search the database by Keyword, City, Zip or provider, or search the Wi-Fi-TF Network on Google.

Hotspot Locations Wireless Directory

This lists wireless hotspot locations in North America, Europe, Asia and Australia. Search by country, state, city or zip code. Click the box to show Only Free Hotspots.

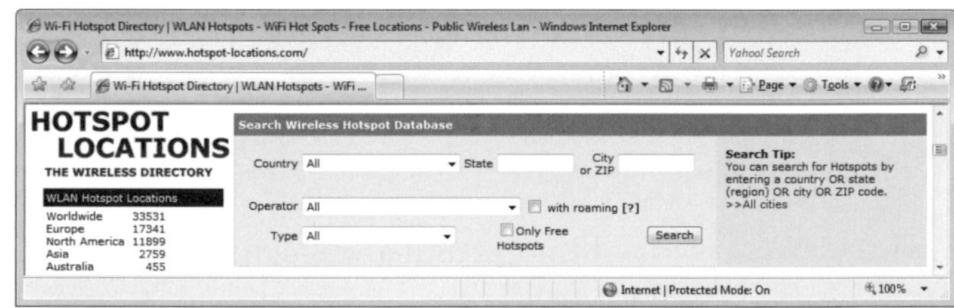

Hot tip

Visit www.jiwire.com, click the Wi-Fi Users button and then click the Wi-Fi Finder entry to display the registry.

JiWire Wi-Fi Finder

JiWire, a mobile audience media company, provides a map-based Wi-Fi registry for 140 countries with over 250,000 hotspots listed. You can also search by criteria such as location, provider or free versus pay.

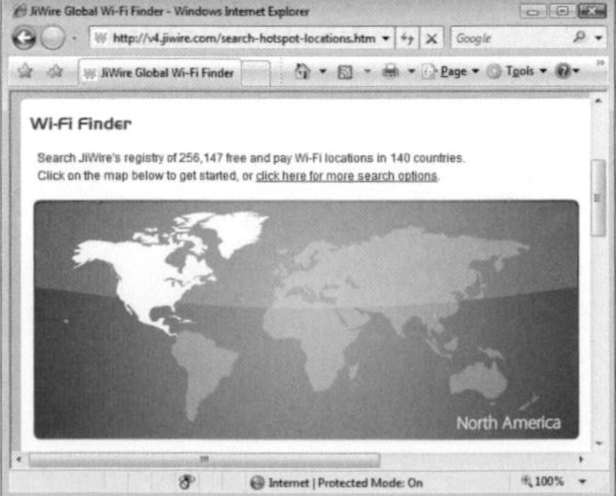

Connect to a Wi-Fi Hotspot

Using a Wi-Fi hotspot is like using your wireless home network. However, before connecting you should disable file and folder sharing, and make sure you are using personal firewall software.

To begin using the hotspot:

1. Select the SSID (network name) from the list of available wireless networks then click Connect

2. Open your Web browser. Most hotspots will automatically display a portal page, for example:

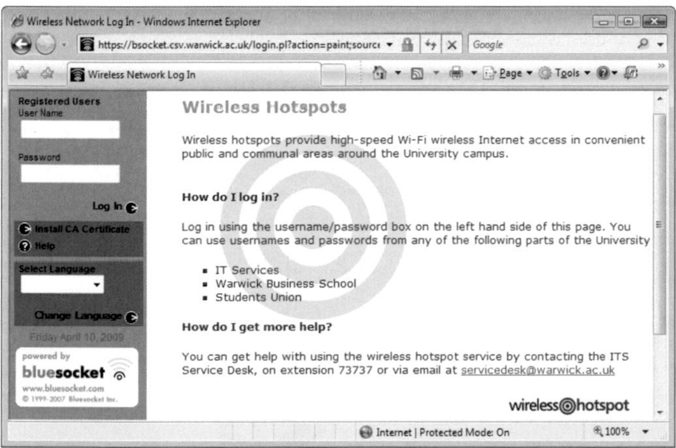

3. Accept T's & C's, make payment or provide security credentials as appropriate, to complete the connection

While you are using the selected hotspot, especially if it is an open network, you must take precautions. For example, only log in to accounts that are on secure websites, using SSL or HTTPS. Your Web browsers should display a padlock icon when the current website is properly secure.

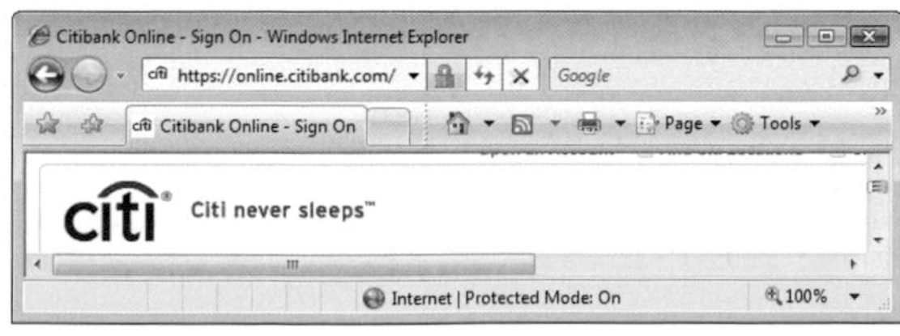

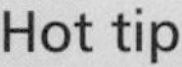

Hot tip

You should also make sure that your operating system is up-to-date at all times so that you receive all the latest security updates.

Don't forget

Some email hosts provide SSL encryption for email accounts, which you have to set up in your email client. If not, most email providers do offer secure access to accounts through a Website.

Hot tip

Make sure any Internet services you use, such as POP3 email and FTP for file transfers, are secured, or use web mail instead to access your email at a hotspot.

Create a Hotspot

Beware

Make sure that you do not inadvertently make your network into a hotspot, by failing to set up network security, or by leaving passwords at their default values.

Hotspots aren't just for companies or municipalities – anyone can create them. For a small area close to your access point, the standard router such as the one supplied by your service provider would do the job.

Since your hotspot may be open to the public, you'll want to separate it from your home or office network while allowing it to share your access to the Internet. The easiest way to do this is to use two routers.

The first router is used for your home. If this router is wireless-enabled, you will need to encrypt the connection. It is used to create a private network, which will only be accessed by trusted and authorized users with a security key for that router.

Hot tip

If you want to provide coverage over a distance, you could upgrade to a hi-gain or directional antenna and perhaps add a signal amplifier.

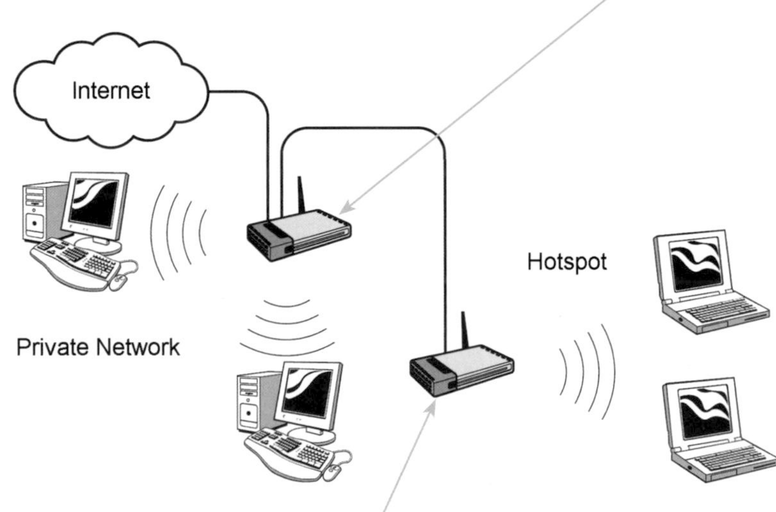

Don't forget

The NAT (Network Address Translation) function enables the network to use one set of IP addresses for internal traffic and a second set of addresses for external traffic.

The second router is the wireless router that you will use to offer access to the public. This router needs NAT function so that it can use the connection to the Internet from the first router, but create a local network of its own, separate from the private network.

If you want to allow all comers to access your hotspot, you can leave it open. If it's aimed at a specific group, you can also control who has access by using wireless encryption and providing the security credentials to the approved users.

Once you have created your hotspot and set up whatever security you want, you can list it in an appropriate hotspot directory, or simply circulate details to the interested group.

FON Spots

You don't have to go as far as setting up your own hotspot, to share your Internet connection. There's a Wi-Fi community set up to share access with one another. This is called FON. For details:

1. Go to http://www.fon.com/ and click on What's Fon

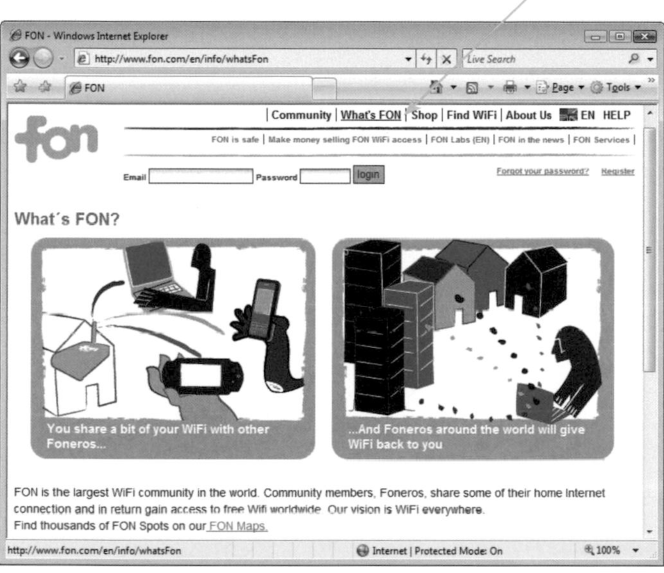

2. To create an account, scroll down and click the Join FON button

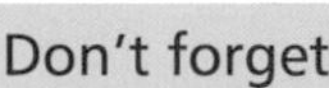

It is a simple concept. You share a small part of your broadband Internet service with the FON Community. In return, you gain free Wi-Fi access at FON Spots worldwide. FON is sponsored by Google, Skype, British Telecom and others, and has grown to nearly a million members and 300,000 hotspots since it was founded in 2006. People that don't share their broadband can still connect to FON Spots around the world by purchasing access passes.

FON has its own, specially designed Wi-Fi router, La Fonera. This is an access point which handles two Wi-Fi signals: an encrypted one for your personal use, and another one that is associated with a portal screen where other FON members can connect.

Hot tip

FON Spots differ from traditional Wi-Fi hotspots in that they are usually located within homes rather than businesses or organizations. This makes them less practical to share, unless you live close by a public location such as a coffee shop.

Don't forget

You can download an upgrade to convert a supported type of router into a FON device. If your ISP supports FON, you may be able to create an account and share your Internet connection using your existing router as is.

Remote Networking

When you get online while away from home, whether via a Wi-Fi hotspot, a FON Spot or using mobile broadband, you may be able to access your wireless home network in a variety of ways.

Beware

The term Remote can be ambiguous, since both computers are remote from one another, so we'll use the terms Home and Away to refer to the computers.

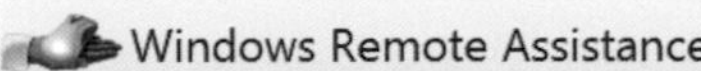

Windows Remote Assistance is designed for an away computer to connect over the Internet and view or take control of the home computer. The home computer must be attended and the home user must authorize the connection. While intended as a way of providing technical assistance, it can also offer you a way to access your home computers while on the road and exchange information. Both of you will see the same computer screen contents, and you will both be able to control the mouse pointer.

Don't forget

Windows Remote Assistance is included in all editions of Vista, while Windows Home Server Console can be installed in any edition of Windows Vista.

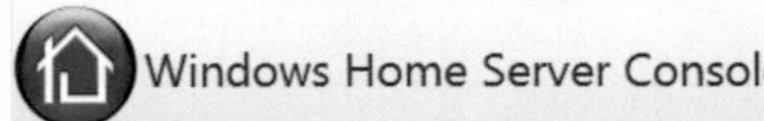

If you have Windows Home Server installed on your home network, and Windows Home Server Console on your away computer, you can access your files and personal computers remotely, using a personalized website, and download and upload files to the shared folders on your home server.

Remote Desktop Connection

Remote Desktop Connection allows you to access a home (or office) computer from an away computer. You will have access to all of your programs, files and network resources, as if you were sitting in front of the computer. While you are connected, the home computer does not need to be attended, and its computer screen will display the Welcome screen (or the Log On to Windows screen, depending on how Windows is configured), so anyone at the home location won't see what you are doing.

Windows Home Server Console also allows remote access to any of the computers on your home network, so you can access their files, and run applications.

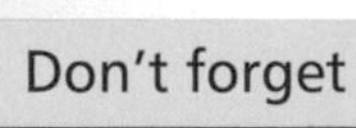

Don't forget

You must have Vista Ultimate or Business edition running on your home computer, in order to use Remote Desktop Connection or the Remote Access functionality of Windows Home Server.

Windows Remote Assistance

Remote Assistance lets a user share the display of their screen and, if they wish, control of their computer, with another user across a network or Internet connection. Thus a user on the home network could let an away user view or use a home computer. The home user could send an invitation via email, via Windows Live Messenger or save it as a file that the traveling user has access to. Alternatively, the away user can offer to connect using Remote Assistance, via Messenger or by starting a connection directly to the home computer.

To turn on Remote Assistance on the home computer:

1. Press WinKey+Break to open the System window, then click the Remote Settings link,

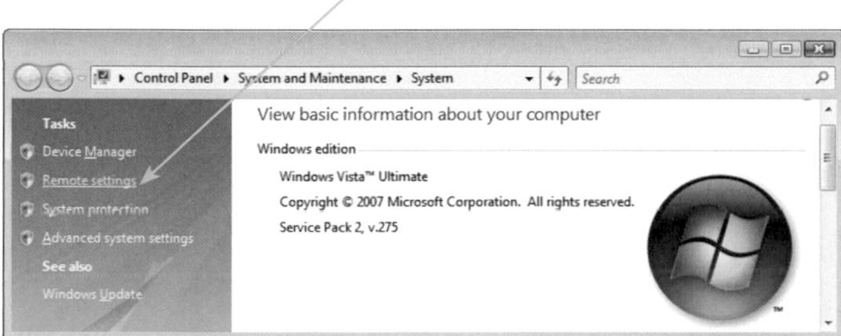

2. If it is not ticked, click the box to select Allow Remote Assistance connections to this computer, then click OK

Vista Home Premium edition

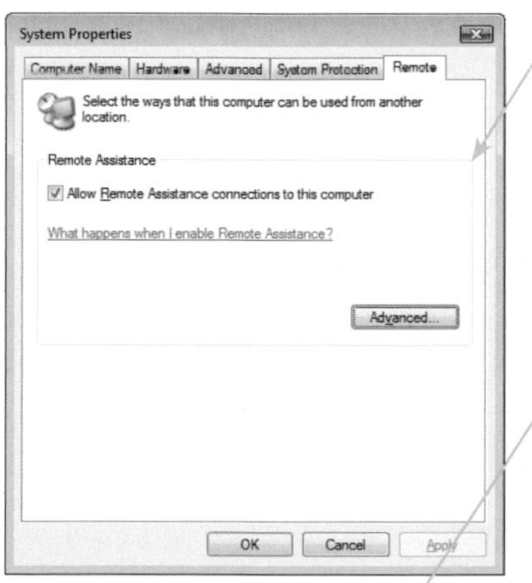

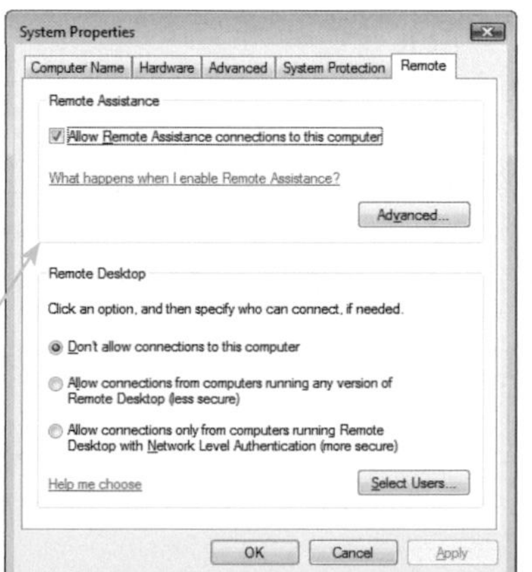

Vista Ultimate edition

Hot tip

For traveling users requiring access to their wireless home network, the invitation file is perhaps the most practical method.

Don't forget

The home user can click Advanced and specify whether others can control the computer remotely, set the length of time invitations can remain open, and restrict connections to computers with Windows Vista or later.

Hot tip

Note that computers with Windows Vista Ultimate or Business editions also show Remote Desktop.

Issue an Invitation

Hot tip

You create an invitation on the home machine to be accessed from an away computer.

1. From Start, All Programs, Maintenance, Windows Remote Assistance select Invite someone you trust to help

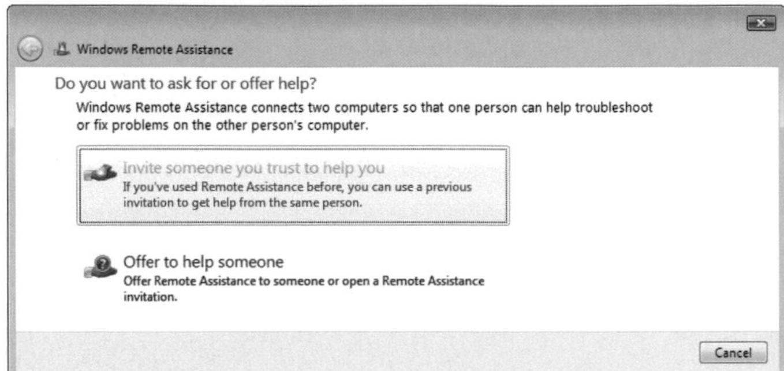

2. Choose to save the invitation as a file

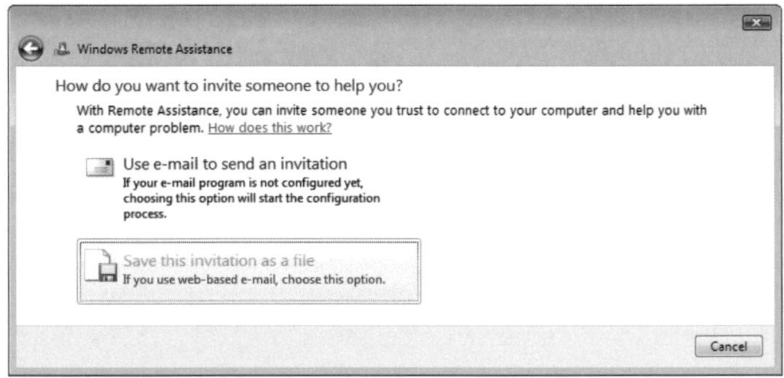

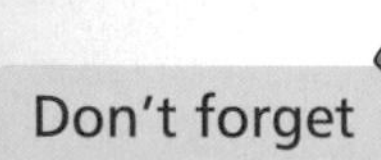

Don't forget

Send the invitation as an email if you are using POP3 mail. You'll need a file if you use Web mail.

3. Enter path, file name and password and click Finish

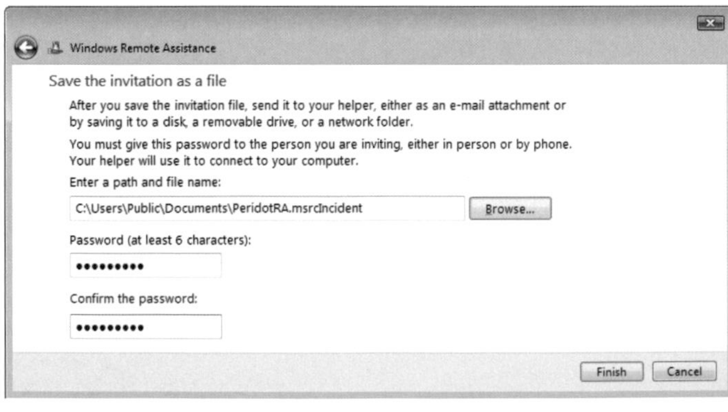

Don't forget

Save the file on accessible public folder space for sharing over the network. Send the file to the remote user for sharing over the Internet.

The home machine waits for contact from the away computer.

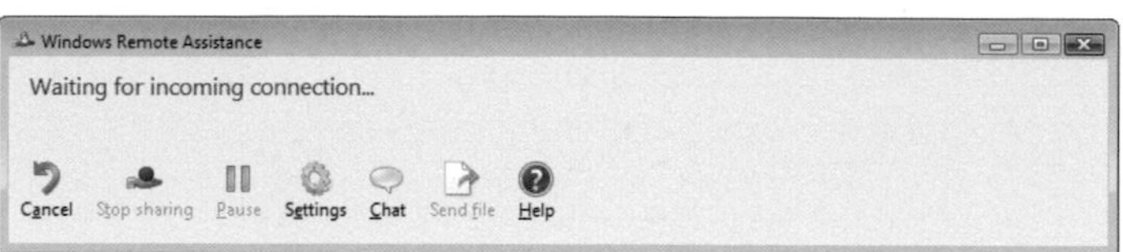

When the away computer has acquired the Remote Assistance file and the associated password, and connected to the Internet, it can request a connection with the home machine.

1. Select Start, All Programs, Maintenance, and Windows Remote Assistance, then select Offer to help someone

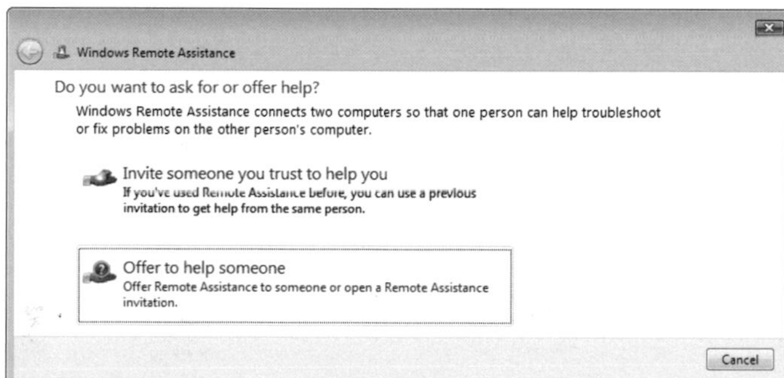

2. Browse to the Remote Assistance file and click Finish

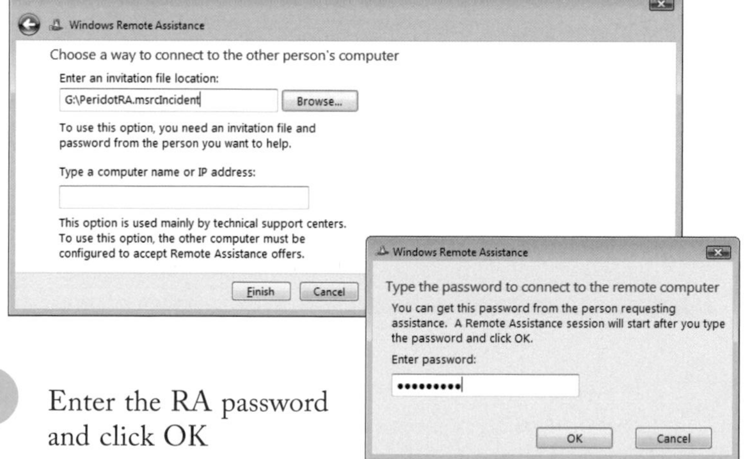

3. Enter the RA password and click OK

The invitation will lapse if the Remote Assistance session on the home computer is closed down. It also lapses after the set period, by default 6 hours.

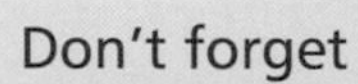

If you know the IP address of your home computer, you can connect directly to it.

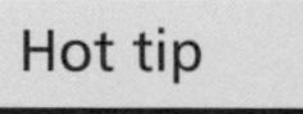

The away computer will await a response from the home computer (or a time out message).

Make the Connection

Hot tip

It is helpful to have a higher resolution screen on the away computer, so that you can view the full home computer desktop without having to shrink the image.

Hot tip

As this screenshot illustrates, the away computer is connected to the Internet via the Vodafone E272 mobile broadband modem (see page 76).

Don't forget

On the home computer, click the box to allow responses to UAC prompts, then click Yes to share control. Either computer is then able to operate the home computer, until control sharing is stopped.

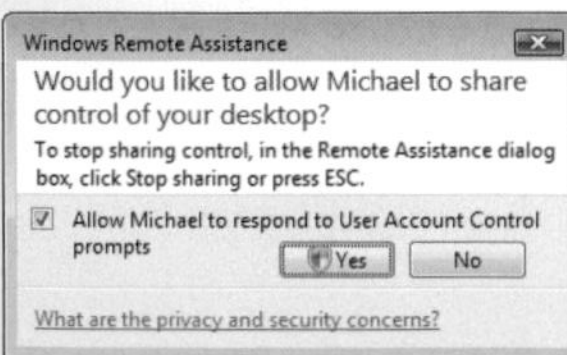

1. On the home computer, choose to allow the away computer to connect and view your screen contents

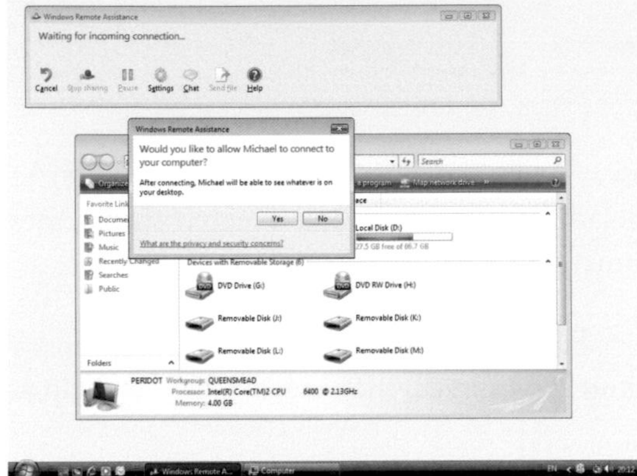

2. On the away computer, the screen now displays the full contents of the home computer

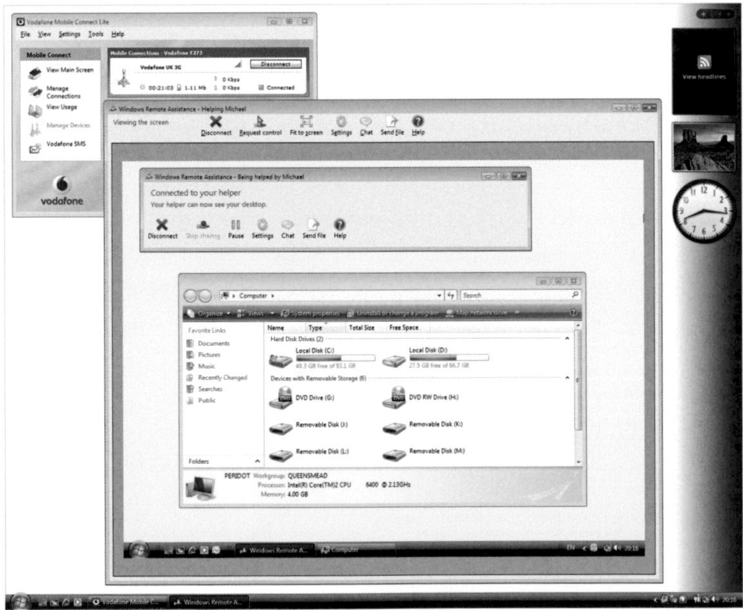

3. If you need to carry out operations on the home computer, select Request Control, and await confirmation

10 Network Monitoring and Security

Task Manager monitors the wireless network. Shared Folders keeps track of sharers. Windows user account and security settings help keep your network safe.

Monitoring the Network

Hot tip

You need to monitor the performance of your network, so you can identify when problems arise and take remedial action.

You can get a basic idea of the capabilities of your wireless network, by opening the Network and Sharing Center and viewing the status.

This example shows you the connection speed as 117.0 Mbps. This compares with 270 Mbps for the wireless adapter (LinkSys WUSB600N Dual Band), and the 130 Mbps of the BT Home Hub (V2).

This indicates that there may be some interference that is restricting the available performance. Repositioning the laptop or the wireless adapter and re-checking the status could help in remedying this.

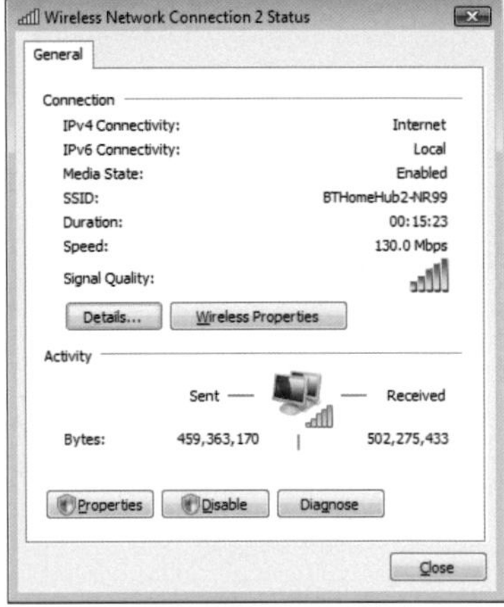

However, this does not give any real insight into the actual performance being achieved through the wireless adapter. For this you need the Task Manager.

Don't forget

Press Ctrl+Alt+Esc to go straight to the Task Manager, or right click the Taskbar and select Task Manager from the menu list.

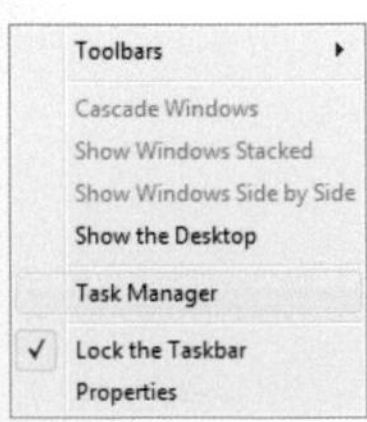

To open the Task Manager:

1. Press Ctrl+Alt+Delete, and select Start Task Manager

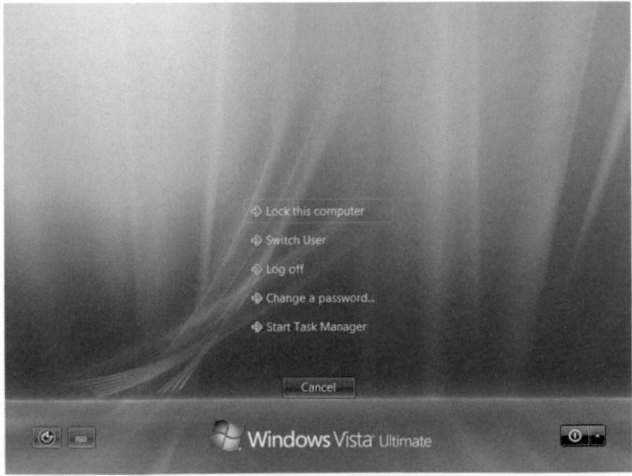

2 Click the Networking tab to display network statistics

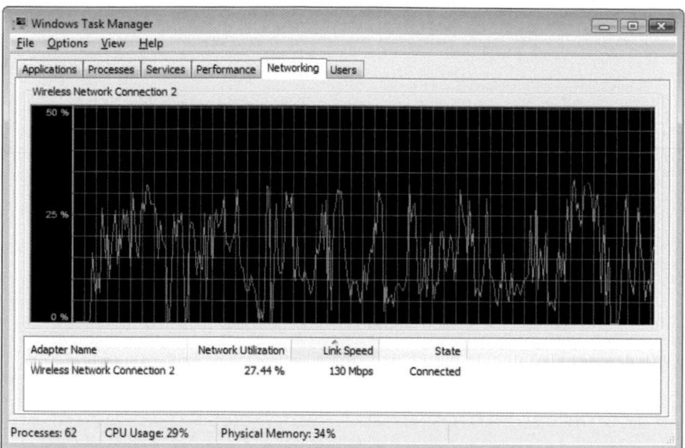

The graph shows the dynamically changing network utilization as a percentage of the adapter speed. In this example, there is an adapter speed of 130 Mbps, and the observed speeds range up to 20% or 26 Mbps total sent and received.

3 Select View, Adapter History and select to display Bytes Received (or Bytes Sent) as well as Bytes Total

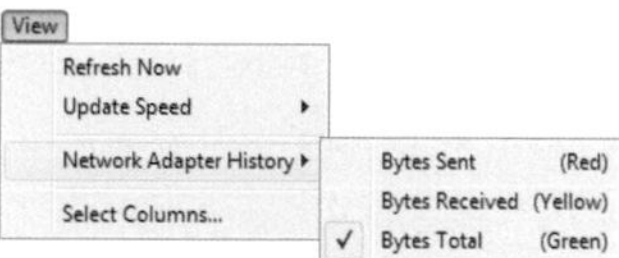

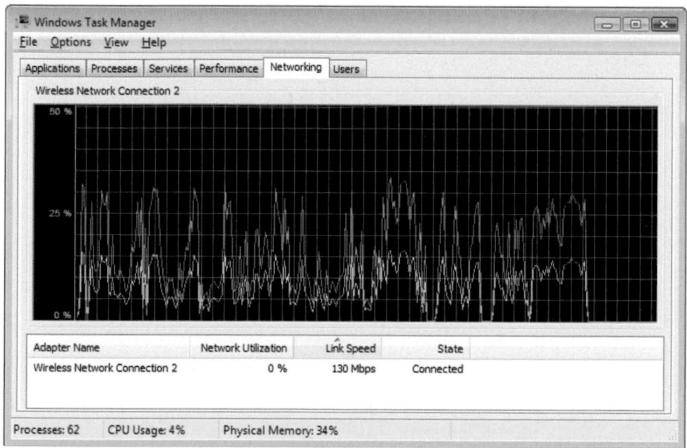

4 To check the activity in terms of processor usage or memory usage, click the Performance tab

Hot tip

Scaling is automatic, so it is adjusted to best fill the display area with the throughput for the current period.

Don't forget

These are toggles, so re-selecting any of them will remove the selection tick from that graph line.

Beware

Sometimes apparent slowness on the network is due to demands on other parts of the system such as memory or processor cycles.

Shared Folders

The Network and Sharing Center will display shared items:

1. Open the Network Center and select Show me all the shared network folders on this computer

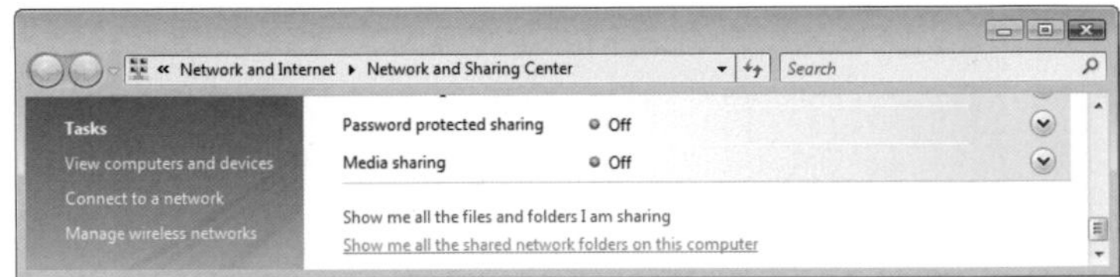

2. The folders (and printers) that have been made available for sharing will be shown, but with no usage details

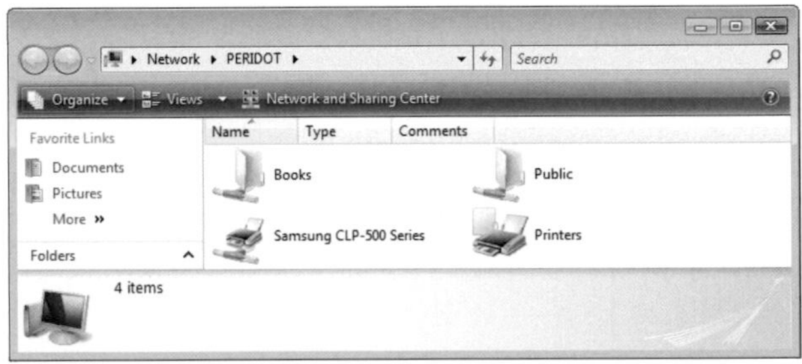

Windows Vista includes a tool called Shared Folders that allows you find which users are connected to your folders, how long they've been connected, and what files they have open.

1. Press WinKey+R (or choose Start, All Programs, Accessories, Run) to open the Run box

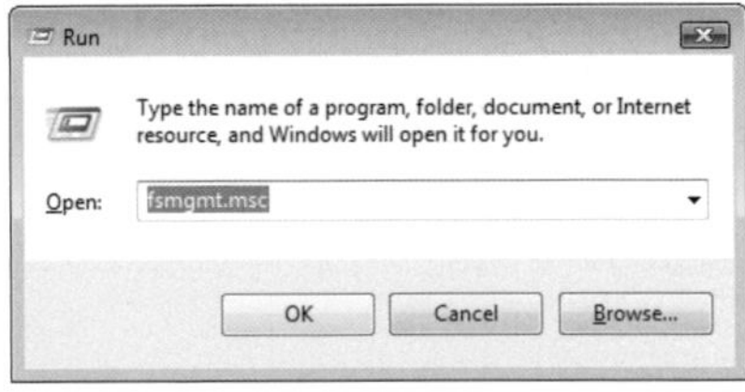

2. Type fsmgmt.msc and click OK to start the Shared Folders tool

Hot tip

It may be useful to know what items are being shared on your computer, and who may be accessing them.

Don't forget

You may add the Run command to the Start Menu (see page 99), or you can click Start, type Run and press Enter to execute the command that Windows Search finds for you.

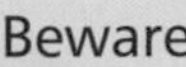

Beware

Windows User Account Control will ask you for permission to carry out this task (see page 176).

3. Click Shared Folders, Shares to display the shared items

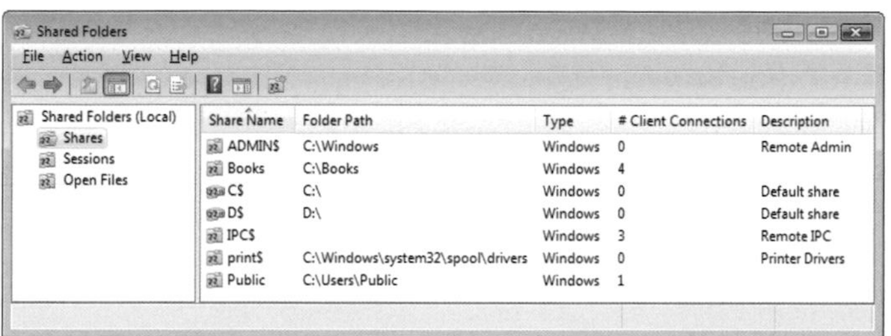

Share Name	Folder Path	Type	# Client Connections	Description
ADMIN$	C:\Windows	Windows	0	Remote Admin
Books	C:\Books	Windows	4	
C$	C:\	Windows	0	Default share
D$	D:\	Windows	0	Default share
IPC$		Windows	3	Remote IPC
print$	C:\Windows\system32\spool\drivers	Windows	0	Printer Drivers
Public	C:\Users\Public	Windows	1	

4. Click Sessions to see the connected users and computers, and the numbers of open files and folders

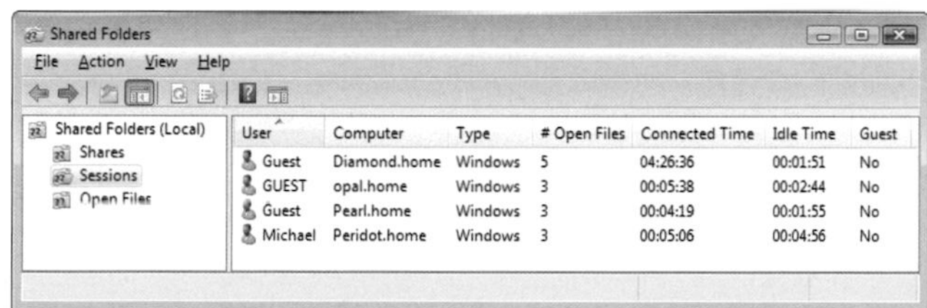

User	Computer	Type	# Open Files	Connected Time	Idle Time	Guest
Guest	Diamond.home	Windows	5	04:26:36	00:01:51	No
GUEST	opal.home	Windows	3	00:05:38	00:02:44	No
Guest	Pearl.home	Windows	3	00:04:19	00:01:55	No
Michael	Peridot.home	Windows	3	00:05:06	00:04:56	No

5. Select Open Files for a list of the open files and folders that you are sharing, showing who is accessing them

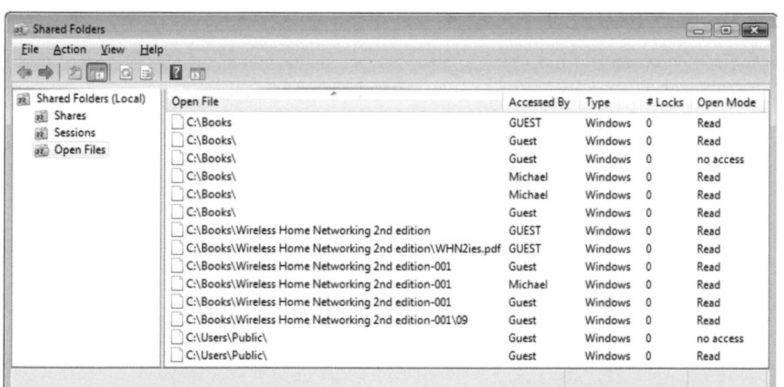

Open File	Accessed By	Type	# Locks	Open Mode
C:\Books	GUEST	Windows	0	Read
C:\Books\	Guest	Windows	0	Read
C:\Books\	Guest	Windows	0	no access
C:\Books\	Michael	Windows	0	Read
C:\Books\	Michael	Windows	0	Read
C:\Books\	Guest	Windows	0	Read
C:\Books\Wireless Home Networking 2nd edition	GUEST	Windows	0	Read
C:\Books\Wireless Home Networking 2nd edition\WHN2ies.pdf	GUEST	Windows	0	Read
C:\Books\Wireless Home Networking 2nd edition-001	Guest	Windows	0	Read
C:\Books\Wireless Home Networking 2nd edition-001	Michael	Windows	0	Read
C:\Books\Wireless Home Networking 2nd edition-001	Guest	Windows	0	Read
C:\Books\Wireless Home Networking 2nd edition-001\09	Guest	Windows	0	Read
C:\Users\Public\	Guest	Windows	0	no access
C:\Users\Public\	Guest	Windows	0	Read

6. Right click a file or folder in the list and select Close Open File to disconnect a share

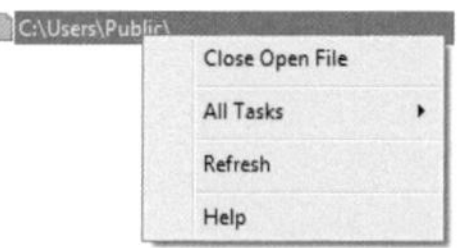

Don't forget

Windows UAC will often ask you for permission to carry out a systems-related task. If you are working with the task specified, you should confirm or enter an appropriate username and password.

Beware

This method of removing a share is for when the user concerned has left the machine, or when you suspect that it is unauthorized.

User Account Control

Don't forget

Windows UAC will often ask you for permission to carry out a systems-related task. If you have requested the task specified, you should confirm, or enter a username and password, as prompted.

When you initiate a task that requires administrator authority, the User Account Control facility will ask you to confirm your authorization. For example:

1. From System folder select Device Manager

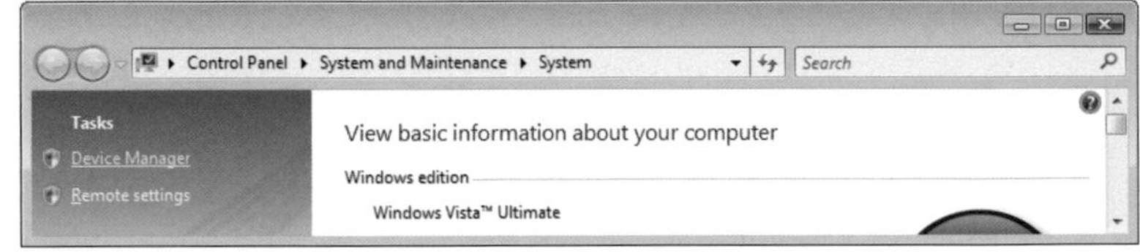

2. If you are signed on with an administrator user name, you just click Continue

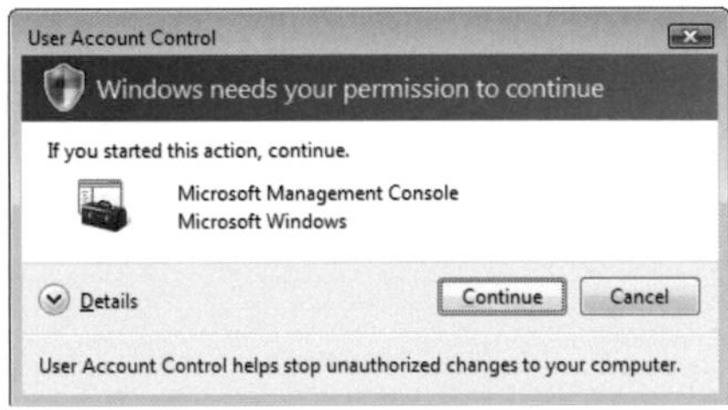

Don't forget

With either response, Windows Vista will then start the requested function, in this case the Device Manager.

3. With a standard user account, you are asked to select a username for an account with administrator authority from the list offered, and type the associated password

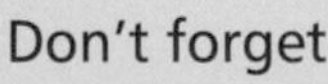

Don't forget

You can right click a system task and select Run as Administrator, and you'll be prompted by UAC for the necessary authorization.

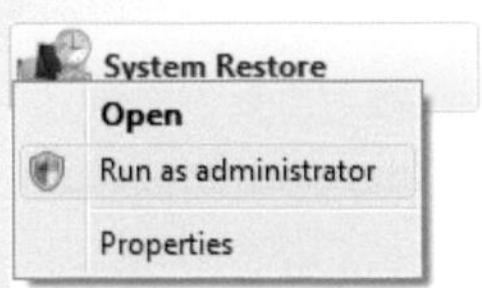

Standard User Account

It may be wise to use a standard user account for normal purposes, especially when you are logging on to public hotspots and potentially insecure sites.

1. Select Start, Control Panel, find User Accounts and Family Safety and click Add or remove user accounts

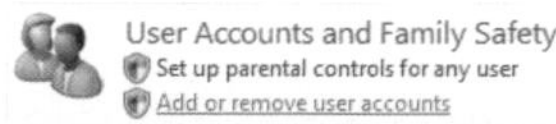

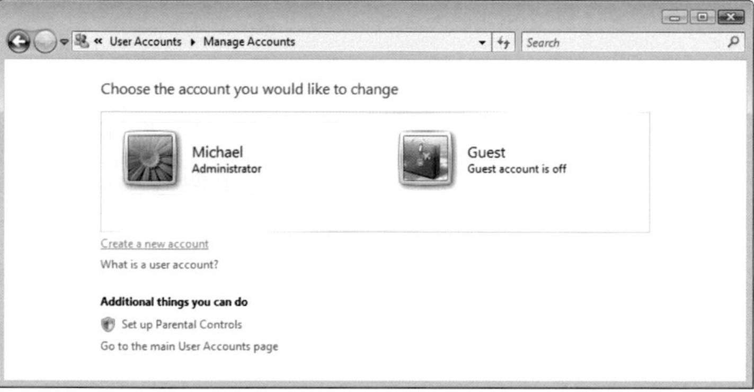

2. Click the link to Create a new account

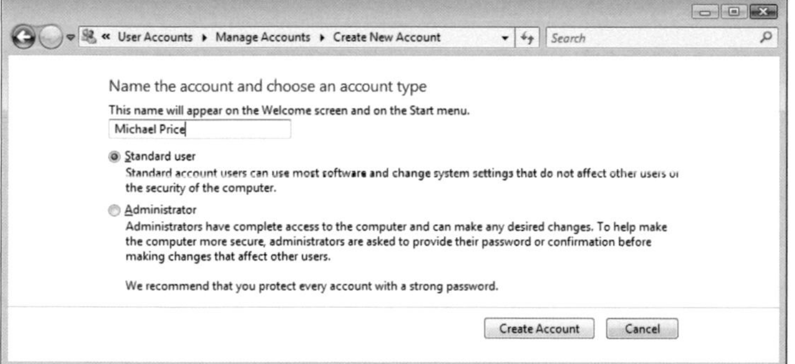

3. Type a new user name, pick Standard user, and click Create Account, then select the new account and choose Create a Password, for better security

Hot tip

You can use UAC as described opposite, or log on with a second user name for a period of time, if you have system tasks to perform.

Don't forget

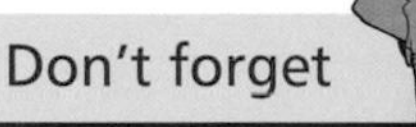

Retain your administrator account for carrying out system tasks when required, but make sure that it also has a password assigned.

Windows Security Settings

Before connecting to a network, whether at home or away, you should ensure that all your Windows security settings are configured correctly.

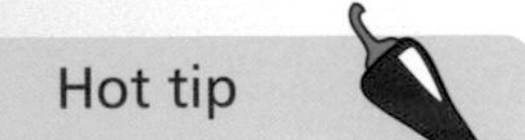

Click Change the way Security Center alerts me, and you can have an icon in the notification area plus a message to warn you when settings may need adjusting.

1. Select Start, Control Panel, Security

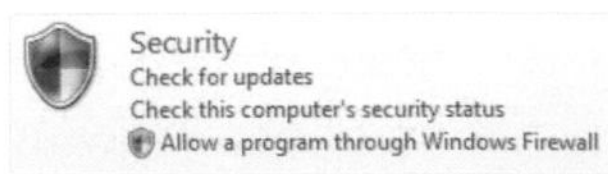

2. Select the Security Center link

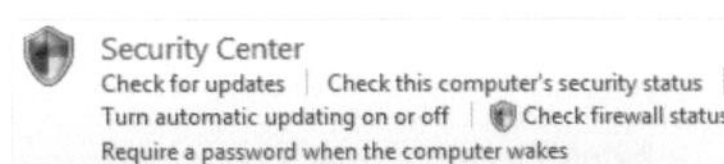

3. Make sure that Windows Firewall and Automatic Updating are turned On

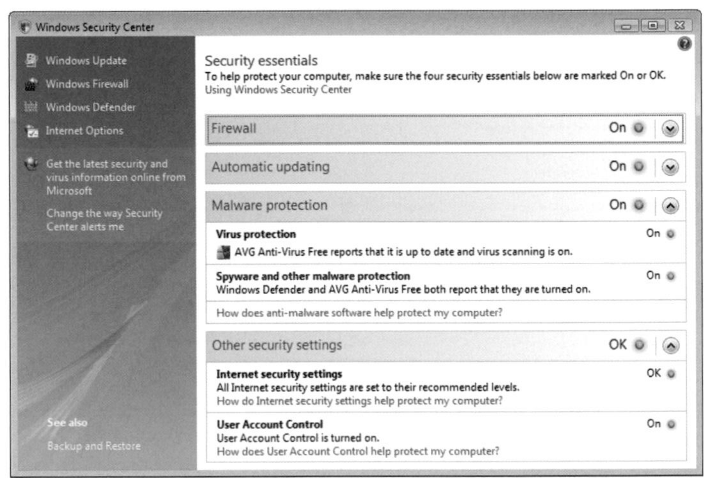

4. Click the arrow next to Malware Protection and check that your Virus Protection is up to date and active, and that your spyware or other malware protection is On

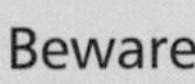
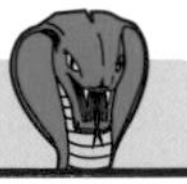

Amber messages give warnings while red messages should be considered as serious error situations.

5. Click the arrow next to Other Security Settings to check that Internet Security Settings are set to recommended levels, and that User Account Control is turned On

When problems are detected, the Security Center will recommend the appropriate actions to take to resolve the situation.

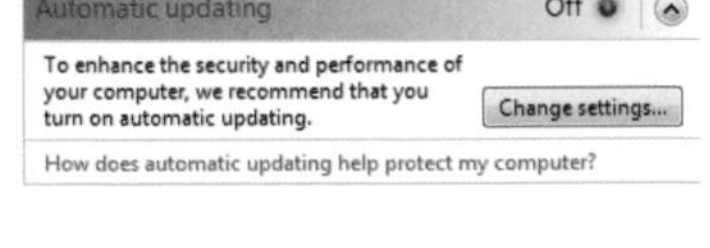

Ensuring Wireless Security

Most wireless routers are supplied with a default administrative username and password, usually admin, admin. It is essential that you change the password and, if possible, the username.

1. Open the router's configuration page (usually 192.168.0.1 or 192.168.1.1). Choose to change the admin password, enter the existing password then enter a new password

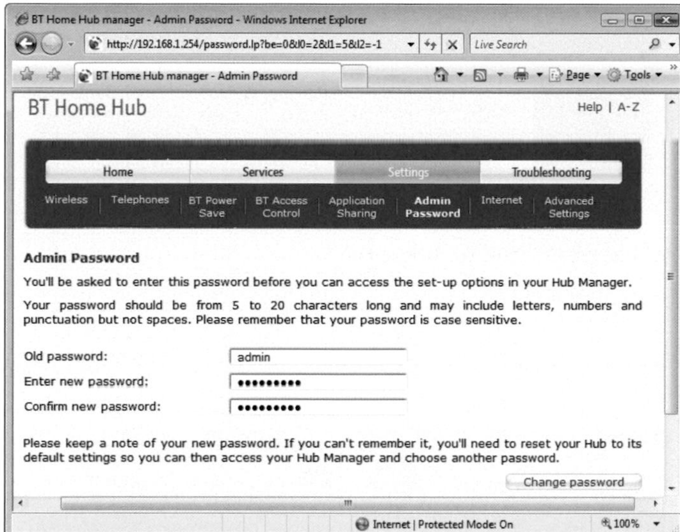

2. Choose to change the wireless encryption key and if possible the wireless network name (SSID)

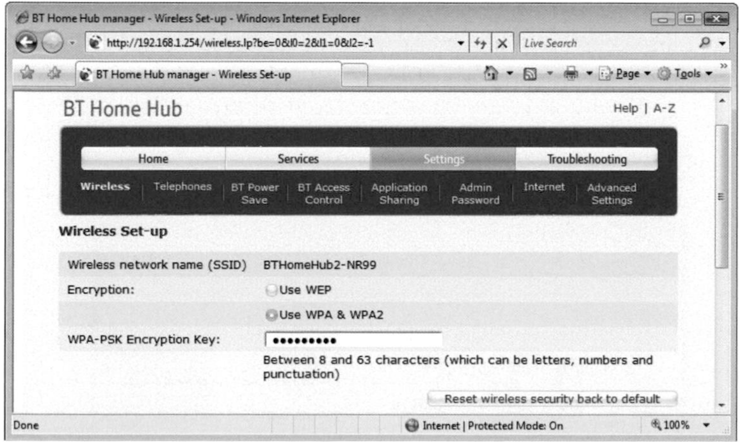

Beware

You should change your wireless passwords and security keys on a regular basis, in case they become known.

Hot tip

If you change the administrative password, then forget the new password, you'll have to reset the router to its factory defaults, and start over again.

Don't forget

Use WPA encryption unless some of your devices oblige you to use WEP encryption.

Help and Guidance

Hot tip

There's an endless source of news, views and advice on the Internet. Just search for Wireless Home Networking or related topics.

Here are just a few of the useful websites you find on the Internet:

www.practicallynetworked.com

PracticallyNetworked provides help for small network builders, including setting up, debugging, Internet sharing and security.

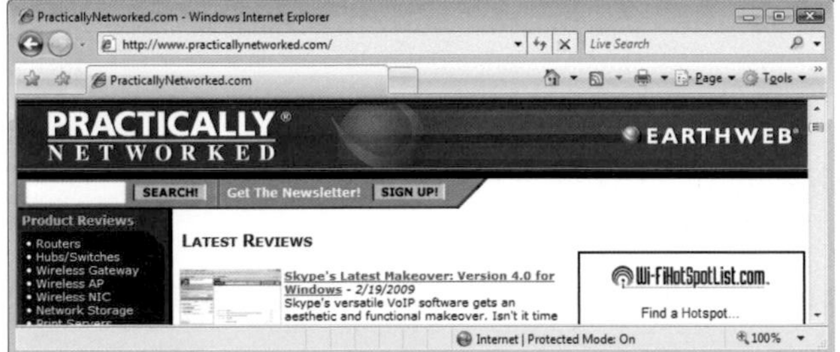

www.homepcnetwork.com

Information and advice on all aspects of home PC networks.

The websites of wireless product manufacturers provide good sources of help and information and can be invaluable when you are trying to resolve problem situations.

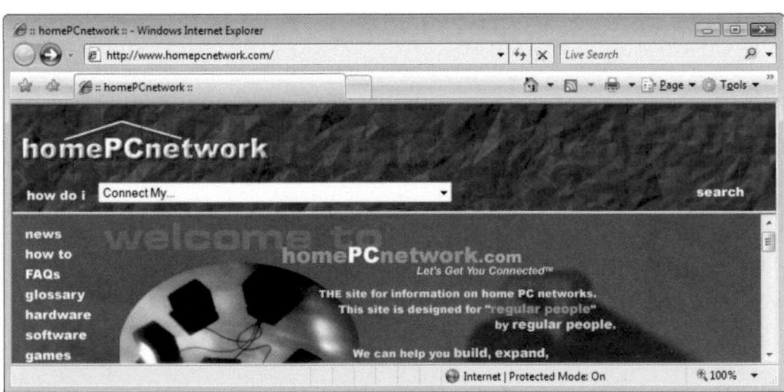

www.wifialliance.org

The Wi-Fi Alliance is a useful source of news articles, FAQs, helpful links, specifications and detailed Wi-Fi information.

For help with Windows Vista networks, go to www.microsoft.com and search on Wireless Home Networking.

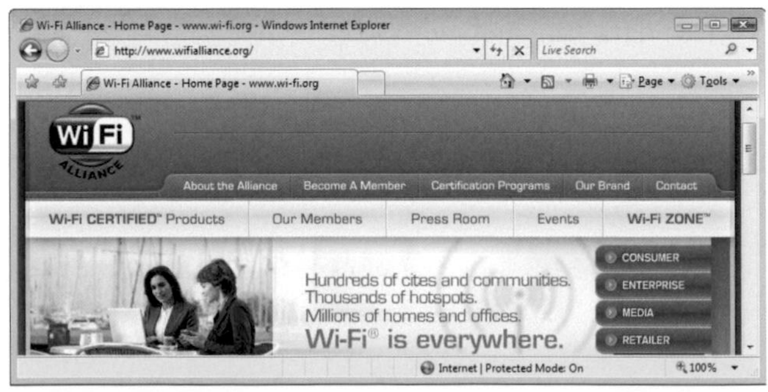

802.11 – Institute of Electrical and Electronics Engineers (IEEE) wireless networking standard, with data speeds of 1 to 2 Mbps, in the 2.4 GHz radio frequency band

802.11a – up to 54Mbps and 75 feet, in the 5.0GHz band

802.11b – up to 11Mbps and 115 feet, in the 2.4GHz band

802.11g – up to 54Mbps and 115 feet, in the 2.4GHz band

802.11n – up to 300Mbps and 230 feet, in the 2.4GHz band (in progress)

Ad-hoc wireless network – wireless network configuration with direct wireless adapter to adapter communication

Adapter Card – card which plugs into a slot on the system board, to add facilities and interfaces for attaching peripheral devices

Administrator – person in charge of a network, with the authority to set up networking hardware and software

ADSL – fast data transfer method that uses normal phone lines to handle phone calls and data transfer at the same time. Download rates of 512 Kbps up to 8 Mbps or more

AirPort – Apple's name for the wireless adapters for the Macintosh computers

Antivirus – program which finds and eliminates computer viruses

Backup – copy of a file or set of files kept in case of data loss

BIOS – Basic Input/Output System, a limited set of instructions to the computer which gets it started up

Bit – short for "binary digit", a single on/off position in a digital number, and the minimum unit of data

Bits per second (bps) – rate at which a modem or other communications device transmits data

Bluetooth – uses short-range radio waves to enable wireless communications between devices e.g. computer, printer, PDA or cell phone

Bridge – network device that provides a path between two network segments to form one logical network

Browser – Software on a computer that allows the user to view Web pages on the Internet

Byte – 8 bits of data, usually a single character

Client – computer that uses the services and resources provided by a server in a client/server network

Client/server network – A network

that divides the computing workload into the front-end clients, and the back-end servers that provide specialized resources, services or information

Commands – special codes or keywords that tell the computer to perform a task

Cookies – Identifiers saved on your hard disk when you visit various Web pages, and used to collect information such as your name, email address and site password, so that the next time you visit that particular site, it will know who you are

Crossover cable – network cable that reverses transmit and receive lines, to connect two computers directly via their network adapter ports

Data Compression – method used to store data in less space or to transmit data in less bandwidth

DHCP server – computer or device that dynamically assigns IP addresses to client computers

Digital media receiver (DMR) – device that accesses a media stream over the network and then plays that stream through speakers, audio receiver, or TV

Directory – grouping of files, more usually known as a folder

Disk Management – program involving formatting and defragmenting your disk

Domain name – A structured name such as www.microsoft.com that is used instead of the IP address assigned to the website, since IP addresses could change

Domain Name Server (DNS) – matches IP addresses with domain names, a process known as name resolution

Download – transfer a file to your computer from elsewhere on a network or the Internet

Driver – file that gives directions to the computer on how to use a device connected to the computer

Email – electronic mail, sending messages over a network or internet connection

Ethernet – A frame-based network architecture that transmits data over twisted pair wires

Executable File – a file which runs a program, also known as an EXE file

External address – IP address that a computer, router, or other device reveals to the Internet. Conversion between external and internal addresses is handled by network address translation

External Device – plugs into a port on the computer or connects via wireless communications to your computer or network

File – something saved on the computer e.g. document or program

File Transfer Protocol (FTP) – method of moving files between computers

Folder – a grouping of files, also known as a directory

Format (Disk) – makes the disk ready for use and removes all existing data

Freeware – program which is given away for free

Full Path Name – lists the route to a file starting with the drive name and naming all the folders/directories, like c:\documents\memos\Report4.doc

Gateway – connects networks of different kinds, for example home network to Internet

Gigabit – one billion bits, in the context of data communications. In the context of memory or data storage, a gigabit equals 1,073,741,824 bits

Gigabyte (GB) – one gigabyte contains 1,073,741,824 bytes

Hard Disk – large capacity data storage device, usually non-removable

Hardware – physical parts of computer or components of network

Hostname – unique name for a network or Internet computer, a human language equivalent of its IP address

Hotspot – A public wireless network that shares an Internet connection, either free of charge or for a fee

Hub – A central connection point for network cables

Hypertext transfer protocol (HTTP) – Internet protocol that defines the URL (Uniform Resource Locator) website address format

Icon – small graphic which when clicked runs a program, executes a command or opens a document

Infrastructure wireless network – wireless network configuration with a wireless access point that receives and transmits signals from wireless computers

Instant Messaging – program which notifies you when your contacts are online. You can write them messages which they receive instantly

Internal address – IP address used by computers, routers and other devices on the local network. Conversion between internal addresses and the external address is handled by network address translation (NAT)

Internal device – plugs into a slot or device bay inside a computer

IP address – The unique address assigned to every host and router on the Internet

Kilobyte – 1024 bytes historically, though often used to represent one thousand (1000) bytes

Local area network (LAN) – network in a contained geographical area, such as home, office or building

Logon – procedure (also called sign on) where user must identify himself to the computer or other device to continue

Malware – generic term for malicious software, including viruses, Trojan horses and spyware

Megabit (Mbit) – equals 1,048,576 binary digits, or bits of data

Megabyte (MB) – 1024 kilobytes (1,048,576 bytes). For data storage devices and telecommunications, it is one million (1,000,000) bytes

Megahertz (Mhz) – one million cycles per second

Menu – a list of available commands which may contain other commands as a submenu

Modem – device which translates between the analog phone line and the digital computer. Comes from Modulate/Demodulate

Nanosecond (Ns) – one billionth of a second. Used to measure memory speed

Nesting – putting directories or folders inside other directories or folders

Network – a set of computers which are linked together for the exchange of information or services, on a temporary or permanent basis

Network address translation – method by which the router converts the public destination IP address for the network into the private address of the computer requesting the data transmission

Network attached storage (NAS) – device with one or more hard drives that connects to a switch or router to allow computers on the network to store files

Node – individual device connected to a network

Notification area – area on the right of the taskbar where Windows displays icons related to the current status of the system. Also known as the System Tray

Operating System – instructions that the computer uses to tell itself how it works

Partition – portion of a hard disk. Disks may have separate partitions for different operating systems or to store data separately

PCI (Peripheral Component Interface) – Intel specification that defines the interface that enables expansion cards to be plugged in to the computer

PCMCIA (Personal Computer Memory Card International Association) – removable card for portable computers, about the size of a credit card, also called PC Card

PDA (personal digital assistant) – Small handheld computer that you can use to schedule time, update address book, make notes and synchronize with your desktop computer

Peer-to-peer network – network in which the computers have equal status and can act as both servers and clients

Print server – printer connected directly to the network so it can be used by any computer on the network

Private IP address – IP address used by your router on your local network. This address is usually either 192.168.1.1 or 192.168.0.1 and not unique to you

Public IP address – IP address that your ISP assigns dynamically to your router. This address is unique across the whole Internet

Queue – the set of jobs waiting to be done, for example Print Queue or Message Queue

RAM – main memory (random access memory), which is volatile memory that is erased when power is turned off

Removable media – storage media that are removed from the computer, such as flash drives, CDs and DVDs

Repeater – device to rebroadcast a network wireless signal so that the extent of the network can be increased

ROM – read only memory which cannot be changed, e.g. for the BIOS

Router – connects networks and controls the traffic of data among devices on the networks

Server – computer which handles network tasks and shared data

Service set identifier (SSID) – name of your wireless network

Shareware – software which you may try for a limited time before purchasing

Shut Down – close all programs and turn off computer

Smart phone – incorporates cell phone, fax, pager, and PDA functions into one multifunction device

Spreadsheet – program for handling numeric data, like budgets, financial statements and sales records

System board – main circuit board of computer, also known as motherboard

Touchscreen – monitor screen that reacts to pressure by finger or pointer

Trojan horse – program that allows others to access and alter your data, and record your logins and passwords

Universal Serial Bus (USB) – type of connection that can be used by a wide range of devices, rather than each device having a unique connector

Upgrade – replace an existing program or device with a newer version

Upload – transfer a file from your computer to a computer or server on another network

User Account Control – Windows Vista gives each user only the minimum level of permissions required to perform day-to-day tasks, and requires that the user authorize tasks that might compromise the computer's security

Utility – program that performs tasks related to the maintaining of your computer's health – hardware or data

Virus – a computer program that performs tasks without your consent. May be harmless but annoying or may be highly damaging

Wi-Fi – most common wireless networking technology, based on 802.11 standard and its amendments

Wi-Fi Protected Access (WPA) – an encryption protocol that protects wireless networks using pre-shared key

Window – a rectangular area of the screen which displays a program's user interface, a document, or a system message

Wired Equivalent Privacy (WEP) – encryption standard for wireless communications, now being superseded by WPA and WPA2

Wireless hotspot – public wireless network that shares Internet connection, either free of charge or for a fee

Wireless range extender – device used to boost signals going to and from a wireless access point

Wizard – an automatic set of steps that lead you through a process

Worm – an unwanted program that duplicates itself across a network. It uses up storage space and resources and can interfere with the ability of the system to function

WPA2 – an encryption protocol that implements the full IEEE wireless security standard. WPA2 Personal is for homes and small offices, while WPA2 Enterprise is for corporate networks

Index

Symbols

A

B

C

D

E

F

G

H

I

J

K

L

M

N

X